Praise for Raymond Bonner's

Anatomy of Injustice

"A genuine whodunit, a page turner, and a tale of redemption. And it's all true. For all that, however, *Anatomy of Injustice* is also a blistering indictment of the death penalty. . . . Bonner delivers a crackerjack feat of storytelling that steadily administers the truth about capital punishment like a slow, toxic IV drip. . . . In his expert hands, the twists and turns of Elmore's appeals, and the gradual discovery of the travesties in the original investigation and trial by Holt's team, make for excruciatingly suspenseful reading."　　—Laura Miller, *Salon*

"Accomplished and meticulously researched. . . . Convincing. . . . As a piece of reporting, the book is masterful. Bonner builds the story, and his argument, carefully, rarely editorializing, mixing in a précis of capital punishment in the United States. . . . Bonner's book is an important addition to the body of evidence against the death penalty."　　—*The Boston Globe*

"Compelling. . . . Bonner makes us feel the frustration and inhumanity of a justice system gone awry."
　　—Wilbert Rideau, *Financial Times*

"Fascinating. . . . *Anatomy of Injustice* moves as swiftly as a great courtroom thriller, and Bonner's astutely observed characters are as memorable as any you're likely to encounter in a John Grisham–penned bestseller."　　—*Richmond Times-Dispatch*

RAYMOND BONNER
Anatomy of Injustice

Raymond Bonner graduated from MacMurray College and Stanford Law School and practiced law for a decade, including as a judge advocate in the United States Marine Corps and as an assistant district attorney in San Francisco. He taught at the University of California, Davis, School of Law and founded the Public Interest Clearinghouse at Hastings College of Law in San Francisco. Later, he became an investigative reporter and foreign correspondent for *The New York Times* and received numerous awards and honors, including the Louis M. Lyons Award for Conscience and Integrity in Journalism, from the Nieman Foundation Fellows, in 1996. He was a member of the *Times* team that won a Pulitzer Prize in 1999 for articles about the sale of American technology to China. He has also been a staff writer at *The New Yorker* and has written for *The New York Review of Books*. His first book, *Weakness and Deceit: U.S. Policy and El Salvador*, received the Robert F. Kennedy Book Award; his second, *Waltzing with a Dictator: The Marcoses and the Making of American Policy*, received the Cornelius Ryan Award from the Overseas Press Club and the Hillman Prize for Book Journalism. He now lives in London.

Anatomy of Injustice

Anatomy of Injustice

A MURDER CASE GONE WRONG

RAYMOND BONNER

VINTAGE BOOKS
A Division of Random House, Inc.
New York

FIRST VINTAGE BOOKS EDITION, JANUARY 2013

Copyright © 2012 by Raymond Bonner

All rights reserved. Published in the United States by
Vintage Books, a division of Random House, Inc., New York,
and in Canada by Random House of Canada Limited, Toronto.
Originally published in hardcover in the United States by Alfred A. Knopf,
a division of Random House, Inc., New York, in 2012.

Vintage and colophon are registered
trademarks of Random House, Inc.

A portion of this work was previously published in
The Atlantic (March 2012).

The Library of Congress has cataloged the Knopf edition as follows:
Bonner, Raymond.
Anatomy of injustice : a murder case gone wrong /
Raymond Bonner.—1st ed.
p. cm.
Includes index.
1. Elmore, Edward Lee—Trials, litigation, etc.
2. Trials (Murder)—South Carolina. I. Title.
KF225.E43B66 2012
345.757'02523—dc23
2011023515

Vintage ISBN: 978-0-307-94854-0

Author photograph © Hazel Thompson
Book design by Robert C. Olsson

www.vintagebooks.com

Printed in the United States of America
10 9 8 7 6 5 4 3 2 1

In memory of my mother,
Marjorie De Mund Bonner
(1912–2000),
who instilled the values in the beginning,
and for
Susannah and Fiona,
who give me hope for the future

[The prosecutor's duty] is not that [the government] shall win a case, but that justice shall be done. . . . He may prosecute with earnestness and vigor—indeed, he should do so. But, while he may strike hard blows, he is not at liberty to strike foul ones. It is as much his duty to refrain from improper methods calculated to produce a wrongful conviction as it is to use every legitimate means to bring about a just one.

—JUSTICE GEORGE SUTHERLAND,
BERGER V. UNITED STATES, 1935

Law enforcement officers have the obligation to convict the guilty and to make sure they do not convict the innocent. They must be dedicated to making the criminal trial a procedure for the ascertainment of the true facts surrounding the commission of the crime. To this extent, our so-called adversary system is not adversary at all; nor should it be. But defense counsel has no comparable obligation to ascertain or present the truth. Our system assigns him a different mission. He must be and is interested in preventing the conviction of the innocent, but, absent a voluntary plea of guilty, we also insist that he defend his client whether he is innocent or guilty.

JUSTICE BYRON WHITE,
UNITED STATES V. WADE, 1967

CONTENTS

Contents

AUTHOR'S NOTE

IN THE FIRST month of the twenty-first century, Governor George Ryan of Illinois dramatically thrust the death penalty into the national debate. Investigative work by reporters at the *Chicago Tribune* and by a joint project at the schools of law and journalism at Northwestern University had resulted in several condemned men having their convictions reversed, one only hours before he was to be executed. Ryan, a longtime proponent of capital punishment, was shaken. "Until I can be sure that everyone sentenced to death in Illinois is truly guilty, until I can be sure with moral certainty that no innocent man or woman is facing a lethal injection, no one will meet that fate," said Ryan. A conservative Republican, Ryan said he still believed in the death penalty, but was compelled to suspend executions in the face of the state's "shameful record of convicting innocent people and putting them on Death Row."

Two weeks later, another conservative Republican governor, George W. Bush of Texas, was asked about capital punishment when he appeared on *Meet the Press* as his party's leading presidential candidate. As governor, Bush had presided over more executions than any state chief executive in history. Indeed, under his watch, from 1995 to 2000, Texas put more men and women to death than the next five states combined (Virginia, Oklahoma, South Carolina, Florida, and Alabama). Toward the end of the hour-long program, the host, Tim Russert, raised the subject of the death penalty.

Would Bush join Governor Ryan in invoking a moratorium until the system could be analyzed "so you don't make a mistake?" Russert asked, noting that Ryan was the head of Bush's campaign in Illinois.

"No, I won't," Bush said without hesitation. "Because I'm confident that every person that has been put to death in Texas under my watch has been guilty of the crime charged and has full access to the courts. I'm confident." He went on, "I've reviewed every case, Tim, and I'm confident that every case that has come across my desk—I'm confident of the guilt of the person who committed the crime."

BUSH WAS THROWING DOWN the gauntlet, in a move reminiscent of Senator Gary Hart's challenge to the media during the 1984 primaries to prove his marital infidelity. But Bush's boast was far more serious: that no innocent man had been executed in Texas, that every death row inmate had enjoyed "full access to the courts."

In response, *The New York Times* sent me to Texas to investigate and report on the matter. My colleague Sara Rimer and I spent several weeks traveling around the state—San Antonio, Brownsville, Austin, Dallas, Houston—talking to death penalty lawyers, prosecutors, victims' families, and members of the Texas Board of Pardons and Paroles, and reviewing cases of men who had been executed. We did not find any case where we could say with certainty that an innocent man had been executed. Our efforts to do so were severely hampered by the fact that once a man is executed, his lawyers and investigators turn their attention to clients who are still on death row, rather than pursuing evidence of a former client's innocence. But we found state officials involved in the Texas criminal justice system who were not as sanguine as their governor that the system was rendering justice in every case. "I worry that we may execute an innocent person," said Paddy Lann Burwell, who had been appointed by Bush to the parole board. "Any person would know that is a possibility. I think our system needs to be improved." Our lengthy article appeared on the front page, and it was accompanied by brief summaries of five cases.

The *Times* editors considered that capital punishment was a topic worthy of further reporting, and Sara and I continued to examine the various issues that marked the debate. We made repeated visits to Texas's death row in Livingston. After passing through security, we'd sit in a rather large room with vending machines dispensing soft drinks, coffee, and candy bars, waiting for a prisoner to be brought from his cell. He'd be on the other side of thick glass, and we'd talk through a telephone. We interviewed John Paul Penry, whose case was twice argued before the United States Supreme Court. It was November, and when we asked Mr. Penry, fifty-six years old, if he believed in Santa Claus, he said, "They keep talking about Santa Claus being down in the North Pole. . . . Some people say it's not true. I got to where I do believe there's a Santa Claus."

One of our front-page articles, "Executing the Mentally Retarded Even as Laws Begin to Shift," was cited by both the majority and the dissent in *Atkins v. Virginia,* the landmark Supreme Court case that held it was unconstitutional to execute a person who was mentally retarded. We were given unexpected insight into the generally poor quality of trial representation provided defendants facing the death penalty when we interviewed a gregarious Houston lawyer named Ronald Mock. He had had more clients executed or awaiting execution than any other lawyer in the country, which didn't seem to shame him at all. Mock boasted that he had flunked his criminal law course and was a heavy drinker. "I drank whiskey with judges," he said. "I drank whiskey in the best bars." He insisted it didn't affect his performance, and judges kept appointing him to represent defendants in capital cases.

We reported beyond the South. I went to Idaho when Charles Fain, who had been on death row for eighteen years, was released after DNA established his innocence.

At some point, I heard about the South Carolina case of Edward Lee Elmore. After a trial lasting seven days, he had been sentenced to death in 1982 for the murder of a wealthy widow, Dorothy Ely Edwards. His conviction was overturned on appeal; he was retried and reconvicted; that sentence was also reversed; after a third trial, he was again sentenced to death. Then, in 2000, his lawyers found evidence that state officials had sworn repeatedly had been lost. The evidence raised questions about Elmore's guilt.

In many ways, Elmore's is a garden-variety death penalty case: a young black male of limited intelligence convicted of murdering a white person after a trial in which his lawyers' performance was so poor that it could barely be called a defense. But the case is also exceptional, and not just because it involved "sex, violence, and racism," as one of Mrs. Edwards's neighbors put it, convinced that this was the only reason reporters were interested. Elmore's story raises nearly all the issues that mark the debate about capital punishment: race, mental retardation, bad trial lawyers, prosecutorial misconduct, "snitch" testimony, DNA testing, a claim of innocence. "While lots of cases have one of these aspects, it's a case that has all of them," John Blume, head of the South Carolina Death Penalty Resource Center, which represented death row inmates, told me.

For this reason, I felt the desire to write Elmore's story more than that of any of the other men Sara and I met on death row. But that wasn't the only factor leading to this book. For me, as a lawyer and as a journalist, what transformed the story was the character, dedication, and determination of his appellate lawyer, Diana Holt, an intense native of Texas whose conversations are punctuated by flailing arms and eye rolls. She's sui generis, her life having more in common with Elmore's than with Ivy League–educated death penalty lawyers. Listening to her speaking with her death row clients is surreal. Using words like "pokie wokie" and "peachie," she talks as if she were at the mall with friends. She is as much a mother, big sister, or friend to these men—most of whom have been abandoned by their families— as she is their lawyer. In the summer of 1993, at the age of thirty-four, Diana, with pure grit and the blossoming of innate intelligence, had overcome Sisyphean odds and finished her second year of law school. As an intern at the South Carolina Death Penalty Resource Center, she was given the Elmore file. By then, he had been on death row for eleven years.

Elmore's case, and Holt's effort to save his life, is a textbook study of how our criminal justice system works in capital cases, as well as how it doesn't. Americans consider their criminal justice system to be the best in the world. Some conservatives may carp that it coddles criminals, and some liberals may believe that there are not enough protections for suspects, particularly indigent ones. By and large, however, the system yields justice. As a former prosecutor and defense counsel, however, I know the system is only as good as the lawyers who administer it— prosecutors, defense counsel, judges. If prosecutors abuse their authority, if defense lawyers are lazy or incompetent, if judges are weak or biased, the result is injustice, and in capital cases that can spell death.

BOOK ONE

Rush to Judgment

CHAPTER ONE

Greenwood, South Carolina, 1982

A FEROCIOUS SNOWSTORM hit the South in January 1982. An Air Florida 737 crashed into the Fourteenth Street Bridge in Washington, D.C., and then plunged into the icy Potomac River, killing seventy-eight people. In Atlanta, temperatures fell to near zero. Some 160 miles east, two inches of snow covered buildings, lawns, and cars in Greenwood, South Carolina. On the front page of the Greenwood *Index-Journal,* there appeared a picture of Emily James, two and a half years old, bundled in a snowsuit, watching "in amazement as her family went sledding." Government offices and schools were closed. In a graceful hand, Dorothy Edwards wrote "Snow" in the squares on her calendar for Wednesday and Thursday, the thirteenth and fourteenth.

Along with some ten thousand homeowners, Mrs. Edwards was without power for thirty-six hours. She jumped rope to keep warm. She was seventy-six years old but could have passed for fifty-six, a petite five foot three, size 6. Every morning, she pulled on her leotards for thirty minutes of exercise. She was a handsome woman, reserved, very much a lady—"elegant in a comfortable sort of way," in the eyes of her daughter, Carolyn. There had been no TV dinners or fast food when Carolyn was growing up; the dining room table was set with china and silver for every meal, breakfast included.

Dorothy's home since the end of World War II was on the north side of Greenwood, on Melrose Terrace; her three-acre wooded plot backed onto Edgewood Cemetery, adding to the feeling of seclusion and tranquillity—except for the nights when young men brought their six-packs for parties among the dead. The west end of the half-mile-long, leafy street is anchored by the First Baptist Church, founded in 1870. The current stately structure with its cathedral sanctuary and stained-glass windows was erected in 1954; the bell tower was added in 1968. Dorothy lived where the boomerang-shaped street curved, at 209. Most of her neighbors were elderly. Christine Henderson, whose husband had died in 1967, lived in a white brick house with a large lawn across the street, at 210; her son was a criminal investigator for the state. The redbrick house at 213 belonged to Mildred Clark, a widow, who was the neighborhood recluse—she didn't even answer the door for trick-or-treaters. At 205 was Roy Raborn, a salesman at Fred Smith Co., a men's clothing store, who had landed at Omaha Beach in 1944. Dorothy's neighbors thought she was a drug company heiress, which was not quite true. She was well-off, having inherited close to $1 million from her mother, while her stepfather had been an executive with Geer Drug Co. in Spartanburg, South Carolina, a lovely town at the foot of the Blue Ridge Mountains. Dorothy's mother, Beatrice Ely, had moved to the South from New York after she divorced; her husband was a jeweler in New York City. Beatrice raised her daughter to be independent and refined. They spent vacations in the mountains, where Beatrice taught Dorothy to ride horses and shoot; years later, Dorothy's neighbors were not alarmed when they heard the crack of a rifle from the yard behind her house. "Did you get it, Dorothy?" a neighbor would shout, knowing she'd spotted another snake.

Beatrice sent her daughter to Converse College, a women's liberal arts school in Spartanburg. The school is strong in music and sends graduates to symphonies and conservatories around the world. Dorothy, a coloratura soprano, won local, regional, and national singing contests. When she was thirty, she took a train to New York to appear on *Major Bowes' Amateur Hour*, performing "Carmena." She took second place. It made front-page news in Spartanburg.

A few months later, back in Spartanburg, she married James Edward Edwards, the son of a well-liked family doctor who would accept a chicken or vegetables from a patient's garden as payment. Dorothy and Ed, as family and friends called him, had met in college when he was at Wofford, a liberal arts college near Converse. They were married on a Thursday morning at the Church of the Advent, in a ceremony marked by "simplicity and dignity," the Spartanburg newspaper reported in a prominent article. The bride, it noted, wore "a becoming fall suit of beige wool with collar of faux fur."

Ed and Dorothy's only child, Carolyn, was born in 1939, and soon afterward, Ed went off to war, a U.S. Navy Seabee. After the war, he moved his family to Greenwood. They bought a marshy plot. Ed drained it, filled it, landscaped it, and built a spacious two-bedroom house; later he added a screened-in porch and a guest room.

He worked primarily in construction and became Greenwood's first civil defense director in the 1950s. He was a generous, big-hearted man who "championed the underdog, and hired the handicapped," his daughter recalled. A heavy drinker, he eventually joined Alcoholics Anonymous and helped set up several groups throughout the state. He died at the age of fifty-eight, in 1966. It was a devastating loss for Dorothy, but she had a strong inner resolve, and gradually she found a strength and independence that impressed close friends. She now put much of her energy into painting, displaying remarkable talent; the walls of her home were decorated with her work. She also made needlepoint pillows and hooked rugs, passing hours in front of a large frame stretched with a rug, peering through a magnifying glass at designs she had bought from New York's Metropolitan Museum of Art. "My brains are in my fingers," she would say jovially to Carolyn.

THE TOWN

GREENWOOD, NAMED IN the early 1800s after a plantation that the owner's wife had called Green Wood, has rich chocolate soil, fertile for small-scale agriculture. But it had grown as a textile town—Greenwood Cotton Mill opened in 1889, a second mill in 1896, and a third in 1897. At its peak, there were 250,000 spindles in the Greenwood environs. In 1897, the town's voters—all white males, of course—approved a $25,000 bond issue for a courthouse and jail. By the turn of the century, the population had soared to 4,828 and nine railroad lines passed through the municipality, bringing twenty-seven trains each day. Traveling salesmen stayed at the Oregon Hotel, the only hotel in town until the 1960s.

Though perhaps today "an hour and a half from everyplace else" (as President Obama would describe it good-naturedly during his presidential campaign), Greenwood residents have much to boast about in their history. After World War I, they saluted Supreme Allied Commander Ferdinand Foch with a huge celebration on Main Street, slightly wider than the length of a football field at the time—before office buildings went up. In 1954, the street was packed with cheering residents turned out to welcome a local girl who had been crowned Miss Universe, Miriam Stevenson. The small town has produced the Swingin' Medallions, modeled on the Beach Boys; a justice of the South Carolina Supreme Court; and three star quarterbacks in succession for Clemson University. Greenwood residents are crazy about their sports. The high school football coach Julius "Pinky" Babb became a legend, winning more than three hundred games between 1943 and 1981. "We were confident in our excellence," said a resident.

It was a white, Protestant community, primarily Southern Baptist. It had very few Catholics until the 1960s, when some northern companies began to relocate in the Emerald City, as the town calls itself. As for blacks, fifteen years after the Supreme Court had declared, in *Brown v. Board of Education*, that separate schools for blacks and whites were unconstitutional, and a year later ordered integration "with all deliberate speed," Greenwood's high schools were still segregated. The segregationists held out until 1969, and then they gave in grudgingly. Greenwood doesn't hide its racial past. A war memorial sits at the corner of Oak and Main, in front of the redbrick, seven-story Textile Building. American Legion Post No. 20 erected it in 1929. A pole carrying the Stars and Stripes extends from a six-foot-high granite base. The bronze plaque on the west side of the base lists the World War I dead in two categories—"White" and "Colored." Thirty-one "whites" and 24 "coloreds" gave their lives. The "colored" include Henry Chin. Another plaque was added after World War II. It also racially divides the men who were killed in action: 131 "white" and 11 "colored." The racial categories were eliminated for the Korean War—12 men from Greenwood are remembered in alphabetical order. Twenty-four men died in the Vietnam War; their names are also listed alphabetically.

At the beginning of the twenty-first century, C. Rauch Wise, a lawyer and probably Greenwood's only card-carrying member of the ACLU, offered to replace the segregationist plaques from the first two wars with plaques that listed the dead alphabetically. He quietly took the proposal to the mayor. After some inquiries, the mayor, an African American, reported back that it couldn't be done. The monument didn't belong to the city, he said. It belonged to the local American Legion post, which opposed the change. A few years later, in 2010, Wise tried again. Again, the legionnaires said no.

Over the decades Greenwood grew out, not up. The eight-story Grier Building, at 327 Main Street, was the tallest in town when it was built in 1919 and is the tallest today. Greenwood's charm gave way to sprawl, and the town became indistinguishable from thousands of others across the country—shopping malls with enormous parking lots, chains replacing independents, fast-food franchises. A small grocery store owned by Dorothy's next-door neighbor Jimmy Holloway was bought by a supermarket chain, which later sold to a chain steak house.

DOROTHY SPENT CHRISTMAS 1981 with her daughter, Carolyn, and her grandchildren. Carolyn had married—she was now Carolyn Lee—and was living in Pensacola, Florida. Dorothy returned home on Sunday, December 27, she noted on her calendar. On Wednesday, Edward Elmore, a lean black man with bright eyes, knocked on the back door. With only a fifth-grade education and of limited intelligence—he could do simple addition and subtraction only if he used his fingers—he worked as a handyman. A few weeks earlier, while working for one of Dorothy's neighbors, he had noticed that the gutters on the house at 209 were full of leaves; he asked Dorothy if she would like him to clean them. Mrs. Edwards said yes. She showed him where the ladder was, underneath the porch. The job took him about two hours, for which he was paid $3. Come back in a few weeks, after the leaves have finished falling, she said.

On December 30 he returned, cleaned out the gutters, and washed the windows as well. While Mrs. Edwards was writing him a check, Elmore told her that the paint on some of the window frames was peeling. He was a good painter, he said. She told him to call in a month or two, when the weather would be better. She slowly spelled her last name and phone number, and he scrawled "Edwards" and "229-4087" on a State Farm Insurance card, which was in his girlfriend's name for her 1976 Mustang; he put it back in his wallet. Dorothy later told Jimmy Holloway what a fine job Elmore had done and showed him the clean windows.

The new year was promising to be a good one for Dorothy. On the calendar square for January 3, she wrote "Lonnie's." Lonnie Morgan was a businessman from Tryon, North Carolina, retired, living comfortably on the proceeds from the business he had sold. He was a member of the Tryon Hunt and Riding Club; Dorothy, a keen rider, was planning to join. They had been introduced by a Converse College classmate of Dorothy's and had been seeing each other for a couple of years; she had recently told neighbors that they were talking about getting married. She visited him in Tryon on January 3. The following Saturday, January 9, she went to a choir party at the Episcopal Church of the Resurrection, a couple of miles away, over on South Main. She attended regularly and was a standout soloist in the choir.

On Thursday afternoon, the fourteenth, when a front-page headline alerted residents, "More snow, sleet heading this way," Jimmy Holloway called around three. He and his wife, Frances, were about to go grocery shopping and offered to pick up some things for Dorothy. The Holloways were her closest friends. They had met at the Oregon Hotel on the eve of World War II, and Jimmy had encouraged Dorothy and Ed to build on the plot next to his.

Jimmy walked over and got her shopping list; then he and his wife drove to the Winn-Dixie supermarket, out on Route 25. When they returned, Dorothy asked Jimmy if he'd lift a five-gallon kerosene canister out of the trunk of her car; she had bought it for a portable heater, which she needed now, with the unusual cold. He carried it through the kitchen and into her den. The three of them chatted for a while.

On Saturday, Jimmy called Dorothy and again offered to go grocery shopping for her. It was sleeting, but the temperature had moved above freezing, melting the worst icy patches. She said she could go herself. She also told him that she was planning to go to North Carolina the next day to visit Lonnie. After hanging up, she drove to Winn-Dixie. In the checkout line she chatted with an old friend, Coley Free. She showed him pictures of her two grandchildren and her two-year-old great-grandson, and then she took her change from the checkout girl, put it in her purse, and drove home. It was late in the afternoon.

THE CRIME

FORTY-FOUR HOURS LATER, the body of Dorothy Ely Edwards was found in her bedroom closet. She was clad only in a reddish-purple housecoat with a ruffled collar, zipped up the front.

There was a horrible bruise on her right knee, and her lower right leg was reddish purple. Her knees were drawn up. A dress boot was wedged between them. Pieces of glass were stuck in the dried blood on her left wrist. Her left ear was nearly severed. The areas around both eyes were black-and-blue. Her hair was matted with blood.

The murder rocked the community. Most of Greenwood's murders were in the black neighborhood—blacks killing blacks in barroom brawls, over money or a woman, or in domestic disputes. The perpetrator was usually caught quickly, often with a gun or knife still in his possession. Those crimes didn't particularly disturb the white community. This one did. "Widow Stabbed to Death" screamed the headline at the top of the front page of the Greenwood *Index-Journal,* accompanied by a picture of policemen at the house. (On that day's front page there was also an article reporting that the Supreme Court, by a vote of 5–4, had overturned the death sentence of Monty Lee Eddings, who at the age of sixteen had been convicted of killing an Oklahoma highway patrolman with a sawed-off shotgun; the court said that the jury had not been properly instructed to consider mitigating evidence.)

THE POLICE

"MYSELF AND PATROLMAN ALVIN COOK were on Smythe Street when we heard a radio dispatched message of a possible Code One, which is an attempted murder," Sgt. John Owen wrote in his official report. (The dispatcher had it wrong—Code 1 is *murder.*) "Myself and Alvin Cook then proceded to 209 Melrose Terrace. And we arrived there at 12:26 p.m. Myself and Patrolman Cook went to the home where we found Patrolman Holtzclaw at the rear of this home." Holtzclaw was talking to Jimmy Holloway, under the carport, next to Edwards's 1976

Cadillac; her large-wheeled bicycle, with handlebars like a gnu's horns, rested against the back door.

Owen noticed what appeared to be an impression of a shoe print to the left of the steps leading into the house. It was reddish. "I believe to be blood," he wrote. He took Holtzclaw's navy blue police hat, with a stiff bill and the Greenwood Police Department seal, and placed it over the print. He walked to his patrol car, opened the trunk, took out a cardboard box, walked back, and placed the box over the print; then he gave Holtzclaw his hat back. "I enformed them of what I had found and advised that this print was not to be disturbed," Owen wrote.

By 12:30 that afternoon, most of Greenwood's forty-five-man police force had descended on the usually tranquil Melrose Terrace, blocking the street with their patrol cars, stirring curiosity and concern among the residents. Sgt. Alvin Johnson, six foot two, two hundred pounds, took charge. He was thirty-two years old and had been on the force for close to eleven years, since being discharged from the Marine Corps with a Purple Heart. Not the smartest kid at Greenwood High, Johnson had joined the marines immediately upon graduation and was still only eighteen years old when he arrived in Vietnam. During a fierce firefight south of Da Nang, his body was shredded by shrapnel and he nearly died, saved only by an alert squad member who hollered for a corpsman.

"What I done when I first got there is talk to Mr. Holloway," Johnson would later testify.

After Mr. Edwards died, Holloway had watched over his widow. He had a key to her house. He liked to slip over in the afternoon for a cocktail. His wife was a straitlaced teetotaler. Dorothy drank, socially. "A southern belle who liked a glass of sherry," said her daughter. Melrose Terrace residents thought there was more to the relationship between Holloway and Dorothy than just being good neighbors. Popular and gregarious, Holloway had a reputation as something of a ladies' man. Neighbors would whisper among themselves about how he would come out of his house, go into his garage, and then look out to see if anyone was watching. Then he'd walk around to the back of his house, stop, look again, and then head across the lawn and over the creek into Dorothy's yard. At that point, the neighbors couldn't see him anymore. But an hour or so later, they'd see him retracing his route. Dorothy spent many days at Holloway's cabin on Lake Greenwood, a reservoir with 212 miles of shoreline on the Saluda River. Dorothy painted while Jimmy worked on his boats.

Holloway told the police officers that he had found Mrs. Edwards's body. It was he who had called the police. He now led Johnson and Owen inside his neighbor's house, retracing the steps he had already taken at least twice that morning. In the small alcove by the back door, the policemen glanced at several of Dorothy's oils: one of Holloway's Lake Greenwood cabin; three of sailboats on the lake, painted from his veranda; a still life of fruit. On the basement door, Dorothy had mounted a metal rack holding three clay flowerpots; it had been knocked askew, pieces of the lower pot on the floor. The three men walked into the kitchen, covered with wallpaper showing green ivy crawling up white bricks. Three wingback metal chairs with floral cushions were carefully arranged around a small circular table; a spoon and a glass mug lay on top. On the floor, Johnson saw a partial denture. A few feet away was a needle-nose pliers. Sticking out of a drawer where Mrs. Edwards kept a Stanley hammer, a screwdriver, nails, a ruler, and masking tape were long-handled bottle tongs, which she used for pulling canning jars out of hot water. A coffee cup had been washed and left to dry upside down on the edge of the sink. On the countertop was a bowl of bananas, oranges, and apples and an empty bottle of Taylor sherry.

There was something odd about this scene. The bottle tongs all but had a sign on them saying "Here, find me." And the kitchen was remarkably clean and neat after such a violent crime. It felt as if someone had been entertaining—witness the empty sherry bottle—and then cleaned up. There was finger-print dust on the sherry bottle, which meant that the police probably had a clue as to who had been in the house if the print wasn't Mrs. Edwards's.

Dorothy's ten-cup General Electric automatic coffeemaker was on a green Formica cabinet. Another Dorothy oil, a ballerina in a pink tutu—it was Carolyn—hung above it. "I have one just like it," Holloway said to Johnson, referring to the coffeemaker. It was set for 6:00 a.m. Holloway explained that Dorothy would have had to set it after 7:00 p.m. the previous night. The coffee had burned dry in the Pyrex pot; Johnson turned it off.

Johnson, Owen, and Holloway passed through the swinging door into the dining room. They noticed a bloody shoe print on the blue carpet at the far end of the dining room, "pointed outward as if someone were walking away from the bedroom area and into the dining room," Owen reported. They turned right, into the den. There was a piano, a grandfather clock, several easy chairs, and a table. On top of a console television set was an elephant carved from expensive black stone with real ivory tusks (which Dorothy had inherited from her mother). In front of the television was an antique settee, covered in silk; a white blanket, which Mrs. Edwards had crocheted, lay on it, rumpled. Her eyeglasses were lying on the coffee table in front of the couch, next to a *TV Guide,* which was open to Saturday night for the shows between 8:00 and 9:00 p.m.: *Joyful News,* a religious show on Channel 16; *Classic Country Music* on 17 and 33; *Resurrection* on HBO; a college basketball game between DePaul and Old Dominion on ESPN. The television was blaring; Johnson turned it off.

Moving back into the foyer, the police and Holloway paused at a drop-leaf table on which Dorothy had placed a silver tray with a decanter and four crystal goblets, several ashtrays, a bowl with artificial fruit, a pair of lined gloves, and a checkbook. This was where Mrs. Edwards put her Aigner clutch purse, Holloway told Johnson. It wasn't there now. They continued to the bedrooms, at the back of the house. On the right was the guest bedroom, with a late-eighteenth-century canopied bed and a small dressing table on which were two porcelain figures, a man and woman in Early American dress, and two family photos in gold-colored frames. Nothing was amiss there.

Dorothy's bedroom was the next room. Her alarm clock, set for 7:00 a.m., was still ringing. Johnson shut it off. The carpet was strewn with a roll of Clorets mints, a penny, some Kleenex, a small leatherette key holder, an AA battery, envelopes, and a "Save 10 Cents" coupon. There was a heavy glass ashtray with an ornate gold rim from which a big piece had been chipped off. Johnson noticed a partial denture, the other portion of what he had seen in the kitchen.

On top of Dorothy's chest of drawers were several sweaters, all neatly folded; a bra; and several family photos in silver frames—one of Dorothy's husband when he was in the navy, one of the two of them, another of Carolyn, and one of her grandchildren. A serrated cake spatula jarred this picture of domestic tranquillity. The handle had dried blood on it; a lipstick-smudged tissue partially covered it. How was it possible that the bloody spatula had ended up there without disturbing anything else?

Dorothy Edwards had slept in a canopied 1800s bed of her own, with four solid posts. There was a night table on each side. From the indentations in the carpet, Johnson determined that the right side of the bed, as he stood at its foot, had been jarred from its normal position against the wall by about six inches. The bed looked recently made, Johnson wrote in his report.

The white carpet near the closet door was saturated with blood. There was more on the wall outside the closet. Johnson opened the closet, and there was Dorothy's bloodied body, just as Holloway had said he'd found it. Her head was almost past the left edge of the door frame, just touching a white chest of drawers in the closet that was streaked with blood.

Johnson quickly walked back through the house and secured the scene. "Cornor Duvall arrived at 12:36," Johnson noted in his report on the investigation, referring to the county coroner, Odell Duvall. Johnson's superior, Capt. Jim Coursey, arrived two minutes later. Like Johnson, Coursey had enlisted upon graduating from Greenwood High, opting for the navy. He was honorably discharged after three years as a parachute rigger third class. Some residents remembered that in high school Coursey had been a hell-raiser and had had his own scrapes with the law. Maybe that made him a better cop, some thought—he understood that every high school boy who drank too much or drove too fast didn't need to be saddled with a criminal record. He also had a reputation for being a redneck, though that did not set him apart at the time.

Johnson filled in Coursey on what he had seen and what Holloway had told him. They went through the house together, and Coursey looked at Mrs. Edwards's body. He knew he was going to need help. This murder would have to be solved and solved quickly to calm elderly widows and, more generally, keep the community at bay.

Coursey went to his car and radioed the police dispatcher. He asked him to notify the South Carolina Law Enforcement Division, in the capital, Columbia, about seventy miles away. SLED, as just about everyone calls it (many South Carolinians don't even know the full name), is the local equivalent of the FBI, coming in to help with complicated crimes. Coursey secured the house; then he, Johnson, and the other Greenwood police officers sat in their cars to get out of the cold while they waited for the SLED agents.

When the call came in at SLED headquarters, two agents from the firearms section, Dan DeFreese and Ira Byrd Parnell Jr. grabbed their 35 mm Nikons, jumped into their state sedan, and sped to Greenwood. When they reached the south edge of the city, on Route 34, Patrolman Holtzclaw was waiting to guide them to Melrose Terrace.

There were no SLED manuals or guidelines for investigations. Parnell and DeFreese took no notes as they went through the house. DeFreese dusted for fingerprints—outside at the screen door, where the killer was thought to have entered; on the kitchen utensils and the wine bottle on the counter; in her bathroom, on the underside of the toilet seat. Parnell squeezed himself into the closet and took pictures of the body and then of the bedroom. Some of the photos showed a pool of blood on the carpet outside the closet. Strangely, there wasn't any blood on the strip of wood under the door, that piece between the carpet in the closet and the carpet in the bedroom. Parnell and DeFreese pulled Mrs. Edwards out of the closet and tied a plastic bag on each of her hands to preserve any evidence under her well-manicured fingernails, such as blood, hair, or skin that she almost certainly would have scraped from her assailant during a struggle. They wedged her into a body bag, robe and all. The agents went through the house, gathering evidence. On the drop-leaf table in the hallway near the front door they found her checkbook. The register, running from September 11, 1981, to January 7, 1982, showed one check for $5, another for $8.75, one for $8, and another for $8.25, written to various payees. And there was check 4031, written on December 30 for $43, made out to Edward Elmore. Holloway told Johnson that Elmore was the handyman who had cleaned the gutters and washed windows recently. In a desk in Mrs. Edwards's living room Coursey found her bank statements, and in the December statement was the check written to Elmore; he had cashed it at the local branch of Bankers Trust before it closed on New Year's Eve.

Late in the afternoon, just before dark, another SLED agent, Tom Henderson, arrived from Columbia. Henderson had grown up across the street from Dorothy Edwards in a lovely ranch-style house on a wooded lot. When his mother, Christine, had seen the police cars and learned that her neighbor had been murdered, she called her son. He jumped into his car and sped to Greenwood.

Greenwood, however, wasn't Henderson's turf; Charley Webber was the resident SLED agent. Webber was a roly-poly, jovial sort who wore his hair long, as he had when he was the trumpet player with the Swingin' Medallions, before he had become a law enforcement officer. He was driving down the street late Monday afternoon when police chief John Young honked for him to pull over. Young told Webber there had been a murder on Melrose Terrace and asked if he would go there. When Webber arrived, he asked Coursey if he needed help. Coursey said no. There was some bad blood between the men since they had both sought the position with SLED and Coursey had been rejected.

Coursey hadn't asked for Henderson either, but *his* offer to help was accepted. Henderson, thirty-nine years old, had been at SLED ten years, after stumbling through early adulthood. "I went to three colleges, five different times, and it took me eleven years to graduate," Henderson said. "Needless to say, I didn't give a damn." He'd also had two stints in the army, including a tour in Vietnam with the Special Forces. The Henderson-for-Webber switch was costly for Elmore. In less than twenty-four hours, Henderson was convinced that Elmore was guilty, a conviction from which he never wavered, while Webber would harbor doubts, which he largely kept to himself.

Robbery did not appear to be the motive for the crime. Mrs. Edwards's $10,000 diamond ring and other valuable jewelry were in plain sight in her bedroom. "Large amounts of silver. Antique silver not disturbed," Johnson said in his report. The only things missing, the police concluded—and this was based on what Holloway told them—were Mrs. Edwards's clutch purse and a .32-caliber pistol, which Holloway said she kept in the nightstand drawer. There was no evidence that she had used the gun, or even tried to, against her attacker.

Indeed, the indications were that she knew her attacker. "It did appear that she was not afraid of the suspect because she had a night chain on the back kitchen door but she did not put it in place and slightly open door but open it wide," Johnson noted in his report. The door had four windowpanes, so she would have seen who her visitor was before letting him in. That alone caused her neighbor Roy Raborn to doubt that Elmore had been the perpetrator. He just couldn't believe that Mrs. Edwards would open the door to a black man late on a Saturday night, even one she knew a bit. "You would be stupid," Raborn said. "I wouldn't do it." And a woman would be even less likely do so if she was dressed in her nightgown.

There was a curious dearth of fingerprints at the crime scene. The SLED forensic investigators found none on the needle-nose pliers lying on the kitchen floor or on the tongs, which were sticking out of the drawer, or on the bloody cake spatula found on the bureau.

Some ten hours after the first policeman had arrived at 209 Melrose Terrace, Sergeant Owen, and Herman Tooley Jr. of the Blyth Funeral Home, took possession of Mrs. Edwards's body from DeFreese and Parnell and took it to Self Memorial Hospital, nine minutes away. Owen recorded this in his report. It was placed in a cooler, at a temperature of thirty-eight degrees Fahrenheit. The cooler was sealed with evidence tape; Owen signed it. The next morning, at 6:00, Owen was back at the hospital. The body was removed from the cooler, and he and Tom McHaney, another Blyth employee, drove it across the state to the Medical University of South Carolina, in Charleston, for an autopsy by Dr. Sandra E. Conradi. They arrived at 10:15.

Six hours later, Owen left the medical school and drove Mrs. Edwards's body to SLED headquarters in Columbia. This was unusual. After an autopsy, a body would normally go to the funeral home. At SLED, Owen and agent Parnell took fingerprints and palm prints from Mrs. Edwards. That explained why the body had been brought to SLED but raised the question of why her fingerprints were needed.

Back in Greenwood, Captain Coursey went to a judge and sought a warrant for the arrest of Edward Lee Elmore. "Probable cause is based on the following facts," Coursey said in his affidavit to the judge. "The deceased body of Dorothy E. Edwards was found at her home at 209 Melrose Terrace, Greenwood, South Carolina, on January 18, 1982, with multiple stab wounds and idencia of her being the victim of rape. A fingerprint of Edward Lee Elmore was found at this residence."

This was shaky. Under the Fourth Amendment, the police may not arrest someone without "probable cause." Basically, that means there has to be enough evidence to convince a reasonable person of the substantial likelihood that the person being arrested committed the crime. Since Elmore had been at Mrs. Edwards's house in December, washing windows for her, it was reasonable that the print was left then. In fact, it might have been there several weeks, or possibly even months. "I can say whose print it was; I can't say when it was put there," SLED agent DeFreese would later testify. Curiously, the police had found only one Elmore fingerprint at the scene. In his request for a warrant, Coursey did not mention the check that Mrs. Edwards had given to Elmore. Even the check plus the fingerprint would not seem to amount to probable cause. Magistrate Charles E. Henderson Jr. issued the warrant.

THE SUSPECT—EDWARD LEE ELMORE

EDWARD LEE ELMORE had grown up in the abject sort of environment that led President Lyndon Johnson to declare a war on poverty. Home was Abbeville, a historic small town fourteen miles west of Greenwood on tree lined Route 72. John C. Calhoun practiced law there from 1807 to 1817 before becoming vice president, secretary of state, senator, and secretary of war. The first Confederate Assembly adopted the Ordinance of Secession here in 1860. A granite plinth rises in the town square, erected by the Daughters of the Confederacy of Abbeville. The inscription on one side: "The world shall yet decide in truth's clear, far-off light, that the soldiers who wore the gray and died with Lee, were in the right." The monument was erected in 1906, destroyed by a fire in 1991, and repaired and put up again by the town in 1996, more than 130 years after the end of the Civil War.

When Elmore was growing up, the "niggers" had their part of town and entered the white areas only to work in the textile mills or as maids or yardmen. They were paid so little that even a middle-class family could afford to employ them. For blacks and whites alike, Greenwood was "the big city," the place to go to the cinema and, in the days before malls and fast-food chains, to shop at Rosenberg's, a clothing store that had been around since 1884, or to eat at The Ranch, a good restaurant. Blacks found Greenwood more racist than Abbeville.

Edward's mother, Mary Ellen Gardner, was the daughter of a

tenant farmer. She was so tiny as a baby, and the family was so poor, that she slept in a drawer. She was sixteen when she had her first child. She'd had a second and was pregnant with her third when she married Henry Odey Elmore. They had a son and a daughter, pneumonia and malnutrition claimed another son in his infancy, then came another daughter, and a year later Mary was pregnant again. In her eighth month, she was diagnosed with toxemia, which can be fatal or result in a mentally retarded child. Mary was hospitalized. After ten days, labor was induced. Edward Lee was born on January 13, 1959.

Henry Elmore was listed as Edward's father, but it is unlikely he was his biological father. Edward had reddish hair and a light complexion. Edward's siblings and playmates taunted him that he had a white father. "His skin was lighter than mine," said Elmore's sister Peggy, whose biological father *was* Henry. When Edward was about two years old, Henry was struck by a car as he walked along Highway 17 in North Carolina. The driver didn't stop. Henry died. The police never did find who hit him. "Probably didn't try very hard," says Peggy. "You know, black man."

After Henry was killed there were always men around Mary, white and black. Some stayed a few hours, others longer. Earl Johnson was around the longest, maybe four or five years, during Edward's early adolescence. He was hardly a role model. He would go into a grocery store and furtively take a package of meat, go off to another aisle, pummel the package a bit, then insist that the grocer give him the meat or sell it at a reduced price.

Drinking and violence were part of the scene, and Edward learned to stay away from his mother's male friends. When Mary got drunk, he would stay away from her as well. She was jailed several times for disorderly conduct. She began giving her son beer at an early age. The family moved from one dilapidated house to another, many without electricity or running water, ahead of the rent collector or after the rent collector had caught up with and evicted them. One day, Eddie and Peggy got off the school bus in front of their public housing apartment and saw their belongings on the street; the family had been evicted again. Shamed and embarrassed, they walked on to a relative's house.

The children picked cotton and peaches and picked up bottles along the roadside. "You'd get five cents from those bottles," Peggy recalled. "We'd buy little stuff to eat, like ice cream." On Sundays little Edward walked barefoot with his mother to Calhoun Falls Baptist Church.

Edward started attending Branch Street Elementary School when he was six. He didn't yet know his colors. Asked to draw a man, he drew two circles, connected them with a diagonal line, and put a squiggly tail on the bottom circle. He was absent more than a third of the time, often because he was forced to scrounge for money, picking up bottles or whatever. He was in the first grade for three years. In the second grade, the kids teased him because he was slow and dim-witted, with speech defects and tics, and his clothes were ragged. His IQ was measured at 61, which psychologists classify as within the range of "mild mental retardation." He quit after the first semester. Edward was twelve years old before he made it to the third grade, at the Langley Milliken School, a quarter of a mile from a large mill. He and Peggy were among the eight blacks sent to integrate the school. They didn't cause any problems. "We got along, we really got along," Peggy said. Peggy and Eddie were close. When she became a teenager and the boys started calling, Eddie would lie on the couch pretending to be asleep, then open one eye and say to the visitor, with a smile, "I got my eye on you."

Edward was "soft-voiced," a teacher noted on his report card. He "likes school—likes playing ball—dislikes spelling most." Even though he couldn't do the work, teachers promoted him through the third and fourth grades. In fifth grade, he dropped out, barely able to read at a second-grade level. He was fourteen but said he was sixteen in order to get a job at the J.P. Stevens textile plant in Abbeville. The machine he worked on would have to be shut down occasionally because of mistakes he made. He didn't like the noise or being inside, and he quit. He wanted to try school again. He was sixteen and school officials thought the other fifth-graders would laugh at him, so they put him into the eighth grade at Wright Middle School. There was no way he could handle that level of work, and after twelve days he dropped out.

As an adult, Elmore would not be able to tell time or draw a clock. He didn't understand the concept of north, south, east, and west or of summer, fall, winter, and spring. He briefly had a checking account but was unable to do the elementary math necessary to have enough in the bank to cover the checks he would write. He never lived on his own. He gave his money to his mother and a girlfriend to pay his bills, as he didn't know how.

He was, however, a steady, trustworthy handyman. He was taken on by Clarence Aiken, a black general contractor who lived on the rough side—he had been shot in a bar brawl and had lost an arm in an automobile accident. Aiken trusted Elmore with the keys to the Abbeville County Courthouse when they were cleaning there. Elmore worked for two weeks cleaning and painting inside the palatial Spartanburg home of Roger Milliken, the textile magnate and one of the richest men in the South. There were never any complaints about his work or his stealing anything.

Elmore worked hard, doing chores around people's homes in some of the most fashionable neighborhoods of Greenwood. In a good week, in good weather, he might earn $600; most of the time he earned between $200 and $300. Many of his customers were elderly widows, friends and neighbors of Dorothy Edwards's. They liked him. "He was a black man that southern women got along with," recalled James Bradford, a lawyer. Elmore painted and did odd jobs for Bradford's mother and his mother-in-law. He was polite, deferential, sweet-natured—in a word, he was "servile," as blacks were supposed to be. Slight of build, he was not at all physically threatening.

Elmore's history was notably void of any clashes with the law. He was never arrested for drugs or drinking. Indeed, he had no criminal record whatsoever, except for a few minor charges arising out of fights with his girlfriend, Mary Dunlap.

They had met at the Depot, a Greenwood nightclub. "Oh, he's so handsome," she said to her girlfriend when she saw him in the crowd. He was taut and had an Afro with a slight reddish tint. She was five foot six, lithe, and beautiful. He came over, introduced himself, and asked her to dance. "That done it, he was my date for the night," she remembered, a glint in her eyes even many years later. She invited him back to her apartment. He was proper. They had a couple of beers, and he left.

A week later, she saw him again at the Depot. "That night he stayed over," she says. Their relationship had begun. She was eight years older and married, with two small children. After she separated from her husband, Elmore moved in. She lived in the Greenwood Gardens Apartments, a small complex of two-story buildings on the south side—the black side—of Greenwood. Mary's apartment, on the ground floor, had two bedrooms, a living room, a kitchen—and three televisions. Elmore brought all his clothes; Mary didn't need a second closet for them.

It was a tempestuous relationship. She was temperamental. He was jealous. "He just wanted me all to hisself," she said. "He didn't want me to do anything unless he was right there." Especially, he didn't like her running around in short shorts and skimpy singlets. That would set off near-childish temper tantrums. But he was a good man. He babysat her children. He gave her money for household expenses. Though he had smoked marijuana as a youngster, he didn't use drugs. He drank beer but didn't get drunk. When he wasn't working, he'd stay at home and watch sports on TV.

They quarreled regularly, and on two or three occasions she complained to the police that he had hit her. She declined to press charges, and some doubted the incidents had ever occurred. There was a correlation between Mary's complaints to the police about Elmore and the failure of her ex-husband to make child support payments. Was Mary taking out her anger at her ex-husband on her new boyfriend? In November 1981, for instance, Mary filed charges against her ex-husband; the next day, she filed a complaint against Elmore, claiming he had hit her. This time she signed a warrant. Elmore was arrested.

He pleaded guilty and was fined $212, all but $40 suspended. Ten days later she called the police and said he had taken her pocketbook out of the car and stolen $60. She declined to prosecute. After that he moved out, but they continued to see each other—and to fight.

On Saturday, January 16, the day the police said Mrs. Edwards was murdered, Elmore had driven from Abbeville to Greenwood, borrowing his sister's 1973 Ford LTD, as he often did, hoping to find work. He first stopped at Kmart, where Mary worked. She told him to come back at four, when she would have her lunch break. He left and drove a short distance to the neighborhood where Mrs. Edwards lived. He first went to Mrs. Wingard's, just around the corner from Dorothy Edwards. Elmore had worked for her before. She didn't need any chores done, but she told Elmore that a neighbor, Mrs. Blaylock, needed her gutters cleaned. He asked Mrs. Wingard to call Mrs. Blaylock to see if she wanted the work done that day. Mrs. Wingard was happy to do so, and Mrs. Blaylock said yes. She was an eighty-seven-year-old widow who for years had taught piano to the neighborhood girls and boys.

The gutters on the Blaylock house were quite small, making it hard to get a hand into them, which meant a lot of cuts. Elmore told Mrs. Blaylock he wanted $30, which she thought was high, but her gutters were quite clogged with leaves and she really wanted them cleaned. She didn't want a black man to think she had that much cash in the house, however, so she said she'd pay by check; he agreed.

He worked only a short time, then left to take Mary to lunch.

Elmore wasn't very happy when Mary came out with two of her coworkers. They all climbed into Elmore's car and drove a few minutes to Po' Folks. She ate; he only drank coffee. He didn't have enough to pay for the meal. She gave him a dollar. He pleaded with her to let him move back in. No. She was firm. They left a few minutes before five, and he drove them back to Kmart. He went back to Mrs. Blaylock's to finish his work.

He didn't do much before it was dark and starting to rain.

"Come inside while I write your check," Mrs. Blaylock said.

It wasn't customary for a white woman to let a black man into her house, but Mrs. Blaylock later testified at Elmore's trial that it was the only humane thing to do; she could not let him stand in the cold. He stayed a few steps inside the door while she went over to the kitchen table and wrote out a check for $15.

He drove to the Kmart shopping center, got out of his car, walked to the pay phone in front of Big Star, and called Mary. She was irritated. She didn't have time to talk, she said. She was doing inventory. But did he have $10? He did, from the $15 check he had just cashed. He walked into Kmart and found her in the shoe department. He gave her the money.

He went back outside and waited. At 9:30, she finished work. She had asked her brother Donnie to pick her up. He was there in Mary's car, a 1976 Mustang, along with his wife, Sue.

Walking to her car, Mary saw Edward parked in front of Big Star. She ignored him. She climbed in with Donnie and Sue, and they drove on Route 25 past the Holiday Inn and McDonald's. They headed to Mary's mother's house, to pick up Mary's daughter. They sat around talking until 10:30 or a bit later, and then they all went to Mary's apartment at Greenwood Gardens.

Around 12:30 a.m., Elmore showed up. When he knocked on the door, Sue opened it. Elmore rushed in and went straight to Mary's bedroom. He'd had a couple of beers. She insisted that he leave. It got louder. Mary's daughter was crying. Mary and Edward were yelling at each other. He asked her if he had left any clothes at her house. No, she said. She had thrown them all away. That set him off again. He took off his coat and started unbuttoning his shirt, then just ripped it off and threw it on the floor. Another temper tantrum.

"Mary, I want you, can't nobody gonna git you," Edward told her.

"I told you to go on, go on, we're through, we've been through," Mary shouted back.

Elmore sat down on the floor. "I ain't goin' nowhere, ain't goin' nowhere without Mary."

He wouldn't leave. So Mary decided she'd leave, go over to her mother's. On her way out, she picked up his shirt and threw it in the kitchen wastebasket, put on her own jacket, turned out the lights, and left. She spent the night at her mother's. Sunday morning, she went back to her apartment. She realized Elmore had spent the night there. He was gone now. She threw his shirt in the trash outside.

Elmore had left about 7:00 a.m., stopped at Fast Fare, a convenience store and gas station, and bought a dollar's worth of gas, enough to get him to his mother's in Abbeville. He spent Sunday drinking beer and watching television.

On Monday, the day Mrs. Edwards's body was found, Elmore went into Greenwood looking for work but decided the weather was too bad and returned home.

THE ARREST

GREENWOOD POLICE, warrant in hand, began looking for Elmore on Tuesday afternoon. He wasn't hiding, hadn't run. He was three blocks away from Mrs. Edwards's house, having resumed his work cleaning the gutters at Mrs. Blaylock's. Less than twenty-four hours before, she had seen the police cars at her friend's house and soon learned what had happened, but she saw no reason to be nervous about Elmore. When he finished, she gave him a check for $15, which he cashed, and then he drove home to Abbeville. That evening, he drove back to Greenwood to see Mary, as if their Saturday fight hadn't happened or they had fought so often that it didn't faze him. It was a repeat of Saturday. Her sister-in-law Sue opened the door and let him in. Mary was in the bedroom. She shouted that she was finished with him and told him to leave. He refused. They argued. He said he was going to buy cigarettes. Mary yelled that when he came back, the door would be locked. That's okay, he said; he would come in the window in the children's bedroom. He'd done that often, and she never objected. He went for cigarettes, came back, and climbed through the window. Again, she demanded that he leave. He wanted to stay.

Mary had had enough. She was going to call the police. She didn't have a phone at home, so she threw her coat on over her nightclothes and stomped out of the apartment. He followed. She got into her Mustang, and he hurriedly climbed in on the passenger side. She drove four blocks to Fast Fare, got out, and walked to the pay phone, which was outside. He was right behind her. She called the police. She told the duty officer that her boyfriend had broken into her apartment and that he wouldn't leave. She and Elmore got back in her car and returned to the apartment. It was after midnight.

The Greenwood Gardens Apartments were only a mile from the Greenwood police station, and within minutes, officers Ray Manley and Randy Miles pulled into the parking lot. They went to building 15, at the south end of the complex, and knocked on the brown door with an *A* on it. Mary let them in and pointed to Elmore. When Manley heard the name, he recalled the arrest warrant that had been issued only a few hours earlier. He radioed for backup.

Detectives Gary Vanlerberghe and Perry Dickenson, who were patrolling nearby, arrived within minutes.

"This is Elmore," Manley told them.

"Are you Edward Lee Elmore?" asked Vanlerberghe.

"Yes, sir."

Vanlerberghe, who had joined the Greenwood Police Department in 1978 after leaving the air force, asked Elmore to step outside, which he compliantly did.

They told him he was being arrested for the murder of a woman on Melrose Terrace. "I didn't do it," Elmore said softly. Elmore's demeanor surprised Vanlerberghe. Elmore didn't resist; he didn't give them any verbal abuse. "Docile" was how Vanlerberghe described him. Maybe he didn't do it, Vanlerberghe thought.

Elmore and four cops, including Manley, a fourteen-year veteran on the force, who was a huge man—280 pounds, with a nineteen-and-a-half-inch neck—walked to the parking lot. The police patted Elmore down, but they didn't handcuff him. They put him in the backseat and drove to the jail, officially called Greenwood Law Enforcement Center, a one-story, sand-colored brick structure built in 1976. It was 2:45 a.m.

Elmore sat at a table across from Detective Dickenson, who was in street clothes. Johnson and Coursey were present. Dickenson read Elmore his Miranda rights, which were printed on a card he carried in his pocket, as police officers around the country have done since the Supreme Court's landmark 1966 ruling in *Miranda v. Arizona* that a defendant's statement to police is inadmissible at trial if the suspect has not been advised of his constitutional rights to a lawyer and to remain silent.

"Do you understand each of these rights I've explained to you?" Dickenson said.

Yes, said Elmore.

"Do you want a lawyer?"

No, Elmore said.

"Do you want to answer questions now?"

He was willing to—but he was befuddled. Who was he charged with murdering? he asked Detective Dickenson again.

"Mrs. Dorothy Edwards."

Elmore said he didn't know any "Mrs. Dorothy Edwards."

"Do you mean to tell me that you do not know Mrs. Edwards, the elderly lady who lives on Melrose Terrace, the street behind the First Baptist Church?" Coursey asked impatiently.

"No, I do not know her," Elmore said.

"You mean you did not do any windows or gutters for Mrs. Edwards?" Coursey said.

"I do windows and gutters, but I don't know a Mrs. Edwards," Elmore said.

There were a lot of seemingly simple things Edward Elmore didn't know or comprehend. He couldn't tell you the street Mrs. Edwards or Mrs. Blaylock lived on, or any of the other people he worked for; he only knew how to get there. He told Dickenson and Coursey he had worked for "Mrs. Henrietta," but Henrietta was the street—near Melrose Terrace—and the woman who lived there was Mrs. Wingard.

Sergeant Johnson showed Elmore the State Farm Insurance card on which he had scrawled Mrs. Edwards's name and phone number; the police had found it in his wallet. Coursey told him that the police had a check for $43 that Mrs. Edwards had written to him and that he had cashed. Now Elmore knew who they were talking about. Coursey asked Elmore if he would give a blood sample. He signed a consent form. Coursey also wanted hair samples. He pulled a comb through Elmore's Afro. He then took him into the shower and ordered him to lower his jeans. He didn't notice any injuries or bruises in the groin area, he would later testify. Coursey pulled on a pair of latex gloves and ran the comb through Elmore's pubic hair. Normally that was all that the police would do; the hairs that were loose and fell out during combing were enough for comparison purposes. But with a tweezers, Coursey yanked out more hairs. Eight or ten hairs, maybe a dozen, are enough for comparison purposes. Coursey collected at least sixty. He put the hairs in a ziplock baggie, which was sent to SLED for analysis.

Tom Henderson took over the questioning. When Elmore was first brought into the police station, Coursey had called Henderson, who was asleep at his mother's. He dressed quickly and was at the jail in minutes. Henderson again advised Elmore of his Miranda rights. Elmore again said he didn't need a lawyer, that he would answer any questions.

Are these your shoes? Henderson asked, showing him the shoes Elmore had been wearing when arrested.

Yes, sir.

How long have you been wearing them?

Long time, said Elmore. He wore them all the time.

All weekend? asked Henderson.

Yes, sir.

On Saturday, the sixteenth?

Yes, sir.

Henderson told him the stains on the shoes looked like blood. Any idea how that got there? Henderson asked.

No, sir, no idea, said Elmore.

Been killing any cows or hogs or any kind of animal, or you

been walking in blood? Henderson asked sarcastically, his signature interrogation technique.

No, sir, Elmore said respectfully.

The interrogation went on for more than two hours. The police had concluded that Mrs. Edwards had been murdered Saturday evening, based on what Holloway had told them, as well as the coffeepot and the alarm clock being on. They asked Elmore what he had been doing that day. He told them about borrowing his sister's car, driving to Greenwood, working for a woman who lived near Mrs. Wingard, driving back to Kmart, eating at Po' Folks with Mary and two friends, finishing at "that lady's house on Henrietta Avenue" (it was Mrs. Blaylock, and she lived on North Street). He went on to say that he had gone back to Kmart and given Mary $10, that she had been picked up by her brother Donnie, that he had gone to her apartment, that she got mad at him and left to go to her mother's, and that he had spent the night. (He did not go into detail about the fight he and Mary had had.)

Henderson dictated a summary of what Elmore had said to a secretary, who typed it up; it was slightly more than a page in length. At 5:05 a.m., Elmore signed it. He'd gone almost twenty-four hours without sleep. Now he was driven to SLED headquarters in Columbia for more interrogation. Henderson and Johnson went with him.

MEANWHILE, the police moved swiftly to gather evidence. It was still dark on Wednesday morning when Dickenson and Vanlerberghe drove to Abbeville. They woke a local judge, Mary Daniels, to countersign a search warrant. Then they went to the Hickory Heights Apartments, where Peggy lived. It was 7:45 in the morning. The police officers knocked on the window of apartment 4F, waking her. Peggy got up and came to the door. Do you have a brother, Edward, she was asked? Yes. They asked for permission to search her car, which was parked in the south lot of the Greenwood Gardens Apartments. They didn't say why. She didn't feel she had any choice. "The police do what they want to," she said later. "I didn't want to go to jail." She signed the consent form. They now told her that her brother had been arrested for murdering a woman. After they left, she drove into Greenwood to see him, to find out what was going on. But he was already in Columbia being questioned by SLED.

The police officers walked over to apartment A, where Edward's mother lived, and Edward, too, when he wasn't with Mary. They introduced themselves and showed Mrs. Elmore the warrant. It authorized them to search for "a ladies clutch purse, money with blood marks, male shoes and male clothing which may contain blood marks and/or hairs of one Edward Lee Elmore or Dorothy E. Edwards, deceased, and a pistol firearm." She couldn't read it, but she wasn't about to say no to any white police officer either, and led them to her son's tiny room, which he shared with his brother. There wasn't much in it. A corduroy jacket and a pair of Levi's were hanging on the door. There were a few small reddish spots on the jeans. The officers took them.

Another Greenwood police team went to Mary Dunlap's apartment in Greenwood. She, too, consented to a search. While there, with the permission they had from Peggy, the police took the LTD and drove it to the station. The police vacuumed the seats and floorboards, front and back, sure they would find some hair or fibers Elmore had picked up while raping and murdering Mrs. Edwards. They came up with half a garbage pail of dirt and debris; Henderson delivered it to SLED for analysis. He described the contents: "Vacuum bag samples from floor of car driven by Edward Elmore on the day he murdered Dorothy Edwards."

Henderson wasn't being careless when he wrote "murdered" and not "allegedly murdered." By that time, he explained during a deposition in the case years later, the police "had firmly reached the conclusion" that Elmore had murdered Dorothy Edwards.

"Area Man Faces Murder Charge" *The Index-Journal* trumpeted in a three-column headline at the top of the page on its Wednesday afternoon paper. And the police considered the case closed. "No other arrests expected," said the police chief, John Young.

The tests on the vacuumed debris revealed nothing. Nor was there any blood in the car. The police found nothing incriminating in Mary's apartment either. They never found Mrs. Edwards's Aigner clutch purse, or the gun, which Holloway said she kept next to her bed. That didn't sway Henderson, the police, or the prosecutor.

THE DEATH PENALTY

Two days after Elmore was arrested, the Greenwood County solicitor, William T. Jones, a powerful and legendary figure, told the court during a hearing following Elmore's arraignment that he intended to seek the death penalty. It was not a surprise, given the history of Jones and the state.

South Carolina has been executing criminals as long as it has existed, as a colony and a state. Hanging rope gave way to the electric chair in 1912, and since 1995, the condemned can choose between the electric chair and lethal injection. The state has the distinction of having put to death the youngest person to be executed in the United States in the twentieth century, George Stinney. An African American, he was fourteen years old when he was convicted, in 1944, of murdering two white girls. The only evidence against him was his supposed confession. An all-white jury convicted him in ten minutes. His arrest, trial, and execution took less than two months.

The American colonies adopted capital punishment from England, where public hanging, burning at the stake, and beheading were the punishments for anyone convicted of a felony, which included shoplifting and stealing a spoon or rabbits, as well as treason, murder, and marrying a Jew. When English juries balked at convicting defendants for petty crimes because they knew it meant death, Parliament steadily reduced the number of capital offenses, until execution could be imposed only for murder and treason. The British government abolished the death penalty altogether in the 1960s, even though polls showed the overwhelming majority of the public supported it.

When it came to writing the Constitution, the Founding Fathers left the issue of execution—along with other punishments—to the states, and hangings continued to be public spectacles. Only a few early American leaders were opposed to the death penalty, most notably Benjamin Franklin and Thomas Jefferson, and the first organized opposition came with the formation of the Society for the Abolition of Capital Punishment in 1845. Many of its members were also active in the antislavery movement. Even back then, and not just in the South, blacks made up a disproportionate number of those executed. It wouldn't happen "to a white man with money," a Boston newspaper wrote about the hanging of a black seaman, Washington Goode, whose case became a rallying cry for abolitionists; some four hundred Concord residents, including Henry David Thoreau and Ralph Waldo Emerson, signed a petition calling on the governor to commute his sentence. Connecticut was the first state to abolish public executions, in 1830, and Michigan was the first state to do away with capital punishment altogether, in 1846, followed quickly by Rhode Island and Wisconsin. (One hundred fifty years later, the Wisconsin district attorney who prosecuted Jeffrey Dahmer, the serial killer who murdered and dismembered at least seventeen boys and men, explained why he was opposed to the death penalty. "I have a gut suspicion of the state wielding the power of death over anybody," said E. Michael McCann. "To participate in the killing of another human being, it diminishes the respect for life. Period.") In the South, punishment by death was tied up with slavery—inciting slaves to run away and the striking of a white person by a slave were capital crimes—and all southern states have the death penalty today.

Executions rose during the Depression, reached a one-year record of 153 in 1947, and then began to taper off as the abolition movement gathered steam, focused now in California and with an assist from Hollywood. Two death row inmates at San Quentin, Barbara Graham and Caryl Chessman, became household names. Graham was a petty criminal, prostitute, and drug addict who was convicted, along with two male friends, of murdering a sixty-four-year-old widow in the course of a robbery; she was put to death in the gas chamber in 1955, two weeks shy of her thirty-second birthday. A movie was made of her case, *I Want to Live!*, with Susan Hayward playing Graham, for which she won an Oscar as best actress. One critic called it a "relentless indictment of capital punishment," while another described it as "a dramatic and eloquent piece of propaganda for the abolition of the death penalty."

Chessman acquired his fame and his role as a cause célèbre for the anti–death penalty movement from his own writings— four books while he was on death row, including *Cell 2455, Death Row.* He never killed anyone and was sentenced to death for a string of assaults on young women on Los Angeles freeways. He earned the sobriquet "Red Light Bandit" for his modus operandi: following young women drivers, he would flash a red light; when they pulled over, he would rob and sometimes rape them. He represented himself at trial and while in prison prepared appeals himself, which earned him several stays of execution. His case attracted international attention, with Pope John XXIII among those calling for Chessman's life to be spared. California governor Edmund G. "Pat" Brown was a devout Roman Catholic, and opposed to the death penalty, but the California legislature rejected a law to abolish the death penalty, and with polls showing that Californians strongly supported Chessman's execution (54 percent to 33 percent), Brown let Chessman go to the gas chamber on May 2, 1960. But the anti–death penalty movement gathered momentum, and a Gallup poll in 1966 found that only 32 percent of Americans supported capital punishment. Support has never been lower, before or since.

Nearly half the individuals being executed were black (even though they made up only some 13 percent of the population), and lawyers at the NAACP Legal Defense and Educational Fund (LDF) were methodically chipping away at capital punishment. Under the direction of two brilliant lawyers, Jack Greenberg and Anthony Amsterdam, the LDF began to lodge appeals in every death sentence case throughout the land. The result was a de facto moratorium. There was only one execution in 1966;

there were two in 1967. State court judges waited to see what the Supreme Court would ultimately say. The answer came in 1972.

Three cases reached the court, those of Lucious Jackson Jr., a twenty-one-year-old black man who raped a white woman, holding scissors against her neck, after escaping from prison; Elmer Branch, a black man of "dull normal intelligence" who raped a sixty-five-year-old white widow in Texas; and William Henry Furman, a twenty-six-year-old black man who murdered a father of five during a botched burglary. Furman had a history of mental problems and was deemed by a state psychiatrist to be mentally incapable of assisting in his own defense; his trial had lasted one day.

The question before the court was limited: Is the imposition and carrying out of the death penalty in these cases cruel and unusual punishment in violation of the Eighth Amendment to the Constitution? The amendment was adopted verbatim by the Founding Fathers from the English Bill of Rights, and it is only sixteen words long: "Excessive bail shall not be required, nor excessive fines imposed, nor cruel and unusual punishments inflicted."

The court had rarely had to consider the clause, and when it did, the issue focused on the method of execution. In 1878, in *Wilkerson v. Utah*, the court upheld execution by firing squad. Twelve years later, in *In re Kemmler*, it upheld the electric chair. One of the more notorious cases to reach the court involved efforts by Louisiana to execute sixteen-year-old Willie Francis for murder. There was no physical evidence linking him to the crime, but he allegedly confessed. On the day set for his execution, he was strapped into the electric chair. The first jolt didn't kill him. The executioner upped the voltage; that also failed to kill him. He was led back to his cell. Appeals followed. The court upheld the right of the state to try again. While what the state was doing was "hardly defensible," Justice Felix Frankfurter wrote, "It is not so offensive to make one puke—it does not shock my conscience." Though he was "strongly against capital punishment," he said that it was a matter for state legislatures, not the Supreme Court.

Those three cases largely represented the state of the law when *Furman v. Georgia* reached the court in 1971. In *Furman,* the issue wasn't the method of execution, but execution per se—was it proscribed by the Eighth Amendment? By a vote of 5–4, the court overturned the sentences.

But the decision was far more complex than it appeared. For starters, the court announced its decision in a very short, unsigned per curiam opinion, something extremely rare. It reflected that the justices were as divided and uncertain on capital punishment as was the general public. Each of the justices wrote a separate opinion, the total coming to more than two hundred pages, one of the longest documents ever produced by the Supreme Court.

Only Justices Thurgood Marshall and William J. Brennan Jr. declared categorically that the death penalty was unconstitutional. "The criminal acts with which we are confronted are ugly, vicious, reprehensible acts," Marshall began his eighty-five-page opinion. "Their sheer brutality cannot and should not be minimized." But the court was not being asked to condone the crimes, Marshall went on; it was only being asked whether the death penalty in each case violated the Eighth Amendment. He then traced the history of capital punishment, noting the decline in the number of crimes for which it was considered appropriate and in its implementation. He concluded that it wasn't a deterrent, and that it was more costly to execute a man than to keep him in prison for life. Finally, he declared, putting a man to death for a crime "is morally unacceptable to the people of the United States at this time in their history."

For Brennan, a punishment was cruel and unusual "if it does not comport with human dignity." And putting someone to death, he wrote, was "fatally offensive to human dignity." The words "human dignity" appear nowhere in the Constitution, and may have sprung from Brennan's Roman Catholic faith.

William O. Douglas was the court's most liberal justice— "the most doctrinaire and committed civil libertarian ever to sit on the court," *Time* magazine wrote in 1975—but he was not willing to go as far as Brennan and Marshall. In his view, it was the arbitrary and capricious manner in which the death penalty was being carried out by the states that rendered it unconstitutional. "One searches our chronicles in vain for the execution of any member of the affluent strata of our society," Douglas wrote. Justice Douglas noted the race, background, and mental faculties of Furman, Branch, and Jackson and, more broadly, that a disproportionate number of blacks, poor, young, and uneducated people, were sent to their deaths.

Justice Potter Stewart saw other evidence of the arbitrary nature of the administration of the death penalty: for the same crime, one person might be executed while ten others were sentenced to life in prison. In an opinion only ten paragraphs long, Stewart said that a death sentence was cruel and unusual "in the same way that being struck by lightning is cruel and unusual."

Among the dissenters was Justice Harry Blackmun. "I yield to no one in the depth of my distaste, antipathy, and, indeed, abhorrence, for the death penalty," he began. "Were I a legislator," he went on, "I would vote against the death penalty." But he was a justice and this was a court, and he could find nothing in history or law or earlier court decisions to justify overturning the death penalty.

The court's decision in *Furman* overturned the death penalty in the forty states where it could be applied and in the District of Columbia as well as for the federal government; across the country some six hundred death row inmates had their lives spared, more than half of them African American. Opponents of capital punishment rejoiced. Prematurely. While the court said the death penalty was unconstitutional as it was being administered, the justices (except for Brennan and Marshall) left open the possibility that capital punishment could be administered in ways that were constitutional.

Death penalty proponents went to work. In California, a ballot initiative to reinstate the death penalty, which was backed by Governor Ronald Reagan, was approved by nearly two to one. Within five months after *Furman*, the Florida legislature had enacted a new death penalty law, and other legislatures quickly followed. The new laws varied from state to state, but in general they limited the death penalty to aggravated murder, rape, and kidnapping; provided for bifurcated trials—first on the question of guilt or innocence, and if the defendant was found guilty, a second phase on the question of sentence—and placed requirements on judges and juries before they could impose it.

The Supreme Court spoke again in 1976, in *Gregg v. Georgia* and companion cases from Texas, Louisiana, North Carolina, and Florida. The new capital punishment laws were upheld. Eventually, when the pro–death penalty legislators and lawyers were finished, the capital punishment map looked a lot like it did pre-*Furman*: executions were permitted in thirty-eight states, primarily in the South and West, and by the federal government.

The first person executed after *Furman* and *Gregg* was Gary Gilmore, who killed a gas station attendant one day and a motel clerk the next. Gilmore, who had spent most of his life in prison or on the run, wanted to die; he did not want his lawyers to seek a stay from the Supreme Court. He was shot by a five-man firing squad in Utah in 1977. The case drew international attention, and Gilmore's life was portrayed in a landmark book by Norman Mailer, *The Executioner's Song*. The death penalty was back. What has become known as the modern era of the death penalty had begun.

THE PROSECUTOR

BEFORE JONES COULD proceed to trial against Elmore, he had to seek an indictment from a grand jury. The grand jury requirement is rooted in English common law and was enshrined in the Magna Carta as a check on the king's power. In the American colonies, grand juries continued to serve as a check on royal powers by refusing to indict individuals who refused to pay taxes and duties imposed by Britain. The Founding Fathers understandably preserved the grand jury. The Fifth Amendment provides that "no person shall be held to answer for a capital, or otherwise infamous crime, unless on a presentment or indictment of a Grand Jury. . . ." The grand jury is no longer used in Britain, and the Fifth Amendment grand jury requirement has not been extended by the Supreme Court to the states (though other provisions of the amendment have been). By their own laws, most states require a grand jury in serious cases. Proceedings are in secret, and neither the defendant nor his lawyer is present. It is also debatable how effective the grand jury is as a shield against abuse of authority. "A competent prosecutor can get a grand jury to indict a ham sandwich," a New York judge once said. (Prosecutors also use the grand jury as an investigative tool, subpoenaing witnesses to help them solve a crime or to find enough evidence to indict an individual. They are often used this way in cases involving organized crime or terrorism.)

A few months before asking the grand jury to indict Elmore, Jones had brought the same panel the case of a prominent member of the community, a white man, who had shot and killed a black man walking across his property at night. In the secrecy of the grand jury room, Jones made it clear that he did not think an indictment was appropriate. The accused was an upstanding member of the community, Jones said, and he asked the grand jurors what they would have done if they had seen a black man on their property in the dark. Wouldn't they have picked up a shotgun? he said to the jurors. The grand jury declined to indict.

Jones didn't present much evidence in the Elmore case—the testimony of a couple of police officers and the gruesome photographs of Mrs. Edwards stuffed in the closet. It took less than twenty minutes. "It was bim, bam, thank you ma'am," recalled Barry Raborn, at thirty-six the youngest member of the all-white grand jury. Raborn told Jones he didn't think he should be serving; he had grown up three doors from Mrs. Edwards—a remarkably attractive lady, he thought—and his father had been a pallbearer at her funeral. He had gone to high school with two of the police officers in the case. Nevertheless, Jones kept him. Raborn abstained from voting for or against an indictment; years later, he would conclude that he had been wrong not to oppose it. It wouldn't have made much difference, except to his conscience.

In addition to murder, the grand jury handed up an indictment for criminal sexual conduct, burglary, housebreaking, armed robbery, and larceny. There was never any doubt the jury would indict. Greenwood grand juries always did what Jones wanted, followed him like sheep, said Raborn. "If he said it was dark outside in the middle of the afternoon, they'd say, 'You're right.' "

WILLIAM TOWNES JONES III was a Greenwood institution—renowned, powerful, and feared. "He was the sort of person for whom the cliché about taking up all the air in the room could have been invented," said a lawyer who knew him. He was about five eight or five nine, of average build. He prided himself on being physically tough and had a firm handshake. Vain about his age, a dapper dresser in a conservative, old-fashioned way—he wore a fedora long after they had gone out of style—Jones was charismatic. At the same time, he appeared to be openly needy, a man who seemed to suffer in front of your eyes. He was born into the landed gentry, in the quaint-sounding Ware Shoals, just up the road from Greenwood. His father had lost the land to drink and the Depression, but by dint of his smarts (Phi Beta Kappa at the University of South Carolina), street savvy, and intensity of will, young Jones had risen. He had a ferocious temper and a reputation as a bit of a bully; no one crossed "Willy T.," as just about everyone called him—though never when he was within earshot. "If he was on your side, you had a friend; if not, you had an enemy," residents said. When Domino's Pizza opened in Greenwood, the phone company gave it the number 229–1111. Jones's law office number was 223–1111. He was soon getting calls for pizza delivery. Annoyed, he demanded that the phone company change Domino's number. Domino's resisted. Jones prevailed.

For years, being county prosecutor was a part-time job in South Carolina, and in his private practice Jones hired talented young law graduates and taught them the practical aspects of the craft. Ron Motley, one of the nation's premier trial lawyers, who earned his name—and millions—suing asbestos and to-bacco companies and years later would represent some of the relatives of the victims of the 9/11 attacks, got his start with Jones. Jones was a "blue dog" Democrat, and at the 1972 Democratic National Convention in New York he met a young southerner who had just finished Yale Law School. He had been so impressed by the recent graduate that he offered him a job. Bill Clinton declined, saying he had decided to go back to Arkansas and enter politics.

Jones was elected solicitor, as South Carolina calls its prosecutors, in 1952 and reelected every four years until he retired in 1984 and was succeeded by his son Townes.

IN THE ADVERSARIAL American criminal justice system, Jones would square off with Elmore's lawyers, with the judge sitting as impartial referee and the jury deciding who won, as it were It is sometimes called "trial by combat." But for the prosecution, for the state, winning is not synonymous with a conviction, or at least it is not supposed to be. The state's interest "in a criminal prosecution is not that it shall win a case, but that justice shall be done," Justice George Sutherland wrote in 1935 for a unanimous Supreme Court in *Berger v. United States*. The court overturned a conspiracy conviction in part on the grounds that the prosecutor had exceeded permissible bounds in his cross-examination. The prosecutor should "prosecute with earnestness and vigor," observed Sutherland, a conservative Republican from Utah. "But, while he may strike hard blows, he is not at liberty to strike foul ones. It is as much his duty to refrain from improper methods calculated to produce a wrongful conviction as it is to use every legitimate means to bring about a just one."

Thirty-two years later, in 1967, Justice Byron White expressed the same view. "Law enforcement officers have the obligation to convict the guilty and to make sure they do not convict the innocent," he wrote in *United States v. Wade*. Though appointed by President Kennedy, White was not a liberal on the court and tended to side with the prosecution over the defense. He had, for instance, dissented a year earlier in *Miranda*.

The American Bar Association sets the standards and ethical codes for lawyers. "The duty of the prosecutor is to seek justice, not merely to convict," says the ABA's Criminal Justice Standards. It elaborates: "Although the prosecutor operates within the adversary system, it is fundamental that the prosecutor's obligation is to protect the innocent as well as to convict the guilty, to guard the rights of the accused as well as to enforce the rights of the public."

At the time Jones was chief prosecutor in Greenwood, his counterpart in Los Angeles, Stephen Trott, was teaching young deputies what this ethical obligation meant. When one of them would come to him and say he was facing an ethical problem because he had discovered evidence that would help the defense, and if he turned it over, the state would lose, Trott would say, "That's not an ethical problem. The ethical answer is easy. Turn it over." Or a deputy would inform his boss that he'd concluded his star witness was lying. Trott, who would go on to serve as assistant attorney general in the criminal division of the Justice Department during the Reagan administration and as a judge on the Ninth Circuit Court of Appeals, would say, "You don't have an ethical problem. You don't have a case. Dismiss it." That's the pinnacle of a prosecutor adhering to his ethical duty. "I wonder how many of today's senior prosecutors tell their juniors stories like that one," said Mark Kleiman, who had worked for Trott.

Apparently, not Jones. After Mrs. Edwards's fingerprints had been taken at SLED headquarters and the hairs found on her body during the autopsy had been examined, the evidence against Elmore was weak at best, and the evidence was stronger that another, unknown, person may have committed the murder. But the police stopped their investigation once they had arrested Elmore, and Jones, far from dismissing the case, proceeded to trial.

CHAPTER TWO

Speedy Trial

J USTICE DELAYED IS JUSTICE DENIED" goes the popular legal maxim, which is traced back to the Magna Carta. But speedy justice can be injustice, too. In Elmore's case, everyone seemed to be in a hurry. Generally, the time between a murder and the opening of a trial is at least a year, and often several. The state has to find evidence, as well as locate and interview witnesses. The defense, lacking the police resources of the state, has an even more difficult and time-consuming job.

But only eighty-four days after Mrs. Edwards's body was found, *The State of South Carolina v. Edward Lee Elmore* opened, on Monday, April 12, 1982, the day after Easter. It was reported on the front page of *The Index-Journal*, but foreign news dominated that day. "Strikes, Arab rioting sweep West Bank" was the six-column headline over a story out of Jerusalem. Beneath that was a story about the war between the United Kingdom and Argentina over the Falkland Islands. In Washington, D.C., John W. Hinckley Jr. was about to go on trial for the attempted assassination of Ronald Reagan. On the West Coast, Mount Saint Helens went quiet after an eruption that had begun three weeks earlier.

The trial was held in the Greenwood County Courthouse, a sand-colored, two-story brick building. In front is a cherry tree donated by Fujifilm when it located its North American headquarters on a leafy campus on the outskirts of the town. The court is located at 528 Monument Street. The monument for which it is named sits in the shadow of a magnificent magnolia tree on the south side of the building and is dedicated to "Our Confederate Soldiers." Erected in 1903 by the Ladies Memorial Association of Greenwood County, and carefully maintained ever since, the monument consists of a Confederate soldier with his rifle standing atop a Greek column and is almost as tall as the courthouse. The inscription reads:

1861–1865

PATRIOTS

Who animated by the same faith, actuated by the same love of country, beset with the same trials and dangers, endured with the same fortitude, and fought as heroically to maintain local self government as did the colonial fathers to attain the same, and with them are immortalized in the same halo of glory.

The courthouse was built in 1968. An open stairwell leads to a second-floor lobby and the courtroom, which has tall, solid double doors. There are no windows—the interior walls are brick—but the high ceiling gives a feeling of spaciousness. It can hold some 250 spectators on church-like pews divided into three sections. The judge's bench is elevated.

THE JUDGE

"Ladies and gentlemen of the jury, if you would give me your attention just for a few minutes," Judge E. C. Burnett III, who had just turned forty, intoned as he opened the trial of Edward Lee Elmore. Black-robed and bespectacled, he was flanked on his right by the American flag and on his left by the South Carolina state flag, a banner with a white crescent and a palmetto tree against a deep blue background that was designed for the South Carolina troops who fought the British. Burnett, an avid golfer and devout Christian, was a circuit court judge from Spartanburg, sixty miles northeast of Greenwood. "I've been assigned to Greenwood for a week of general sessions court, which is commonly referred to as criminal court," he explained to the men and women who had been summoned for jury duty.

After graduating in 1964 from Wofford College, the small liberal arts school Dorothy Edwards's husband attended, Burnett served in the army, including a tour in Vietnam. Following his military service, he earned a law degree from the University of South Carolina, then returned to his hometown, engaged in the private practice of law, and served one term in the South Carolina House of Representatives. He was appointed a probate judge in 1976 and later a family court judge. He would go on to serve thirty years as a judge by the time he retired from the Supreme Court in 2007, a longevity record in South Carolina. He was politically conservative, and he had occasionally allowed his politics to triumph over the discipline expected of judges. Some years after the Elmore trial, he signed an anti-abortion ad, which brought a reprimand from the South Carolina Supreme Court for taking a public stance on an issue that might come before the court. The South Carolina Bar Association rated him "least qualified" when he was later being considered for a seat on the state's Supreme Court, but politics trumped merit. The legislature appoints circuit court judges and Supreme Court justices, and black lawmakers cut a deal: they voted for Burnett for the Supreme Court in exchange for white legislators agreeing to a black judge on the circuit court.

While sitting on the high court, Burnett embroiled himself in another controversy. His daughter, a Spartanburg schoolteacher, sent him an e-mail that mocked blacks. The subject was "Vocabulary Words." A student named Leroy is asked to use the words in a sentence.

"AFRO—I got so mad at my girl, AFRO a lamp at her."

"KENYA—I needed money for the subway, so I axe a stranger KENYA spare some change."

"DIMENSION—I be tall, dark, handsome and not DIMEN-SION smart."

There were eighteen examples in all.

"I don't see anything racially offensive in it," Burnett told *The State*, Columbia's largest-circulation newspaper, which got hold of the e-mail. "I just thought it was funny." Only after black lawmakers held a news conference and demanded an inquiry did Burnett apologize.

As a trial judge, Burnett was to be an impartial arbiter on matters of law, a role that evolved in the seventeenth and eighteenth centuries, when judges were responsible for adducing the facts of a case, examining and cross-examining witnesses for the prosecution and defense. Today, judges in most European countries, except for Britain, supervise investigations, gather facts and evidence, and examine witnesses. An American judge may overturn a jury's finding of guilty if he deems the evidence does not support the verdict, but he may not find a defendant guilty if the jury has returned a not guilty verdict. At the time of Elmore's trial, Burnett had been a trial judge for only seven months, and this was his first capital case.

THE DEFENSE LAWYERS

THE TWO BEST criminal defense lawyers in Greenwood were James Bradford and Rauch Wise, both in their early thirties. Wise could not represent Elmore because he had a conflict: the victim's daughter, Carolyn, had once worked for his law partner. Besides, he and Bradford had just finished a capital trial and were not emotionally or financially ready to take on another.

Therefore, the public defender became Elmore's lead lawyer. Geddes Dowling Anderson was a lanky six-foot-four swashbuckler with a smart mustache and a fondness for Panama hats. Some thought he looked like Gregory Peck or was even more handsome. Most good trial lawyers have a bit of actor in them, and while a student at the University of South Carolina—where he enrolled after being tossed out of Clemson—he performed the lead male role in *Bus Stop,* playing Bo Decker, the cowboy who chases Cherie (played by Marilyn Monroe in the film version). Bitten by the acting bug, he dropped out of school and headed to Hollywood, driving day and night across the country in a 1950 Ford. He studied at the Pasadena Playhouse, got bit parts in the ABC series *Bronco,* and befriended the musician David Crosby, who had yet to team up with Stephen Stills and Graham Nash. After a year and a half, Anderson returned to South Carolina and tried again at Clemson, where a brother, Joe, was now the star quarterback. Geddes didn't excel at anything, except maybe partying, and he was thirty-two before he finally managed to complete law school, at the University of South Carolina.

By his own account, he should have stayed in California. "I probably would have been a lot happier, as well as a hell of a lot more successful," he said many years later, sitting in his office with threadbare carpet. Creditors and the IRS seemed to knock on his office door more than clients did. He sought the public defender job, which would guarantee him a steady income of $12,000 a year.

Anderson was as affable as they come, and in truth, he was pretty good in the courtroom—when he was sober. Around town, bartenders called him "the bourbon cowboy." (They were sure they had seen him on television as the Marlboro man; they hadn't.) He was busted twice for drunk driving, once while he was the public defender, which caused some of the cops to laughingly wonder what it would be like for a prisoner to find himself sharing a cell with Anderson. During the trial, Elmore smelled alcohol on Anderson's breath every day, and his behavior in the courtroom reinforced the suspicion that he had been drinking when he should have been preparing. Anderson insists he was "perfectly sober" throughout the trial. "I wasn't even hungover one day," he said. SLED investigator Tom Henderson scoffed at that: "Geddes Anderson was drunk through the whole trial."

Under South Carolina law, because Elmore was facing a possible death sentence, he had to have two lawyers (a requirement in most death penalty states). Finding a second chair for Elmore wasn't easy. There were some thirty lawyers in Greenwood, all white and male, save for Solicitor Jones's daughter Selma. None rushed to take the case of a black man accused of killing a prominent white woman. When the town's lawyers realized the court was going to appoint one of them, they raised $5,000, which they offered to any lawyer who would take the case. It was kind of like buying your way out of the military during the Civil War.

John Beasley stepped forward. He was an undistinguished criminal defense lawyer, known around town for boasting that he really didn't care much for work. Saturday was his favorite day of the week, he would tell friends; he liked it so much, he got up earlier that day, he said. His father, Hugh, the county prosecutor for the twenty-six years before Jones took over, was a staunch segregationist, and routinely used the word "nigger." His son was more guarded, but he once slipped, referring to Elmore as a "redheaded nigger."

Anderson and Beasley couldn't comprehend Elmore. He was courteous and polite, but he was so uncommunicative. He wasn't like other men Anderson had defended, who'd scream, "I didn't do it, I didn't do it! Here's what happened." Elmore just quietly kept saying he hadn't killed Mrs. Edwards. Anderson never considered that Elmore's reticence, his inability to articulate what happened, might reflect his mental limitations. Even less did he imagine that perhaps Elmore was telling the truth, that he was indeed innocent. "In my judgment the son of a bitch did it," Anderson said years after the trial. "I was convinced of that at the time, and I still am."

Nonetheless, Anderson had an ethical obligation to defend Elmore vigorously. Even if he puts no witnesses on the stand and presents no evidence, a defense lawyer in a criminal trial must test the state's case, require it to prove the defendant guilty beyond a reasonable doubt. The obligations of the defense counsel and prosecutor are notably different. The prosecutor "must be dedicated to making the criminal trial a procedure for the ascertainment of the true facts surrounding the commission of the crime," Justice Byron White wrote in 1967, in *United States v. Wade*. "But defense counsel has no comparable obligation to ascertain or present the truth." White continued: "Our system assigns him a different mission. He must be and is interested in preventing the conviction of the innocent, but, absent a voluntary plea of guilty, we also insist that he defend his client whether he is innocent or guilty." Ethical restraints that operate on the prosecution do not apply to the defense counsel. He need turn over nothing to the state that will help the state's case, while the prosecution is required to turn over all evidence to the defense. During cross-examination, a prosecutor is not supposed to seek to undermine a witness who he knows is telling the truth; a defense lawyer may. "As part of the duty imposed on the most honorable defense counsel, we countenance or require conduct which in many instances has little, if any, relation to the search for truth," Justice White wrote.

In capital cases, the obligation of the defendant's lawyer is even greater. "While defense counsel has the obligation to render effective, quality representation in all criminal cases, defense counsel in a capital case must, given this extraordinary penalty, make extraordinary efforts on behalf of the accused," the ABA says in its Criminal Justice Standards. With his client's life at stake, "defense counsel should endeavor, within the bounds of law and ethics, to leave no stone unturned in the investigation and defense of a capital client."

Anderson and Beasley did virtually nothing. They consulted no independent experts, no pathologists, no fingerprint specialists. They didn't search for witnesses; didn't talk to any of Mrs. Edwards's neighbors; didn't interview Mr. Holloway, who had found the body. They didn't even read the police interviews with the witnesses, which the prosecution had turned over to them as required by law. Ever since the time that defense lawyers first began to appear in criminal cases under English common law, their obligation has been to force the state to prove its case. Anderson and Beasley accepted the state's case more than they challenged it. They stipulated to the admissibility into evidence everything Jones wanted to introduce—hair, fingerprints,

Elmore's blue jeans and coat—ninety-eight items altogether. This meant that Jones didn't have to establish the "chain of custody," that is, who had had possession of each item and where it had been, in order to rebut any chances of tampering. "I have respect for the SLED team, and they're the best we have in South Carolina, and I assumed they were not going to contaminate the evidence," Anderson explained.

THE JURY

WITH THE SIXTH AMENDMENT, the Founding Fathers guaranteed an accused the right to trial by an impartial jury, and in 1968, the Supreme Court said this right applied to cases in state courts as well. "The guarantees of a jury trial in the Federal and State Constitutions reflect a profound judgment about the way in which law should be enforced and justice administered," Justice White explained in *Duncan v. Louisiana,* which held that even if a person was charged with only a misdemeanor, he had the right to a jury trial if he wanted one.

The Constitution says nothing about how an "impartial" jury is to be selected. It is the judge's responsibility to ensure an unbiased jury, and he is helped in getting one through a process known to lawyers as voir dire: The judge, prosecutor, and defense counsel question the men and women who have been summoned for jury duty. Many questions are routine: Do you know any of the police, the prosecutor, the defense counsel? Have you heard anything about the case that would prejudice you in reaching a verdict? How do you feel about capital punishment?

Jones and Anderson also asked members of the jury pool about their religious affiliations and views. Did they go to church? If so, which one? How did they feel about the biblical axiom of an eye for an eye, a tooth for a tooth? Or were they more New Testament, prone to turning the other cheek?

Solicitor Jones was a member of the same Episcopal church as Dorothy Edwards. But he wasn't looking for Episcopalians, because their church is opposed to the death penalty. Jones wanted Southern Baptists, members of the most conservative church in a conservative region, among the staunchest believers in capital punishment. Get more than four Southern Baptists on the jury, and once your client is convicted, he's doomed to be sentenced to die, death penalty lawyers say. Whites tend to support the death penalty more than blacks, men more than women, married persons more than singles, wealthy people more than poor people, suburbanites more than urbanites. And individuals who believe in capital punishment are generally more inclined to convict, to believe the police and the prosecutor.

Frances Carolyn Mann was the first member of the panel to be questioned. She fit the profile of a pro prosecution juror: ninth-grade education; owned several guns—a stainless steel .357 Magnum, an Ithaca riot gun, a .22 Magnum, and a .25 automatic; her current husband ran the Central Detective and Security Agency.

"Mrs. Mann, I don't want to embarrass you, but isn't it a fact that your husband has a pending indictment against him in this court?" Anderson asked.

"Yes, sir, he does."

Anderson asked Judge Burnett to disqualify her. "She doesn't want to have him on her husband, I can tell you that," Anderson said, referring to Jones. Burnett disagreed. She could sit.

The law gives the prosecution and defense preemptory challenges, the right to dismiss a potential juror without giving any reason. In South Carolina at the time, Anderson had ten; he exercised his first to dismiss Mrs. Mann. He used his second and third against the next two on the panel.

Then came Elizabeth Pinson, fifty-five years old.

Have you formed an opinion about this case? Judge Burnett asked.

Just about everyone had, she said. It was a revealing observation about the press coverage of the murder and the chances of Elmore getting a fair trial. More candor and insight followed. Do you feel like you could give Edward Lee Elmore a fair and impartial trial? Beasley asked. "I feel that I have an obligation to the people that I know real well who are terrified because of this, and I think if I were on the jury, they would expect me to feel for all of them who were close to her and who saw the situation and who—and whose lives did change because of this."

Did she believe in an eye for an eye, a tooth for a tooth? Beasley asked.

"I'm not a vindictive person, but I still—I feel some obligation to the little old ladies of the community."

Beasley argued to Judge Burnett that given these views, Mrs. Pinson could hardly be a fair and impartial juror, and asked that she be disqualified. Burnett declined to do so. Beasley exercised another preemptory challenge.

The defense had only one left when Joseph Chalmers was called. He looked like a good juror for the defense: Methodist and one of the most educated members of the jury pool, with a BS in industrial engineering from Clemson, '49. He lived in the fashionable Belle Meade neighborhood, a couple of miles from Melrose Terrace.

Anderson asked him if he had read about the case.

Yes.

Had that caused him to form an opinion?

His answer reinforced what Mrs. Pinson had said. "Well, the newspapers pretty much put the facts on you," he said, "that they'd found the guilty person, and certainly I went ahead and believed that."

Still, Anderson accepted Chalmers for the jury; by virtue of his education and religion, he might vote for a life sentence rather than execution. Chalmers was sent off to wait while the jury selection continued.

The process of selecting a jury had already been long and taxing when forty-seven-year-old Augustus Covington was called. Would you be prejudiced against the State of South Carolina or the solicitor because they asked for the death penalty? Judge Burnett asked Covington, as he had other potential jurors.

"I wouldn't be prejudiced, but I don't approve of no death penalty," Covington answered.

"You do not approve of the death penalty?" Burnett repeated.

Covington answered with a shake of his head.

"My religion teach me, the Bible says, 'Thou shalt not kill.' "

Mere opposition to the death penalty wasn't enough by itself to disqualify Covington from serving. In a landmark case, *Witherspoon v. Illinois,* the U.S. Supreme Court held that an Illinois statute allowing the prosecution to remove a potential juror who had "conscientious scruples against capital punishment" was unconstitutional. A jury should reflect a cross-section of the community, and in every community there are individuals who oppose capital punishment, the court said. Only if a potential juror said that under no circumstances could he impose the death penalty could he be removed for cause, the court ruled.

Judge Burnett had to probe further.

"If the evidence in the case and the law supports the death penalty, could you bring back a recommendation of death by electrocution for this defendant?" Burnett asked Covington.

"No, I don't—I don't see—I don't approve of the death. The Bible says 'Thou shalt not kill.' "

"So, no matter what the evidence and no matter what the law is, as I understand you, you could not recommend that this defendant be sentenced to death?"

"No, sir. My mother didn't teach this."

After more questions, Judge Burnett decided that Covington should not sit on the jury. He dismissed three others because they were opposed to capital punishment.

One juror was still to be selected when the bailiff notified Judge Burnett that Mr. Chalmers wanted to speak to him. He was brought back into the courtroom. He'd neglected to tell the court something when he'd been questioned earlier. "Selma Jones is a very close friend," he now told Burnett. "She is my daughter's closest friend."

Not only was Selma the solicitor's daughter, but the twenty-six-year-old was right there in the courtroom, at the counsel table, sitting next to her father. She was the assistant prosecutor.

William T. Jones didn't think a thing like personal friendship should keep someone off the jury. "This is a small community," he told Judge Burnett. "As a matter of fact, we all feel pretty close; even when we square off in battle we feel pretty close, Judge." To disqualify Chalmers because of his daughter's friendship with Selma "would be prejudicial to the state," Jones argued. Burnett ruled that he would not disqualify Chalmers.

It took two days to pick the jury of five men and seven women, two of whom were black. The foreman was a thirty-two-year-old assistant treasurer at Greenwood Savings and Loan, James Sherrer. He was a member of South Main Baptist Church, and agreed with the biblical injunction "an eye for an eye." While in the army in Vietnam, he "killed five or six, I don't know," he said during the voir dire.

Jury selection ended at 7:45 p.m., and SLED agents then escorted each juror to his or her home to pick up clothes and toiletries, and then to the Holiday Inn, a few miles away. Telephones and televisions were removed from the rooms.

THE OPENING STATEMENTS

"Is the state ready?" Judge Burnett asked on Wednesday morning.

"Yes, Your Honor," said Jones.

It was time for opening statements. The state goes first. It is the opportunity for the prosecution to lay out the state's case, to alert jurors to what is coming, making it easier for them to follow the evidence as it is presented. A prosecutor has wide latitude in the opening argument, as does the defense counsel when his turn comes. He must only be careful not to promise the jury something that he does not later deliver; he has to be careful, that is, if the defense lawyer is alert.

Jones was to the courtroom born. He was theatrical and damn good. He would cry. He would pound on the heavy wooden counsel table so hard it would jump. As would the jurors. He carried a pocketknife. While making an argument, he'd pull it out and begin cleaning his nails, glaring at the defendant, his back to the judge and jury. He limped, telling the jury that as a child his family had been so poor that his diet had been deficient in calcium and one of his legs was deformed. Even his own children weren't sure if this was true or a bit of the lore around the man; his limp was noticeably less pronounced when he wasn't in front of a jury.

Jones was said to have prosecuted more cases than any man in South Carolina history. He was livid if he lost, and he rarely did. "When it came to prosecuting a case, nobody could touch William T. Jones," the South Carolina General Assembly declared in a tribute when Jones died in 1998, at the age of seventy-six. "He will long be remembered as a master at courtroom rhetoric—many a legal opponent learned that the hard way," the homage read. "They dreaded having to match wits and wisdom with him, and the records show why." William Townes Jones suffered from Lou Gehrig's disease; one of the finest orators in the South lost his voice before dying.

The courtroom was crowded as Jones gave his opening statement. He was wearing a dark suit, a white shirt, a narrow tie, and shoes that looked like they needed a polish. The courtroom spectators were noticeably divided by race throughout the trial. On the right, behind the prosecution table, sat Mrs. Edwards's neighbors and friends from the Episcopal church, as well as police officers and ordinary citizens, all white. They easily outnumbered Elmore's supporters—his mother, sisters, and brothers, along with Elmore's pastor, Rev. Emanuel Spearman, and members of his Mt. Olive Baptist Church. Some members were afraid to come to the trial, however. "The Klan is gonna blow your ass up," a member of the congregation told him. When Spearman's support for Elmore became known around Greenwood, the white owner of the restaurant where he had been eating breakfast regularly for more than a year—a member of his congregation was a cook there—told him he was no longer welcome.

An easel had been set up. It held four sketches of Mrs. Edwards's house, drawn to scale for Jones by Susan Smith, a city employee. He walked to the easel and, using a pointer, meticulously led the jurors through the state's case, room by room. This is the carport, this is the back step, this is the kitchen, this is the stove, this is the sink, he said, moving his pointer as he talked. He presented a blowup of the back door and kitchen. The crime had begun there, he said. He pointed to a drawing of the needle-nose pliers, of the partial denture, of the tongs sticking out of the drawer. He took that one down and put up a drawing of the bedroom. His pointer moved to the bed. "And in this area, we will attempt to show this: that there were found fifty-three hairs," Jones told the jurors. He paused dramatically. "During this trial, may I say that I hope we're not too timid to deal with talking about exactly what we have to talk about, such as pubic hairs, and all of that." That gave the jurors something to anticipate—pubic hairs on the victim's bed?

Jones orated and exhorted for an hour, without a note.

What a performance, thought Ed Eubanks, a young law student from nearby Abbeville who had come specifically to observe Jones. Reading the newspapers at the time of the crime and Elmore's arrest, Eubanks had no doubt Elmore was guilty. After listening to Jones, Eubanks thought, "Hell, he could convince me that *I* did it."

Jones began calling his witnesses, starting with the policemen and SLED investigators—Holtzclaw, Cook, Owen, Johnson, Parnell, DeFreese. Collectively, they told the jury how they were called to 209 Melrose Terrace on Monday, January 18; how they had found Holloway there; how he had told them he had gone to check on his neighbor because he saw her car in the driveway when he thought she was going to be out of town. When Jimmy Holloway was on the stand, answering Jones's questions, he verbally walked the jurors through the house, just as he physically had led the police officers: denture and needle-nose pliers on the kitchen floor, coffeemaker set for 6:00 a.m., ringing alarm clock in Mrs. Edwards's bedroom, blood in the bathroom, Mrs. Edwards stuffed into the closet. Anderson hadn't interviewed Holloway.

Serologist John Barron, who had worked at SLED for eight years, was called to the stand. Answering questions from Jones, he testified that he had found only five small spots of blood on the blue jeans that had been taken from Elmore's room. Three were type A, Mrs. Edwards's blood type. Elmore had type B blood, Barron told the jury. He had tested scrapings from the bottle tongs: type A. He had tested scrapings from under Mrs. Edwards's fingernails. All he found was her blood.

When SLED agent DeFreese was on the stand, the state's case unexpectedly headed toward a constitutional derailment. Jones asked him about the fingerprint he found at the back door and how it had been linked to Elmore. Anderson objected: DeFreese should not be permitted to testify about this because the police had not had probable cause to arrest Elmore. Judge Burnett sent the jury out.

Jones was in trouble. It was arguable that a single fingerprint and a canceled check did not constitute probable cause to arrest Elmore, given that he had worked for Mrs. Edwards. Jones explained there was more. "Your Honor, I would like to state for the record for the edification of counsel for the defense that I was in court on the nineteenth when Captain Coursey came to me." Coursey told him that Dr. Conradi had found "Negroid hair" on the victim's body, Jones went on. "Putting all that together, I gave the advice to Captain Coursey that he had sufficient grounds for probable cause to issue the warrant against Edward L. Elmore." Coursey had never mentioned this "Negroid hair" when he had sought an arrest warrant from the magistrate.

Jones did not introduce it into evidence. In reaching its verdict, a jury may only consider matters that have been admitted into evidence by the judge. This requires the introducing party to demonstrate the item's authenticity and establish that it has not been tampered with. In this case, Jones would have had to have Dr. Conradi testify that she had in fact found a "Negroid hair," that she had placed it in a baggie of some kind, and that the baggie Jones was seeking to introduce was that one. Jones was spared having to do any of this, because Anderson did not ask to see the "Negroid hair."

Burnett was satisfied there had been probable cause to arrest Elmore, and the jury was called back in.

The jury was now arranged differently. All the women jurors

were in the second row. Those who had been in the front row had asked to be moved. They didn't want to sit so close to Jones; they had been frightened by his dramatic outbursts. Once, he kicked his briefcase.

DeFreese was still on the stand. Jones asked him about the fingerprints he had found at the scene. None were found on the needle-nose pliers, or on the chipped ashtray, or on the paring knife, or on the bottle tongs. Altogether, he testified, he had found six fingerprints, only three of which had enough ridge detail for comparison purposes: one of these was found by the back door and was Elmore's; a second was on the swinging door between the kitchen and the dining room, and that belonged to Mrs. Edwards; and the third, a palm print, was found on the top of the toilet.

Strikingly few for a crime scene, DeFreese agreed. The only explanation was that "Mrs. Edwards, or whoever kept her house, was a very meticulous housekeeper. The place was extremely clean and extremely neat."

Jones finished with DeFreese. Anderson's cross-examination was brief, mostly about the method DeFreese had used to lift and compare the prints. Even if Mrs. Edwards had cleaned before the perpetrator arrived, the house would certainly not have been "extremely clean and extremely neat," with so few fingerprints, after the struggle that had ensued. And how did she manage to remove the fingerprints from the tongs in the kitchen drawer, from the coffeemaker, and from all the doors, walls, and other surfaces she surely would have touched while trying to escape?

It was early evening when DeFreese stepped off the stand. It had been a long day, but Burnett wanted to keep going. After a ten-minute recess, Jones called Dr. Conradi. She had reached Greenwood after a harrowing journey from Charleston, where she taught at the Medical University of South Carolina. A SLED agent had picked her up, and even before they were out of the parking lot, he turned on his siren as well as the blue light on top of the car. Soon they were hurtling along at a hundred miles an hour. When they had to go through towns, he drove on sidewalks to get around traffic. Apparently, it was all for show: when they reached Newberry, thirty miles east of Greenwood, the SLED agent said he was hungry and they stopped at McDonald's.

THE PATHOLOGIST

TELL THE JURY what a forensic pathologist is, Jones began his questioning of Conradi. "A forensic pathologist is really a medical-slash-legal pathologist, who examines bodies that died of unnatural types of death," she answered. A smallish woman, forty-four years old, Conradi was a transplanted New Yorker who had moved to South Carolina with her doctor husband in 1973. Jones asked her to describe the injuries that had been inflicted on Mrs. Edwards. Anderson objected. Dr. Conradi should simply state the cause of death. The gruesome detail about the injuries was solely intended to arouse the passion of the jury, he argued. Judge Burnett said Jones could go on.

Conradi was clinical. "There was, involving her lower left leg, bruising at the knee in an area one point two by point eight inch in dimension, and there was patchy bruising of the inner aspect of the left calf, also blue in color, in an area two by two inches. Examination of the right leg revealed bruising of the right knee and the right lower leg, bluish and reddish purple in color, and medial, or in the inner aspect of the right knee, and also the right lower leg. On the front of the shin of the right lower leg was a cut, or laceration, measuring a third of an inch in length, and lateral to that on the outer aspect of that, about a half inch additional abrading, which is scraping away of the skin, with a band of intervening superficial purplish abrading. In other words, between the cut, or laceration, and the abrasion was an initial abrasion. And those, basically, were the injuries to the legs."

Mrs. Edwards had thirty-three wounds on her chest, abdomen, and back, Conradi testified. Two-thirds "were red-based and were obviously a premortem injury," she said.

"So you are saying that approximately twenty-two of them were administered before death and approximately eleven of them after death?" Jones said, reinforcing to jurors the notion of how vicious Elmore was to keep beating her after she was dead. Jones was playing to the jurors' guts and emotions, not their intellects. He was looking ahead. Confident the jury would convict Elmore, Jones was implanting the horror of what had happened, the brutality, so that the jury would impose the death penalty. It was the strategy of any good prosecutor.

"Your Honor, I don't see what that has to do with anything," Anderson said, rising. "It's plainly calculated to inflame the jury."

Overruled. It was relevant to the issue of malice, Burnett said. As a legal matter, in order for Elmore to be convicted of murder, and therefore subject to the death penalty, Jones would have to prove that Elmore had acted with malice; the killing of a person without malice is the lesser crime of manslaughter.

Thirteen of Mrs. Edwards's ribs had been broken, Dr. Conradi told the jury. There were two stab wounds behind the left ear, made with a sharp instrument, such as a knife. "Or even pointed-nose, needle-nose pliers could have produced injuries such as that," she said. Mrs. Edwards had thirty-three "small injuries" on her chest and abdomen, she testified. "By small, I mean up to two point five inches in length, but generally about a third of an inch in length."

On the back of the body there were nineteen injuries, again most of them one-third of an inch. None of the stabs hit an artery or vein. Altogether, there were fifty-two wounds, most of them no more than a third of an inch deep. That was curious, since most killers slashed their victims, leaving long, deep gashes. This did not sound like the work of a person who had gone to rob, rape, and murder Mrs. Edwards. What's more, most of the injuries had been inflicted by the bottle tongs, which measured slightly over a third of an inch in width, according to Dr. Conradi. The killer, whoever it was, seemed to have an obsession with the tongs. He used them to kill the victim and then carefully put them in the kitchen drawer after cleaning them of fingerprints. That, too, was odd.

Was there any evidence of sexual assault? Jones asked Conradi. There were abrasions on the vagina, Conradi said. But she found no traces of sperm in any of the "oral, rectal, and vaginal orifices."

This wasn't the answer Jones wanted and needed. A black man raping a white woman was a crime worse than murder to many southerners. Besides, if Elmore hadn't raped Mrs. Edwards, some jurors might wonder why he had broken into the house, the police having concluded that robbery wasn't a motive.

Is it possible for semen to be expelled into the vagina without there being sperm? Jones asked.

Possible, said Conradi.

That was too equivocal for Jones.

"I would ask you this, then, as a forensic pathologist: Was the injury to her vagina consistent with the insertion of an erect human penis?" Jones said.

Anderson could have objected. It was a leading question. On direct examination a lawyer is not allowed to ask leading questions, which are questions that suggest the answer. Generally, questions that can be answered yes or no are leading questions. A nonleading form of the question could have been: As a forensic pathologist, could you tell us what might have caused the injuries to the vagina? But Anderson didn't object.

"Yes, sir," Dr. Conradi answered.

Satisfied, Jones moved on to the crucial question of when Dorothy Edwards was murdered. Again, he had trouble getting the answer he wanted.

It is difficult to determine the time of death with any accuracy, Conradi explained. Mrs. Edwards could have been murdered anywhere from twelve hours to three days before she examined the body, Dr. Conradi said.

Jones wanted one time—Saturday evening. This is when the police had determined Mrs. Edwards had been murdered, based on what Holloway had told them. And Jones knew from police interviews with Elmore's girlfriend, Mary, her brother Donnie, and Donnie's wife, Sue, that Elmore would have trouble accounting for a two-hour period late Saturday night.

Conradi wanted to avoid being pinned down to a specific time. Determining time of death is not an exact science, and South Carolina pathologists were not well trained in conducting death investigations.

Jones was persistent.

"All right, then, I'll ask you this question. Is that wide range of estimates consistent with the possible death between ten and twelve o'clock p.m. on the night of January the sixteenth?"

Another leading question. Anderson did not object.

Yes, said Dr. Conradi.

Jones was satisfied and was finished with questions for the pathologist. "Thank you, ma'am," Jones said, sitting down. "Answer questions counsel will ask you." He hadn't asked her about the "Negroid hair" he had told the court she had found on Mrs. Edwards's body, which seemed surprising. But it wasn't an oversight by Jones; he knew something about that hair that he did not want Elmore's lawyers to know.

John Beasley stood. He didn't ask her about the "Negroid hair" either. He asked only six questions and did more to harm than help Elmore. Didn't you say that you could not say with certainty that there was sexual assault? he asked Conradi. That was not what she had said, and this gave her a chance to reiterate. "I can say with certainty that there was sexual assault." What she could not say with certainty was whether Mrs. Edwards had been raped. The penetration of the vagina might have been with "a foreign object," she said. That was tantalizing, but Beasley didn't ask, "Such as what?" On the time of death, Beasley didn't ask Conradi if it could have been Sunday, which was within her parameters. He did ask her whether Mrs. Edwards might have been murdered as early as three o'clock Saturday afternoon. Conradi answered that while it might be possible, her estimate, which was based in large measure on what the police had told her, was that Mrs. Edwards had been murdered sixty-five hours before she examined the body, which would make it Saturday evening.

On recross, Jones used his questions, and Conradi's answers, to drive home to the jury that Mrs. Edwards had been murdered

Saturday evening. This became a critical given in the case, accepted by virtually everyone.

When Conradi finally finished testifying, it was very late. Burnett apologized to the jurors and let them go to the Holiday Inn.

THE GIRLFRIEND

"GOOD MORNING, ladies and gentlemen. I hope you had as pleasant an evening as you could under our circumstances. Y'all do look very fresh and ready for another very difficult day," Judge Burnett cheerfully greeted the jurors when they returned at 10:00 a.m. on Thursday, April 15, the fourth day of the trial.

Jones called Mary Alice Dunlap, Elmore's estranged girlfriend, to the stand. Jones was wary, not certain whose side she'd be on. She was sworn in and took the witness chair. She was nervous as she looked at the crowded courtroom but seemed to relax once she started giving testimony. Jones asked her about her relationship with Elmore: how long they had dated; their on-again, off-again living together in her Greenwood Gardens Apartments; how she would ask him to leave, he'd move out, then she'd take him back. Jones came to Saturday the sixteenth. Her story largely matched what Elmore had told the police. She added a few details. On the way from Kmart to her mother's they had passed him on Baptist Street. It was around ten. She and the other members of her family had arrived at her apartment around ten thirty. Around midnight, or maybe twelve thirty, Elmore showed up. She told him to leave. He refused. He said he wanted to get the clothes he had left at her house. She told him she had thrown them away. She turned off the lights and everyone left, except Elmore.

Jones had more questions.

"Was there any conversation concerning the condition of his lip?" he asked Dunlap.

"He asked was his lip swollen. I said it was swollen a little bit."

"That's his upper lip."

"Uh-huh."

Jones didn't ask the obvious question. He knew the answer. As part of their investigation, Greenwood police detective Perry Dickenson and SLED agent Tom Henderson had questioned Warren Martin, the live-in boyfriend of Elmore's sister Peggy. He had seen Elmore on Sunday morning. He was limping and his lip was swollen, Martin told the officers. "Did he tell you what happened?" they asked. Yes. Elmore said he had slipped on some ice coming out of Mary Dunlap's apartment, Martin told the police officers. The jury never heard this. Jones preferred to leave the inference that Elmore had cut his lip struggling with Mrs. Edwards.

Jones asked Dunlap what Elmore was wearing. A brown jacket, an off-white shirt, and jeans, she answered.

"What, if anything, transpired with regard to the jacket, white shirt, or jeans?" Jones asked.

"What you mean, 'transpired'?"

"What took place? What happened to it? What happened to the coat, shirt, or britches?"

Elmore had started to unbutton his shirt, then just ripped it off, she said. "I picked it up and threw it in the trash."

Again Jones left the obvious question unasked. He preferred leaving jurors with the inference that the shirt had blood on it and that Elmore was getting rid of incriminating evidence. "Your Honor, that's all I have at this time," Jones said, and sat down.

Anderson had only a few innocuous questions. When did Dunlap and Elmore begin dating? When did she get divorced? How many children did she have? Did she want to marry him? Yes. Had they had lovers' spats? Yes. Did she still love him? Yes. That was it. If Anderson had read the police interviews of Martin and Dunlap, which Jones had given to him, as he was required to, he would have known the questions to ask, and the answers would have helped Elmore.

Like a good prosecutor, or defense lawyer, Jones wasn't going to let a critical piece of evidence—where Elmore was at the time the state said Mrs. Edwards had been murdered—rest on one witness. He called as a witness Frances Moseley, Mary's mother. She, too, could testify that Elmore had not been seen between 10:00 p.m. and midnight—if Jones could get her to speak so that the jury could understand what she was saying.

Where do you live? Jones asked.

He couldn't understand her answer.

"It might help a little bit, if you don't mind, if I could take your gum. Do you mind?" She was a habitual gum chewer.

"No, sir."

"Can I have your gum?"

"Okay."

Jones took a piece of paper off the counsel table, walked a few steps, and gave it to Mrs. Moseley. She took the gum out of her mouth, put it in the paper, and held it while Jones took up the questioning. He still had difficulty getting the responses he wanted.

"Do you know when it was that you went back down there to your daughter's house?" asked Jones.

"I don't understand."

"Well, now, I thought the four of you went down to your daughter's house first."

"Yes."

"And y'all stayed down there—"

"Yes, sir."

"—for about an hour?"

"Yes, sir."

"Well, wouldn't that put it up around eleven, or later?"

"Yes, sir."

Beasley objected. Jones was leading the witness. But Judge Burnett was sympathetic to Jones's plight in dealing with an uneducated black woman. "I think in this case some leading is going to be necessary," the judge said. Jones continued to lead his witness. Eventually, he got all he could from Mrs. Moseley.

Then he put Mrs. Moseley's daughter-in-law Sue Moseley on the stand.

She also was uneducated, and Jones had the same problems.

"Before you got to your mother-in-law's house, did you meet somebody?" he asked.

"Yeah, we did. We met Lee."

"And where did you meet him?"

"I get mixed up with the streets."

"You get mixed up?"

"Yeah."

"Well, was it on the street before you turn into the little street where your mother-in-law lives?"

"Yeah."

"What did his car do, if anything?"

"What you say now?"

Jones was frustrated and again resorted to leading questions. Anderson objected. Burnett was as exasperated as Jones. "You understand we have a problem with this one, also," the judge said. Not a problem with "this witness" or with "Mrs. Moseley." With "*this one.*" He let Jones continue to ask leading questions. Jones finished. Anderson had no questions.

In spite of the difficulties with the witnesses, Jones seemed to establish a gap in Elmore's activities on the evening in question. Mary and her brother had seen him around ten and not again until about midnight. In those two hours, the state argued, he had driven over to 209 Melrose Terrace, knocked on Mrs. Edwards's door, and raped and killed her.

HAIR ON THE BED

JONES WAS METHODICALLY building the case against Elmore. Conradi had testified that Mrs. Edwards was murdered Saturday evening. Elmore's girlfriend and family had testified that they had not seen him late that evening. But Jones had yet to give the jurors any evidence that conclusively placed Elmore inside the house when Mrs. Edwards was murdered. The fingerprint by the back door might have been left when Elmore was legitimately working there.

Jones called Ira Parnell, one of the two SLED investigators

at the crime scene. Jones had the easel set up. He walked over to it and, using his pointer, directed Parnell's attention to the victim's bedroom. He asked Parnell to direct him to where the bed was.

"The upper-right-hand area of the drawing, right there," Parnell said, as Jones moved his pointer.

Jones asked Parnell to step down from the witness box and approach the easel. He asked him to describe the condition of the bed. There was a small pillow in one corner, and the top cover of the bed had been folded back, Parnell said.

Had Parnell found anything on the bed?

"Yes sir, I did," he said.

"And what did you find?" Jones asked.

"I found a quantity of human hair."

"A quantity of human hair?" Jones repeated, stressing the point to the jury.

The hairs had been spread over an area approximately eighteen inches long and three feet across, Parnell said. Parnell said he had collected the hairs, put them in a baggie, and delivered it to SLED chemist Earl Wells for examination.

Jones finished his questioning of Parnell. He had now presented evidence that was damning—and new. Neither Johnson nor Owen had mentioned finding any hairs on the bed in their reports, nor had anyone else, nor had there been any reference to hairs on the bed in any of the proceedings prior to the trial. Anderson had no questions.

Parnell's testimony about finding hairs on the bed was tantalizing, but the jury had to wait until later in the trial for the rest of the story.

On Friday, the fifth day of the trial, Jones called Earl Wells. He began with routine questions about Wells's background— a BS in chemistry, five years in the textile industry before joining SLED as a forensic chemist. Wells said he had conducted "several hundred" tests and had testified in many trials. Jones asked Wells if he had received samples of the victim's head and pubic hairs. He had. Had he received samples of the defendant's head and pubic hairs? Again, he had.

"I ask you furthermore if you received a sample of hairs that were collected from the bed of the victim by SLED agent Ira Parnell, brought to you by SLED agent Dan DeFreese."

"I did."

Items of physical evidence that either side wants to introduce into evidence are given a number. The baggie with the hairs Parnell said he found on the bed was State Exhibit 58.

"I hand you State Exhibit 58, and I ask you if they contain fifty-three hairs gathered from the bed of the deceased, Dorothy Edwards?" Jones said to Wells.

"I think the total count on the hairs is forty-nine, Solicitor," Wells said.

Jones was taken aback. During his opening argument, he had told the jury fifty-three hairs had been found on the bed.

"Would you check your records," Jones now said to Wells.

"I do not recall the number, but as I recall there's forty-two in here and seven of which I used to prepare microscopic slides with."

"Forty-nine?" Jones asked, surprised.

Wells, a thirteen-year veteran, was uncomfortable. He knew there was a cardinal rule: You never challenge Willy T.

Wells answered honestly, "Yes, sir." Forty-nine.

Jones knew better than to get into a disagreement with his own witness in front of the jury, and he let the matter of the number drop.

Wells testified that he had taken seven hairs out of the bag, mounted them on slides, and examined them under a microscope. Two were probably Mrs. Edwards's pubic hair; two were her head hair, he said. Three were Elmore's pubic hair. The remaining forty-two? "My opinion is that there's a very high degree of probability that these hairs originated from the defendant in this case," Wells testified.

Jones asked Wells a few more questions—how could he distinguish head hairs from pubic hairs, cut hairs from yanked hairs?—and then turned the witness over to Beasley for cross-examination. Could Wells say with absolute certainty that the hairs found on the bed came from the defendant? he asked.

No, said Wells, though with a "high degree of probability." Beasley made nothing of the inconsistency about the number of hairs in the baggie, or of the fact that Wells said DeFreese had given him the hairs, while Parnell had testified that he had delivered them to Wells. Beasley asked three questions in all.

THE JAILHOUSE INFORMANT

IN CRIMINAL CASES, the state must convince the jury of the defendant's guilt "beyond a reasonable doubt." This standard of proof "dates from at least the early years as a Nation," the United States Supreme Court noted in *In re Winship*, which held the standard applied in a juvenile delinquency hearing for a twelve-year-old boy who had stolen $112 from a women's pocketbook. Trial lawyers and legal philosophers debate the meaning of the phrase, which is not defined in the Constitution. One of the most often cited definitions was by the renowned chief justice Lemuel Shaw of the Massachusetts Supreme Judicial Court in 1850. The standard does not require the state to eliminate "mere possible doubt," because everything in human affairs is open to some doubt, he wrote. But it must do more than "establish a probability" that the facts are true. The jurors must be convinced "to a reasonable and moral certainty," he wrote.

The case against Elmore seemed to be loaded with doubt. If there was a moral certainty after two days of testimony from some twenty witnesses, it might have been that Elmore was innocent. How did the state explain that only one of Elmore's fingerprints was found at the scene? And that could have been left weeks before the murder. How was it that there was an absence of any semen, even though the state was charging Elmore with rape? The police had concluded nothing valuable was taken from Mrs. Edwards's house, so what was the motive? Yes, Jones had presented testimony that Elmore's hairs were found on the bed, but given the inconsistencies about the number, some jurors might have had reasonable doubts about the veracity of that testimony.

As his penultimate witness, Jones called the man who could plug the holes: James Arthur Gilliam Jr. He was thirty-nine years old, with eight kids, a big man at six seven. He had a rap sheet that ran to several pages: burglary in Brooklyn, New York; a string of fraudulent-check charges in South Carolina; receiving stolen property; prison escape; disorderly conduct; resisting arrest; assault and battery. He was currently in the Greenwood County jail for violation of probation on a conviction for receiving stolen property. He was facing eighteen months in state prison.

A few days before Elmore's trial was to open, the guards put Gilliam in a cell with Elmore. A day or two later, Gilliam scrawled a note to Sgt. Alvin Johnson, well known to Gilliam from numerous encounters:

> *My name is James Gilliam. I am in the county jail. I think we should have a talk. Mr. Elmore has did a lots of talking to me about killing that lady. I would like to talk to you and Mr. W.T. Jones if I can. Thank you.*

A jailer mailed it. Two days later, Gilliam was taken to Solicitor Jones's office on the second floor of the Grier Building. Sergeant Johnson and Detective Vanlerberghe were there. For two hours on Friday evening, as he tapped ashes and ground out cigarette butts into the ever-present, always seemingly full ashtray on his desk, Jones went over Gilliam's testimony with him. When the lights were turned off and everyone had left, Gilliam was ready for trial time.

It was permissible for Jones to go over Gilliam's testimony with him prior to trial, and indeed, it was part of good trial preparation. However, a lawyer may not encourage a witness to lie nor put him on the stand knowing that he will lie. But lawyers, trained to argue about the number of angels that can dance on the head of a pin, find their ethical consolation in the difference between "knowing" someone is lying and merely "suspecting" that he is.

Anderson objected to Gilliam's being allowed to testify to what Elmore had allegedly told him. The jury was sent out.

The guards at the jail had placed Gilliam in the cell with Elmore to ask him questions, and that made him a state agent; he was thus required to give Elmore his Miranda warning, Anderson argued to Burnett. He apologized for making the argument. "I'll be frank with you, Judge, I think they've got good evidence. I think that the evidence that has been elicited at this trial has been certainly evidence that has been forthright. But, now, I think this is a distraction, frankly, on what they're trying to do here and it's unnecessary and prosecutorial overreach."

Jones feigned offense.

"Now, Your Honor, I don't like that at all. It ain't no prosecutorial overreach. I'd be derelict in my duty if I didn't bring him in here."

Judge Burnett ruled that Gilliam could testify. "I find specifically from the evidence that there was no intention of any law enforcement personnel to place this witness, Mr. Gilliam, with this defendant for the purposes of eliciting any statements. Voluntary admissions and statements of the defendant are his prerogative and deserve no constitutional protection, and there is no violation in this case."

Jones told Burnett that Elmore had confessed to other men in the jail, but in the interest of saving time, he was calling only Gilliam. Anderson didn't challenge this, didn't ask for the names of the others.

The jury was brought back in.

"How did this conversation about this case come up with him?" Jones asked Gilliam, who was casually dressed.

"I don't know. I guess he just needed somebody to talk to him," Gilliam said.

JONES: All right. Tell us some of the things he said.
GILLIAM: Well, he said he went there to rob the lady, you know.
JONES: He went there to rob her?
GILLIAM: Right.

JONES: Did he say he knew her before?

GILLIAM: Yes, he did. Said he did some work for her, cleaning windows and ducts, and all that stuff.

JONES: All right, then, he said he went there to rob the lady. And what did he say to you about it.

GILLIAM: Well, then he said he didn't want to hurt her, but he knocked her down when she—

JONES: But, he knocked her down?

GILLIAM: He knocked her down.

JONES: And what?

GILLIAM: She wouldn't quit screaming.

JONES: She wouldn't quit screaming?

GILLIAM: Right.

JONES: And then what?

GILLIAM: He said he had to kill her, then—

JONES: He said he had to kill her?

GILLIAM: Right.

JONES: All right. Is there anything else that you recall that he had to say to you?

GILLIAM: Well, he asked me then if you have sex with a woman and you wash up, would it show any signs that you've had sex with her.

JONES: If you have sex with a woman and you wash up, would it show any signs that you've had sex?

GILLIAM: Right.

JONES: All right, was there anything else you can recall?

GILLIAM: And he said he knew the police couldn't have no fingerprints of his because he had wiped everything down when he left.

JONES: He knew the police couldn't have no fingerprints of his because he wiped everything—

GILLIAM: Wiped everything down before he left.

JONES: Wiped everything down before he left?

GILLIAM: Right.

JONES: I see. Can you think of anything else he said?

GILLIAM: That's about it.

JONES: All right, answer questions of counsel if you will, Mr. Gilliam.

Anderson didn't believe Gilliam. He thought he saw a jail-house snitch who was testifying to save himself. Besides, why would Elmore, who was so reticent that Anderson couldn't get anything out of him, spill his guts to a stranger? Anderson asked Gilliam about his previous convictions, his long criminal record. Hadn't he concocted all this because he was facing prison and was hoping to cut a deal? No, said Gilliam.

Jones still had one legal issue to address. To convict Elmore of larceny, which was one of the charges, the state had to establish that something of value had been taken from Mrs. Edwards's house. Jones called Carolyn Edwards Lee. Answering questions from Jones, she testified that her mother had an Aigner clutch purse worth between $40 and $50, and that she usually kept at least $50 in cash in it. When Carolyn had gone through the house on the Tuesday after her mother's body was found, she had not been able to find the purse or any money, she testified.

Carolyn was on the stand for only a few minutes. It hadn't been as bad as she had feared, and she was greatly relieved that she wasn't asked any questions about her mother's relationship with Holloway.

Jones told the court he had no more witnesses. It was Friday afternoon. It was time for the defense case.

THE DEFENDANT—EDWARD LEE ELMORE

ANDERSON AND BEASLEY had almost nothing to offer. They called only one witness—Elmore. Some jurors showed their surprise.

It is rare for the defendant in a murder case to testify. The Fifth Amendment, which was adopted in response to abuses of authority by the British Crown, provides that no person "shall be compelled in any criminal case to be a witness against himself." Judges instruct juries that no inferences are to be drawn if a defendant does not testify.

No one of sound mind, guilty or innocent, would subject himself to cross-examination from a lawyer like Jones. "That man could get the pope to confess," said Greenwood police detective Vanlerberghe. "He was downright scary. He was a very feared man." But Anderson told Elmore he *had* to testify. Elmore obeyed, as he always did.

Elmore, wearing dark pants and an open-collared white shirt, his hair medium length, was sworn in. Anderson asked him about his work washing windows and cleaning gutters in Greenwood's fancy neighborhoods. Anderson came to Saturday, January 16. Elmore recounted the events of the day, as he had to the police, and his testimony was the same as what his ex-girlfriend, Mary, had testified.

While Elmore was answering questions from Anderson, Jones was rocking back and forth in his chair, grimacing, making faces, relaying to the jurors only a few feet away his scorn for Elmore and his story.

It was after five o'clock when Anderson finished questioning Elmore. Once again, Burnett wanted to keep going. He wanted this trial over with.

Edward Lee Elmore, shy, quiet, uneducated, was now at the mercy of William T. Jones, and Jones showed no mercy.

Jones asked Elmore how often he had worked for Mrs. Edwards.

The first time had been "when the leaves was falling," Elmore said.

"Well, when was the second time? That's what I'm asking you about."

"That's what I'm saying, a month before—before the—before the, you know, the first time."

Now Jones was confused. "What's that?"

"It was a month or so before the first time I worked for her."

"You mean the second time that you worked there is a month or so before the first time?"

"Yeah."

Elmore spoke so softly that Judge Burnett, sitting next to him, had trouble hearing his answers. "Would you speak into the microphone and speak out, please, sir, so we can all hear you," he said to Elmore.

With the next question, Jones employed a classic trial lawyer's tactic on Elmore, firing off questions in an effort to rattle the witness into contradicting himself or admitting knowledge that would undercut his denials, reveal his lies. It was the stuff of *Perry Mason,* crime novels, and movies, but with a person of Elmore's IQ, Jones could reasonably believe it would work.

He showed Elmore a picture of Mrs. Edwards's den, with the couch and TV.

> JONES: And that's what she lie on and watch TV?
> ELMORE: I don't know. I couldn't tell you.
> JONES: You couldn't tell us, huh?
> ELMORE: No.
> JONES: Was she lying there that night?
> ELMORE: What night?
> JONES: The night we're talking about
> ELMORE: I don't know.

Jones paced while asking questions. He stopped, then moved to within inches of Elmore. Jones had a reputation for being a bit of a bully, and that side of him was on display now. "He was intimidating," said a juror. "If it had been me, I would have been real scared."

> JONES: When you went around there and killed Mrs. Edwards it would have been after dark, wouldn't it?
> ELMORE: I didn't kill Mrs. Edwards.
> JONES: If you had, it would have had to have been after dark, wouldn't it?
> ELMORE: I didn't—I didn't—
> JONES: Well, did you go around there in the daylight?
> ELMORE: I didn't go at all.

JONES: Did you go in the daylight?
ELMORE: I didn't go at all.
JONES: Well, I asked you did you go in the daylight?
ELMORE: No, sir.

Elmore's mother began to sob and left the courtroom. Elmore's sisters sat impassively, petrified. Watching Elmore getting pummeled by the questions, Reverend Spearman thought he looked like a scared child. "It was like he didn't know why this was happening. He knew he was on trial, but he didn't realize the magnitude of the situation," Spearman recalled. "The expression on his face was, Why is this happening to me?"

Jones led Elmore through the evening of the sixteenth, his trips to Kmart, his pleas with Mary, her rejections, his following her to her apartment, passing each other on Bishop Street. They were the same facts the others had related.

Then Jones asked about the shirt Elmore had ripped off at her apartment. "The main reason you took it off is because you didn't want to go around with it bloody?" he asked Elmore. It was a statement to the jury as much as it was a question.

"No, sir, there wasn't no blood on it."

"The truth of the matter is that she saw the blood and made some comment about it, isn't it?"

Anderson could have objected. There was no evidence in the record that Mary had seen blood on the shirt. Anderson's objection might have been overruled—on cross-examination, an opposing lawyer has considerable latitude and is allowed, for example, to ask leading questions, which he may not ask on direct examination. But by objecting, he would have been reminding the jury that no one had testified that there was blood on Elmore's shirt. Instead, Jones got away with planting the inference that there was.

Jones turned to mockery. "Now—now, anytime during that month of January, whether Mrs. Edwards was in there or not, did you ever stand around her bed and reach down in your pubic area and start pulling out hairs and throwing them on the bed?"

It wasn't a serious question. Elmore didn't know any better than to answer it straightforwardly: "No, sir."

Jones had been hammering Elmore for more than an hour. He was almost finished. By putting Elmore on the stand, Anderson had handed Jones an opportunity to lay a trap, and now the solicitor set it. He turned to Sergeant Johnson, who was seated among the spectators.

"Stand up, if you will," Jones said.

Remember him? Jones asked Elmore.

Yes, sir, was the response.

"I'm going to ask you if you told him that if you went there and killed Mrs. Edwards you just didn't remember it?"

"No, sir."

"You are saying, now, you deny on Wednesday, January the twentieth, around three p.m., or shortly thereafter, telling Officer Al—Sergeant Alvin Johnson that if you went there and killed the lady you couldn't remember?"

"Yes, sir."

Jones turned to Tom Henderson. Stand up, please, Jones said. Elmore said he remembered him as well.

Same question to Elmore: "Will you admit, or deny, that you told him that if you killed Mrs. Edwards that night you didn't remember it?"

"No, sir."

Finally, at 7:25 Friday evening, Elmore limped off the stand. He looked like a "frightened child" to one juror.

EVERYONE was back in the courtroom at 10:00 a.m. on Saturday.

"I hope you had enough time this morning to watch some of the Saturday morning cartoons before coming up," Judge Burnett said to greet the jurors.

"Does the defense rest?" Burnett asked Anderson.

"Yes, sir. Yes, sir," Anderson replied.

It was time for the state's case in rebuttal. Jones now sprung the trap he had set for Elmore.

He called Sergeant Johnson as a witness, reminding him that he was still under oath. Jones had only two questions for him.

"Mr. Johnson, I ask you this, whether or not on January twentieth, 1982, at the South Carolina Law Enforcement Headquarters, sometime after three p.m., the defendant, Edward Lee Elmore, told you that if he went there and killed Mrs. Edwards he couldn't remember?"

"Yes."

"Did he do so repeatedly?"

"Yes."

On cross-examination, Anderson asked a few perfunctory questions: Where did this happen? SLED headquarters. What time? Three p.m. Who else was present? Henderson. He didn't ask Johnson to explain how the conversation had come about. Had Elmore just blurted this out? Or had Johnson planted the idea? Had Johnson said, Now, Mr. Elmore, is it possible that you did this, but you didn't know what you were doing? Might he even have said, Look, if you did it but don't remember, you can't be held responsible?

Henderson was next.

Same two questions from Jones.

"Mr. Henderson, I will ask you to state whether or not the defendant, Edward Lee Elmore, on January the twentieth, 1982, at the South Carolina Law Enforcement Headquarters, sometime after three p.m., told you that if he went there and killed Mrs. Edwards, he couldn't remember?"

"Yes, sir, he did."

"Did he do so repeatedly?"

"Yes, sir, he did."

Anderson asked no questions.

The state rested.

The defense rested.

IT WAS TIME FOR closing statements. It was the moment for Elmore's lawyers, and then Jones, to argue their case to the jurors, summarizing the evidence most favorable to their side, highlighting what they saw as the weaknesses in the other. The order is the reverse of opening statements, with the defense going first. Beasley led off.

It was Saturday, a day he did not like to work. "I promise to be brief," he told the jurors. He was. Anodyne. He had represented lots of criminal defendants, but he had never seen one as nice as Mr. Elmore, he told the jury. "For him to be charged, really, is just for me—it's sort of shocking because, of course, I did not know him before this time, but I know him now. And really, he seemed to me like such a nice fellow to be up here and charged with such a serious crime." He gave the jurors a high school civics lesson: the burden was on the state to prove the case beyond a reasonable doubt. It is the last resort for a defense lawyer who has given the jury no evidence to raise doubts. Beasley asked the jurors to dispense justice to Elmore just as they would to any member of their own family.

"Thank you," he said, and sat down.

THE PROSECUTOR'S CLOSING ARGUMENT

WILLIAM T. JONES got up, and everyone knew he wouldn't be short and he wouldn't be bland.

"Mr. Foreman, ladies and gentlemen, a book can never be judged by its cover," he said. "You could ask the question, How could someone as young and someone as nice-looking and someone who can sound nice and cooperative do such a thing. Mr. Foreman, ladies and gentlemen, don't expect yourself to know that. You're not supposed to know that."

Someone entered the courtroom. Jones was not pleased. He did not want anything to divert the jury's attention from what he was saying. He asked Judge Burnett to prevent anyone else from coming or going until he had finished.

"I apologize, ladies and gentlemen, but I'm—inept enough without other things," he said with his well-practiced feigned modesty. "We've got a job to do here. I'm trying to do mine the best I can and I apologize to you for all of my ineptness. And I'm not trying to sound humble when I say that, because I know I am in many respects inept. I just don't know how many." He had the jury spellbound.

Jones turned to the issue of malice. It could be implied from the use of dangerous instruments—the needle-nose pliers, the paring knife. "And particularly, Mr. Foreman, and particularly, there are times I think when a man, who keeps himself in shape, doubles up his fist even and rams it into the face and the fragile little bones and into the—to the rib cage of a human being no taller than four feet, five and a half inches, weighing no more than a hundred and thirty pounds, not later to break them, but crush them where they go into the entrails, certainly, the heart and the lungs are entrails as well as things in our abdomen, and puncture them, causing them to collapse and bleed." Jones was using Mrs. Edwards's height and weight as recorded by Dr. Conradi in her autopsy report; she was actually several inches taller and many pounds lighter. Still, it was not hard to imagine jurors blanching at this scene, though there was no evidence in the record to suggest this was what happened.

To drive home the horror, Jones talked about the instruments that had been used to batter and kill Mrs. Edwards—exhibits that had been introduced into evidence and the jurors would be able to have with them during their deliberations. "I want you to feel it," he said about the ashtray. "Just feel the weight of it." Then there were the bottle tongs. "Look at them. They had blood on them, even back in there in the drawer."

Abruptly, Jones shifted to the night Elmore was arrested. He knew what common sense would lead some jurors to wonder.

"Some people ask you, Why would he wait down there with her that night on the early morning hours of Wednesday the twentieth when he heard her call the police, and stay down there. You can't answer that, because your brain doesn't work like a person who would do this act. You might ask the question, Why would he take this back and put it in that drawer and let it be hanging out. You can't answer that. No way you can answer it. Your brain doesn't work like one. You can't fathom why he did this act in the first place. It's so repulsive to you. If you're not the one who has the ability to kill, you can't understand why one would kill, or why he'd do certain acts before or after doing it. You just can't do it. It's improper to ask you to put yourself in his place."

Jones addressed another question he knew a reasonable person might have: If there had been a rape or a sexual assault and there was all this blood elsewhere, why was there no blood on the bed? His answer, to the jurors, was, "She could have been swallowing the blood."

He was now ready to explain how those hairs had got on the bed. "Give me your attention, ladies and gentlemen. When he put his part of his body into the part of her privates, it was so repulsive to the lady that she, then, grabbed down there for the first time and came out with forty-something of his pubic hairs." He picked up the tempo. "And it hurts him, then. He hurt her, first, but that hurts him. Then he jumped up and she tried to get up, but he caught her. He caught her in the corner and he beat her to death. For two or three reasons, because he has not only the capacity to kill but to overkill. Understand that mind? Don't let anybody try to make you, because you can't. You're not a killer, you're not a murderer. Yes. Yes."

The jury was hushed. Jones had only a few more things to say. He came back to the image Elmore had projected sitting there and on the stand. "Well, we all know the choirboys can do wrong, who have been models up to a point. You never know when that fuse, or where there is an explosion inside that might go off."

He asked the jury to convict. This was the man who had murdered Dorothy Edwards.

He had been talking nearly two hours and now sat down.

It was 1:30 and Burnett recessed for lunch. Before sending the jurors out, he cautioned them that even though the lawyers had finished with their witnesses and arguments, the jurors were not to begin discussing the case, not until he had instructed them on the law.

After lunch, Judge Burnett charged the jury, following the standard instructions drafted by the state judicial authorities. He began by reminding the jurors that the defendant was presumed to be innocent and that on each count of the indictment the state had to prove his guilt beyond a reasonable doubt. "A reasonable doubt is not a whimsical doubt, nor is it a slight, fanciful, or weak doubt," he said. "Proof beyond a reasonable doubt must be proof of such convincing character that you would be willing to rely upon it unhesitatingly in the most important of your own affairs." He then explained each element of the charges in the indictment. "In order for the State to prove the Defendant guilty of murder, it must be proved beyond a reasonable doubt that the Defendant did kill a person and that the killing was done with malice aforethought, express or implied," he said. "Malice aforethought is the deliberate and well-formed purpose to do the unlawful act. Aforethought simply means that the intention to do the unlawful act was conceived, or planned, sometime before the actual commission of the act, and the length of time is not important."

Lawyers for each side may ask for specific instructions, and Anderson asked for an instruction related to Gilliam's testimony. He wanted Burnett to instruct the jury: "If the jury believes from the evidence that any person was induced to testify in this case by any promise of immunity from further punishment, or that any hope was held out, or entertained by him that he would be rewarded or in any way benefit if he implicated the defendant in the crime charged herein, the jury must take such fact into consideration in determining what weight should be given to the testimony, closely scrutinize it, and unless they can reconcile it with truth, completely reject it." Burnett declined to do so.

At 3:50, the jurors filed out of the courtroom, into a spacious adjacent room with a large conference table and a coffeepot. The bailiff brought them all the exhibits that had been introduced into evidence. They began to discuss the evidence. They talked about how poorly Elmore had been represented. "Why doesn't this guy get another lawyer?" they asked one another. They discussed the evidence, the fingerprints, the hair found on the bed, the blood found on his blue jeans. One of the jurors said she thought one of the more incriminating pieces of evidence was Elmore's bloody shirt. That was a reflection of how successful Jones had been and how ineffective Anderson and Beasley were: No witness had actually testified to seeing blood on the shirt. Jones had created the inference when he got Elmore's girlfriend to testify that Elmore had torn his shirt off and she had thrown it away. Elmore's lawyers never asked her if there was blood on the shirt, and never pointed out during their closing argument that there had been no testimony that there was.

An hour into their deliberations, the foreman advised the clerk that the jury had a question. Judge Burnett went into the jury room, accompanied by Jones and Anderson, leaving Elmore in the courtroom with police guards hovering near. A question had arisen among the jurors about whether Elmore would have had time to go from Mary's apartment over to Melrose Terrace, murder Mrs. Edwards, then return in the two-hour space of time in which he had not been seen. The jurors wanted a map of Greenwood. Because a map had not been introduced into evidence, Judge Burnett could not give them one.

Another hour passed, and the jurors took a vote.

At 6:20, the foreman advised the bailiff and the bailiff advised Judge Burnett that the jury had reached a verdict. The jurors filed back into the courtroom. They found Elmore guilty of murder, criminal sexual conduct, housebreaking, and burglary. He was found not guilty of armed robbery and larceny.

"It was an open-and-shut case," said James Walker, a thirty-four-year-old worker at Greenwood Mills. Elizabeth Hackett, one of two blacks on the jury, wanted to find him not guilty. "We felt he was innocent. We thought he was framed. But we had to go by the evidence, not by how we felt," she said. "He didn't have a good lawyer," she added.

"His lawyers didn't give us anything that would help him," said another juror, Susan Burnett. "There was nothing that could sway us, that could create any doubt."

WHEN THE SUPREME COURT reinstated the death penalty in 1976, in *Gregg v. Georgia*, it ruled that a defendant charged with a capital offense must be given a bifurcated trial. First, the jury must decide on guilt or innocence. If it finds the defendant guilty, then comes the second, or sentencing, phase. It is a trial of sorts: The prosecution puts in evidence of aggravation, to convince the jurors that the defendant is such a terrible, evil, dangerous person that he does not deserve to live. The defense offers mitigation, evidence of the defendant's good character or childhood traumas, in effect arguing to the jury that even if he committed the crime, his life should be spared.

By statute, Elmore was entitled to a twenty-four-hour period before the second phase could begin. Anderson and Beasley urged him to waive it, and of course he did. Judge Burnett went into the jury room and asked the jurors whether they wanted to work Sunday or take the day off and start again Monday morning. Everyone's attitude seemed to be the same: This guy's guilty; let's get it over with.

DELIBERATION ON DEATH

ON SUNDAY MORNING, when many of the jurors normally would have been in church, they were back in court. They wouldn't miss a sermon. "He could have been a preacher, the way he was going," Elmore's sister Elease said of Jones's performance that day.

Jones wanted to persuade the jurors that Elmore had not only murdered Dorothy Edwards but had tortured her as well. He called Dr. Conradi to the stand. He showed her the photos of the victim's bloodied, battered, and bruised body, then passed them to the jurors. Doctor Conradi again described the thirty-three stab wounds on the front and the nineteen on the back. Forty-one had been administered before death, she said. Plus there had been blows to the head, neck, and legs. Mrs. Edwards had still been alive when many of those wounds were inflicted, Conradi said. In other words, she had gone through a slow, painful death.

Slowly, painstakingly, body part by body part, injury by injury, blow by blow, Jones created images in the jurors' minds. How about the left ear? he asked.

"The blow to the left ear was of a severe nature and severe enough to partially tear the ear away from its attachment in the back," Dr. Conradi replied.

"And could you give us the degree of pain?"

"I would say severe."

When Jones had finished, Anderson had no questions but rather a request of the judge. Could the court recess so that he could attend a luncheon engagement? Judge Burnett agreed to it.

After lunch, it was time for Elmore's lawyers to try to save his life with evidence in mitigation. Anderson put on a nominal case. He called members of Elmore's family. They were terrified at having to be in a courtroom facing white prosecutors, a white judge, white jurors, and white cops. But they would do whatever was necessary to help their son and brother. Anderson first called Elmore's mother. Like her son, she talked softly, and Anderson asked her to speak up. The illiterate daughter of a tenant farmer, she said Eddie was the sixth of her eleven children. (He was actually her eighth.) She said he finished the eighth grade. (He had dropped out in the fifth.) She said he had turned twenty-three years old in February. (His birthday was in January.) She said he went to church every Sunday, helped with the chores around the house, was a good boy. "I never had no trouble out of him."

Jones objected. "Your Honor, I don't think she's got the right to say anything she wants to," he said, jumping to his feet.

Anderson said he was trying to get Eddie's mother to explain her son's personality.

"I think the jury is aware of the two types of personalities we may be dealing with," Judge Burnett said. If the jury wasn't, Burnett was helping them, suggesting this was a classic case of a split personality, a choirboy and a murderer, as Jones had portrayed him in his argument to the jury.

Anderson called Elmore's sisters. Mary Crawford, twenty-seven years old and the mother of six children, was the only one with a high school education. She testified that Eddie had been an obedient child, brought in firewood, didn't get into fights, had gone to church. She said she was the closest in age to Eddie.

On cross-examination, Jones didn't spare her.

"How old is Peggy?" he asked.

"I don't know right off," Mary said.

"Oh, now, you know just about how old."

"Twenty-five, or twenty-six."

"About twenty-five, isn't she? Is that right?"

"Uh-huh."

"Peggy is next to him, isn't she?"

"Uh-huh."

"And you're on beyond Peggy, aren't you?"

"Yes."

"So, when you said just a little while ago that you were the one closest to him in age, that's not quite right, is it?"

Mary said nothing.

Anderson finished with the family members and put Elmore on the stand again. Anderson knew it was not going to be easy. He would have to draw him out. He asked simple questions, the kind Elmore could answer yes or no. You don't remember your daddy, do you? No. You gave money to your mother, didn't you? Yes, sir. You worked for Clarence Aiken, didn't you? Yes, sir. You did a good job, didn't you? Yes, sir. Worked in Roger Milliken's home, didn't you? Yes, sir.

Jones was up. Objection. Anderson was asking leading questions.

Burnett agreed. "Don't lead your witness," he admonished. Anderson said that he was handling Elmore just as Jones had dealt with Mrs. Moseley and Sue Moseley, which Judge Burnett had allowed. Burnett cut him off. It was not necessary to ask Elmore leading questions. "He's an intelligent young man," Burnett said (again assisting Jones, who was trying to convince the jury of just that).

Burnett wanted a word with the lawyers, and the jury was sent out. Both sides were guilty of leading their witnesses, he said. His harshest rebuke was of Anderson. "Now, don't come back after one of my rulings and go back and do the exact same thing, Mr. Anderson," he said. Anderson countered: "I want the record to reflect that I am being prevented from eliciting some remarks that need to be heard here by virtue of a very nervous person on trial for his life. He's scared to death to . . ."

"Tone yourself down," Burnett interrupted. Anderson was talking so loudly that Burnett feared the jury, which was in the other room, might hear. During that lunch break Anderson had requested, he had apparently consumed more alcohol than he should have.

Anderson lowered his voice. He tried to explain to Judge Burnett that given Elmore's personality, his quiet, reticent nature, it was hard for him to defend himself. "He's never talked to me hardly about the case, about anything," Anderson advised the judge.

The jury was brought back in, and Anderson continued questioning Elmore. When he had finished, he said, "Is there anything else you want to say about this matter, about this case, about your life?"

"Yes, sir. I'd like to say I didn't—I didn't kill Mrs. Edwards."

"All right. Answer any questions the solicitor might have."

Now it was Jones's turn.

"Put your feet on either side of that and pull it up closer to you, like that," Jones began, gently enough, telling Edwards to get closer to the microphone. "Speak into that and speak up." He was positioning him for the kill.

The jury might have sympathy for a man as quiet and meek as Elmore, might even think he was simply not capable of such a grisly crime. Jones had to destroy the choirboy image. He showed Elmore the drawings of the house, which he had set on the easel in his opening argument, and asked questions. Elmore had difficulty understanding.

"Remember that breezeway between her house and the guest room back there? You remember that, don't you?"

"Breezeway?"

"You know what a breezeway is, don't you, Mr. Elmore?"

"No, sir, not right now."

The tempo accelerated—questions, charges, objections, rulings.

JONES: You want this court to believe you were always this quiet, don't you?

ELMORE: Well, I, you know—you asked me something, I answered it.

JONES: Uh-huh. Well, you want them to always believe you're real quiet and polite, and yes, sir, no, sir, isn't that right?

ELMORE: No, sir.

JONES: Well, where did you get this ashtray here?

ELMORE: That's—

Anderson jumped up. Objection.

ELMORE: —not my ashtray.

JONES: Well, where did you—

THE COURT: Overruled

JONES: —pick it up?

ELMORE: I didn't pick it up.

JONES: Well, why did you hit her with it?

ELMORE: I didn't hit her with it.

JONES: Why did you stick her with this knife?

ELMORE: I didn't stick her with no knife, sir.

JONES: Tell us your thoughts while you were sticking her in the neck?

ELMORE: I didn't—

ANDERSON: Same objection, Your Honor.

ELMORE: —stick her in the neck.

ANDERSON: It's been tried before.

THE COURT: Overruled.

JONES: What was your thoughts when you stuck this in there?

ELMORE: I didn't stick that. I ain't never seen that before.

JONES: Well, you hit her right on this side of the head with this, didn't you?

ELMORE: No, sir.

JONES: When you were jiggling this into her body, your attitude is a little bit different than what it's been—you've put up here on this stand, isn't it?

ANDERSON: Same—

ELMORE: I didn't—

ANDERSON: —objection, Your Honor.

JONES: —jig that in her body, sir.

THE COURT: Overruled.

JONES: What's that?

ELMORE: I did not jiggle that in her body.

JONES: Your attitude was a lot different then, wasn't it?

ELMORE: I didn't have no attitude, but I wasn't at nobody's house to do that to nobody's body.

JONES: I see. Well, if you had been there doing it, your attitude would have to have been a lot different to stick her as many times as you heard the lady say she was stuck, wouldn't it?

ELMORE: I don't know.

JONES: You couldn't—nobody could have been doing it with the attitude you've been showing up here on this stand, could they have?

ELMORE: I couldn't answer.

JONES: What's that?

ELMORE: I couldn't answer that.

JONES: Oh, you couldn't?

ELMORE: No, sir.

JONES: I see. Uh-huh. You wiped off all your fingerprints out there, so they couldn't find any, didn't you?

ELMORE: No, sir, I haven't been in there.

JONES: Would you tell us why you picked up her body out of that puddle of blood and put it into the bed, or into the—into the closet.

Jones had almost slipped. He had told the jury during his closing argument that there was no blood on the bed because Mrs. Edwards had swallowed it.

ELMORE: I didn't pick up no body, sir.

JONES: You pulled it out of there about ten, or fifteen after twelve and took on down to your girlfriend's, didn't you?

ELMORE: No, sir.

Jones showed Elmore State Exhibit 58, the baggie with the hairs Agent Wells said were Elmore's and Jones had argued Mrs. Edwards had pulled from Elmore when he had thrown her on the bed.

JONES: Now, tell us how it felt when she reached down and jerked them out of that area? It hurt you, didn't it?

ELMORE: Sir, she didn't jerk them from me because didn't nobody—I wasn't there.

JONES: And it made you mad, didn't it?

ELMORE: No, sir, I wasn't there.

JONES: And she tried to get up off of the bed and get out of there, didn't she?

ELMORE: I wasn't there, sir.

JONES: And you caught her and started pounding her with your fist, didn't you?

ELMORE: No, sir.

JONES: Right into the wall, didn't you?

ELMORE: No, sir.

JONES: Stomach and all.

ELMORE: No, sir.

JONES: Did you kick her?

ELMORE: No, sir, I wasn't there.

JONES: That's all I have to ask him.

Jones was finished. It was 6:00 p.m. On Sunday. Closing arguments commenced—the defense, then the state, and then the defense would get a rebuttal.

Beasley stood up. "I'll be brief," he said. First, he told the jury that he had "no criticism whatsoever" of their having found Elmore guilty. But he argued that the evidence was circumstantial—no one had seen Elmore murder Mrs. Edwards. With circumstantial evidence, he said, you can never be sure with absolute, moral certainty that you could be right in imposing the death penalty. Then he sat down. He had spoken for only five minutes.

Now Jones was ready once more to whip up the jury, to feign humility, to ask for sympathy—for himself, not Elmore. "I beg of you not to allow the tone of my voice, my general appearance, whatever kind of clothes I've got on, and the shoes I wear to interfere with your dispensation of justice. I'm confident that you won't—you won't do that. But allow me to beg of you not to do it. I do the best I can do and everybody is handicapped."

It was Sunday, and Jones, wearing a dark suit, white shirt, and thin tie, was in his pulpit. He believed in an eye for an eye and in vengeance; he knew that most of the jurors did as well. He focused on those jurors who had religious scruples about the death penalty. "It's not for us to get into the religious aspect of it," he said. "We're here to do our duty. And I don't feel there's any religion on the face of God's earth that calls upon us not to be a citizen in the country that we live and stand by and carry out our duty, according to law."

He turned spiritual. Mrs. Edwards is "not here today where we can see and touch her, but she's somewhere around here. I have that faith. When I was little, I used to think heaven was up that way and hell was down this way. But I think both of them are all around us. I think it's just a different state. And I've got faith that those who have gone on are looking at us and watching us every day."

He shamed them, challenged them, taunted them. "Either you have the fortitude and the manhood to do it, or it is a blight upon our jury system."

He sat down.

Anderson, in a suit slightly less conservative than Jones's, stood up. It was Elmore's last chance. The courtroom was packed.

"Mr. Foreman, members of the jury, certainly the solicitor has the ability, the oratory, to work you into a frenzy. I hope that he hasn't done that. I hope that you can maintain calm deliberations as you enter the jury room to begin your deliberations."

Anderson was hoping to get just one juror to hold out against the death penalty. That's all it would take to spare Elmore's life. He argued against the death penalty in principle. He gave the jurors a brief survey of the death penalty. In England, they used to hang people for stealing a horse, for witchcraft, for petty theft, he told them. The public was invited. "They put you on a high hill and the point was, they'd hang you up there and hang you by the neck until you were dead and the point was that the people who would walk up there, come on, let's watch the hanging." The theory was that a public hanging would be a deterrent. "You were supposed to be good. Just there he is hanging by his neck. The reaction is, I sure don't want to do that." It didn't work. "You know what it does? It breeds it. That hard feeling breeds more cruelty, breeds it, engenders it, fosters it. There's no deterrence here."

He didn't neglect religion. "I'm more of a New Testament man," he said. He embraced forgiveness, not an eye for an eye.

"I'm going to sit down now, and let the judge charge you, but I want to tell you one more time if I haven't reached all of you about this killing business, I hope I've reached some of you. If I've reached some of you, hang in there, and come back with a recommendation of life and let him spend the rest of his days behind bars. No sense in taking his life."

It was nearly 7:30 on a Sunday evening. Most evenings during the trial, The Ranch, the best restaurant in town, had catered the jurors' meals, but it and other restaurants were closed on Sunday, leaving the jurors to choose between McDonald's or Hardee's, Judge Burnett told them. Hamburgers were brought in.

At 7:50 p.m. the jury began deliberating Edward Elmore's life, whether he would spend the rest of his days in prison or whether he was to be strapped into the electric chair. Anderson had reached a couple of the jurors. After two hours, the foreman notified Judge Burnett that at least one juror was holding out for a life sentence. In fact, two were: Elizabeth Hackett and Georgia Moten, the two African Americans on the jury.

Judge Burnett brought the jurors back into the courtroom. He reminded them that during jury selection, when a potential juror said he was opposed to capital punishment, he had been asked if he could put aside those views and impose the death penalty if that is what the evidence required. All had said yes, Burnett reminded them. He urged them to go back into the deliberations and reach a verdict "according to the oath that you took, each of you, and the duty of a juror as I explained to each of you to render a verdict that is supported by the law and the evidence in this case."

It was nearly 10:30. The jurors continued to discuss the evidence. Hackett and Moten were against executing Elmore. But the two black women, thirty-one and twenty-four years old, respectively, were no match for the ten whites. "This could have been anybody's mother," juror Susan Burnett said at one point. "We have to think about the innocent." She was thirty-three years old, taught Sunday school at the Methodist church, and believed in capital punishment. She was uncomfortable with sentencing a man to die, as were other jurors. "But we didn't feel we had a choice as far as the law was concerned."

Another juror, James Walker, who had considered the case against Elmore open-and-shut, wasn't at all uncomfortable with sentencing him to die for what he considered a most heinous crime. Walker planned to attend the execution.

An hour later, there was still no verdict. It was nearly midnight. Burnett had no choice but to let the jury go for the night. They were taken to the Holiday Inn.

AT 10:00 A.M. Monday, April 19, 1982 (the day Sally Ride was announced as the first woman astronaut and Guion Bluford the first black), the jurors tried again.

This time, their deliberations were short. At 10:50, they reached a verdict, advised the court, and were led back into the courtroom. Elmore rose, hands in his pockets. The courtroom was about half full. The foreman passed the verdict to the clerk. She read:

> State versus Edward Lee Elmore: We, the jury, in the above entitled case, having found beyond a reasonable doubt the existence of the following statutory aggravating circumstances, to wit: one, criminal sexual conduct first degree; two, physical torture, now recommend to the court that the defendant, Edward Lee Elmore, be sentenced to death.

Burnett asked Elmore if there was anything he wanted to say.

"I'd like to say I did not commit that crime Your Honor said I did," Elmore said, calmly. Again, it seemed to Reverend Spearman that Elmore simply did not comprehend what was happening.

Burnett asked if there was anything else.

"Yes, sir. I'd like to say I'll be—no, sir, that's all."

Once again, Burnett could barely hear Elmore and asked him to repeat himself. No, "that's all," Elmore responded.

"I'm satisfied from this evidence that you, without question, committed this most horrible and inhuman crime," Judge Burnett told Elmore. "This jury, in my judgment, has been swayed by no passion, no prejudice, nor any other arbitrary factor."

Again, he asked Elmore if he wanted to say anything before he imposed sentence.

Elmore said he did not.

Judge Burnett spoke: "It is, therefore, the judgment of the land and the sentence of this court that this defendant Edward Lee Elmore, be taken to the county jail of Greenwood and thence to the state penitentiary, henceforth to be kept in close confinement until the twenty-first day of June, 1982, upon which day between the hours of 6:00 a.m. and 6:00 p.m., the defendant Edward Lee Elmore, shall suffer death by electrocution in the manner prescribed by law. Take the defendant."

Elmore's mother and three of his sisters broke into sobs as friends led them from the courtroom.

Beasley turned to Anderson as they were walking out of the courthouse. "That damn son of a bitch will live longer than I will," Beasley said, expressing his contempt for the long appeal process he knew was ahead. That indeed would be the case.

CHAPTER THREE

Replay

TWENTY MEN WERE ON South Carolina's death row when Edward Lee Elmore arrived in April 1982: thirteen whites, seven blacks. Given this ratio, South Carolina could argue it was not guilty of racism in the application of the death penalty. But all the victims in the cases that put those men on death row were white, save three. This same pattern held in other death penalty states. In Illinois, when the victim was white, it was three times more likely that the defendant would receive the death sentence than if the victim was black. Altogether, across the country, in cases where a person was executed, more than three-quarters of the victims were white.

Elmore's lawyers appealed to the South Carolina Supreme Court, which appointed a thirty-four-year-old prematurely gray lawyer of quiet brilliance, David Bruck, to represent him. It was Elmore's first break. "Almost Gandhiesque" was how a South Carolina prosecutor described Bruck to David Stout, author of *Carolina Skeletons,* a fictional account of South Carolina's execution of George Stinney, the fourteen-year-old put to death after a trial that took only seven hours.

A serene man, Bruck generally maintained a low profile, but he acquired national prominence in 1995 when he represented Susan Smith, the woman who strapped her two small boys into their car seats and then drove her car into a lake. (Dr. Conradi performed the autopsy.) The jury needed only two and a half hours to find Smith guilty of two counts of murder. During his closing argument in the sentencing phase, Bruck opened a Bible and read from John 8:7: "He that is without sin among you, let him cast the first stone." She was given life.

When Bruck looked at the death penalty, he saw what the Supreme Court had seen in *Furman:* most of the men on death row were black and poor. The administration of the death penalty was too capricious, too loosely governed, too inconsistently applied. It was, he said, like a fisherman reaching into his bait box and pulling out a worm for his hook.

Bruck's career was a by-product of the Vietnam War. At Harvard, where he had graduated magna cum laude, he had demonstrated against the war and decided to become a lawyer in order to represent conscientious objectors to the draft and soldiers who refused to go to Vietnam on similar grounds. Accordingly, he chose the University of South Carolina, in Columbia, for law school because it was near Fort Jackson, one of the country's largest army training bases, where he could combine study with practical work. Then the Vietnam War ended, and he felt himself "beached like a flopping fish by the receding waters of the Vietnam antiwar movement." Searching, he headed west. In New Mexico, he worked with the Navajo to stop uranium mining at a sacred tribal site. A Canadian by birth, he then set off for Vancouver, where he planned to represent labor unions. While back in Columbia to gather up his books and few possessions, he learned that hundreds of protesters were being prosecuted for a sit-in at the Savannah River bomb-manufacturing site. He agreed to represent some pro bono and took a job in a welding shop while waiting for the trials to begin. One day, during his lunch break, he read a newspaper story about the resentencing trial of two black men who had been convicted of killing a white gas station owner. On appeal, the South Carolina Supreme Court had reversed the death sentence on several grounds. For Bruck, the case underscored the importance of good appellate work in capital cases where the defendant's lawyer at trial had been ineffective, bordering on incompetent. He went to the state appellate defense office and offered to handle all the death penalty appeals in exchange for an office and a modest salary. He was extremely effective. Of the fifty or so death row inmates whose cases he would handle, he lost only three.

Elmore's case was one of his first. He drove to Greenwood and met with Anderson and Beasley. Bruck asked them about the pubic hairs that the SLED agent claimed to have found on the bed and that were said to have a reddish cast. "If that don't take the cake, a redheaded nigger," Beasley replied, chuckling. Bruck didn't find it funny. Beasley would later say he didn't recall making that remark; he didn't even remember ever meeting Bruck.

In the South Carolina Supreme Court, Bruck argued that Judge Burnett had erred in allowing Joseph Chalmers to sit on the jury, because his daughter was a close friend of Solicitor Jones's daughter, and in excluding Augustus Covington because of his opposition to the death penalty. The court disagreed. The trial judge has wide latitude in deciding who may sit on the jury, it said, and his discretion would not be overturned without a showing that it was totally unsupported by the evidence.

The court was disturbed, however, by how Judge Burnett handled the situation when at least one juror was holding out against the death penalty. His reminder to the jurors that during voir dire, each of them had said under oath that whatever their personal views might be, they could impose the death penalty if the facts warranted it was improper, the court said, because it was directed solely at those jurors who were voting against the death penalty while implicitly approving the decision of those jurors who were voting for it. Judge Burnett had "effectively urged agreement at all cost, rather than reminding the jurors of their right to retain conscientiously held views," the court said.

Elmore had a new trial.

IN MARCH 1984, the State of South Carolina tried Elmore again. It did so in the same courthouse, with the same prosecutor, William T. Jones, again assisted by his daughter Selma.

There was a new judge, however—James E. Moore, a gregarious Greenwood native who had been student body president at Greenwood High in his senior year, an accomplishment he considered so significant that forty years later, when he was a justice on the South Carolina Supreme Court, he was still citing it on his résumé.

When Elmore's conviction was overturned and it was announced that he'd get a new trial, a juror from the first trial, Elizabeth Hackett, thought now "they'd give him a good lawyer." But Judge Moore assigned Elmore the same lawyers, Anderson and Beasley.

In a rare display of assertiveness, Elmore told Judge Moore he wanted "Mr. *Brooks*" to represent him. "I think it would be in my best interest to have some new attorneys," he told the court.

Judge Moore didn't agree. Anderson and Beasley were experienced attorneys who had handled many trials, he told Elmore. "The court is of the opinion that you are represented by two competent attorneys."

Elmore asked if he could at least have some time to get in contact with Mr. Bruck.

Moore was in no mood to delay. "The case, Mr. Elmore, is scheduled for trial to begin on Monday," he said. "Mr. Anderson and Mr. Beasley are your attorneys."

This trial was like watching a video replay of the first one. Jury selection took just over two days, as it had the first time. The entire trial lasted eight days, as had the first one. The state's witnesses were the same—police, SLED agents, Conradi, the neighbor Holloway, and the jailhouse informant, Gilliam. Again, Anderson and Beasley put forward no case, and told Elmore to testify.

Again, when it was Jones's time for cross-examination, he tore into Elmore. The pummeling had just begun when Elmore turned toward Judge Moore and asked if he could speak to him. He spoke so softly that the court reporter couldn't hear.

"For the record, gentlemen," Judge Moore said, speaking to the lawyers, "the defendant requested that he be allowed to speak to me about his nerves being bad; and I've told him that if he desires to make any such statement, it should be part of the record and not off the record."

He turned to Elmore. "You were attempting to tell the court that your nerves are bad. Do you wish to tell me anything further about that?"

"No, sir. I'm not going to say anything."

Jones was fed up. "He's guilty," the solicitor shouted.

Elmore timidly asked if he could talk to his attorneys. No, said Judge Moore. When a witness is being cross-examined, he cannot talk to his lawyers about his testimony.

"I ain't going to talk about testimony," Elmore said.

Moore was puzzled. "About your being nervous? Is that what you want to talk about?"

"Right. Well, yes." He was embarrassed, humiliated, and awkwardly tried to explain. "You know, I been talking about—you know my nerves and all. You know, went to the bathroom."

Edward Lee Elmore, twenty-five years old, had wet his pants.

It took the jury of eight whites and four blacks two and a half hours to find him guilty, exactly the amount of time it had taken the first jury. It took them three and half hours to sentence him to death, beating the first jury by an hour.

Execution was set for June 22, 1984, two years and one day after he was first supposed to be executed.

THE CASE WENT BACK to the South Carolina Supreme Court. The state fared better this time. During the sentencing phase of the trial, Anderson had wanted to call three prison guards as witnesses. They would testify that Elmore had been a model prisoner, had not caused any problems, and could be rehabilitated. Jones had objected, and Judge Moore kept the testimony out. The South Carolina Supreme Court said that the testimony should have been allowed. But because Elmore's mother and four sisters had testified to his good character, it was a "harmless error," the court said. The "harmless error" doctrine, which is the law by statute or high court rulings in all states, stipulates that not all errors during a trial are reversible. Appellants must show that but for the error, the outcome of the trial would likely have been different.

"Mrs. Edwards was savagely attacked and brutally raped," the South Carolina Supreme Court concluded in a two-page opinion.

As his lawyers started the appeals through the federal courts, Elmore was back in prison. He was nervous around other prisoners and would often go days without being able to sleep. He was diagnosed by a prison psychiatrist with acute anxiety and mild depression, and was medicated with Sinequan and Inderal. He was allowed an hour a day for recreation five days a week, a shower five days a week, one visitor a week, and church on Sundays. Fellow inmates affectionately nicknamed him "Brown Bear," from the little animals Elmore made from the arts-and-crafts supplies given to prisoners. He was no trouble for the guards. "Mr. Elmore was always very polite," Calvin Claypoole, deputy warden at the Central Correctional Institution, said. "I see him in the morning, 'Good morning, Mr. Claypoole, how are you this morning?' In the afternoon, it was the same type of greeting. With the behavior of some of the others, the greetings were much more hostile, if you will." Some death row inmates, he said, "in order to get your attention there's spit in your face, there's human waste in your face, there's flooding of cells, setting of fires." Elmore had never done anything like that.

It was just the kind of testimony that Judge Moore had not allowed. Even if Claypoole and prison officials had testified, however, it is unlikely the jury would have been persuaded to spare Elmore's life. His fate seemed sealed. But David Bruck was still representing Elmore in his appeals, and Elmore's case was part of a grand legal strategy. It wasn't by chance that Anderson had sought to introduce testimony about Elmore's good behavior in prison. Bruck had recognized that the U.S. Supreme Court, while unwilling to abolish the death penalty outright, was circumscribing the instances in which it could be imposed and ensuring that defendants found guilty had every opportunity to present evidence in mitigation. Bruck became convinced that eventually the court would say that evidence about a defendant's adaptability to prison—shown by his good behavior there—was a mitigating factor. Thus, he had sent memos to every lawyer handling a capital case to make sure they offered such evidence; it would be excluded, as he knew, but that would provide the basis for an appeal. He was right. In 1986, the case of another of Bruck's clients, Ronald Skipper, was before the United States Supreme Court. He had been convicted of murder and rape. During the sentencing phase of his trial, his lawyer, following Bruck's advice, had sought to introduce testimony of two jailers who would say that during Skipper's pretrial confinement he had been well-behaved and had adjusted to prison life; therefore, the lawyer argued, he would not be a threat to other prisoners if he was sentenced to life in prison, as opposed to execution. The trial judge had not allowed the testimony, and the South Carolina Supreme Court upheld his decision. The United States Supreme Court reversed it. All relevant mitigating evidence must be considered by the jury, including testimony of the prisoner's good behavior in jail, the Supreme Court said.

In light of *Skipper v. South Carolina,* Elmore would get another trial. Not on the question of guilt or innocence, only on the appropriate sentence.

By this time, it would have been hard to find many residents of Greenwood who didn't know that two juries had found Elmore guilty of murdering Dorothy Edwards, so the trial was moved to Newberry, thirty miles east. William T. Jones was no longer the solicitor. After the second Elmore trial, Jones, then sixty-two, had begun to talk about retiring. His son William T. Jones IV, known as Townes, urged him to do so. Jones waited until the last minute to announce that he would not stand for reelection, so it was too late for anyone else to mount a campaign. Many in Greenwood thought Jones's daughter Selma was the brighter and more qualified; several police officers had written in her name. (In a few years, she would abandon the law, move to Boston to study acupuncture, and return to Columbia to practice.)

After graduating from Erskine College, a small Christian liberal arts school in the idyllic town of Due West, South Carolina, Townes had drifted—bartending, waiting tables, working on highway crews, selling vacuum cleaners. He had a reputation for rowdiness, becoming a public embarrassment to his father on one occasion. The senior Jones was prosecuting an evangelical preacher for attempted arson of a policeman's house (the policeman had arrested the preacher's daughter for speeding). The preacher took the stand in his own defense, and on cross-examination, Jones asked him what a man of God was doing hanging out at Jackson Station, where there was drinking and gambling and dope smoking. The preacher-defendant shot back, You ought to know. Your son Townes is there all the time. Spectators had never seen Bill Jones turn so red, the veins in his neck bulging. Townes pulled his life together and went to law school, at the University of South Carolina, then worked as an assistant solicitor in nearby McCormick before returning to succeed his legendary father.

Presiding over Elmore's third trial was a former solicitor from nearby Greenville, forty-nine-year-old William B. Traxler Jr., who had excelled in law school and would later be named to the federal district court by President George H. W. Bush and elevated to the Fourth Circuit Court of Appeals by President Clinton. The judge who had presided over Elmore's first trial, E. C. Burnett, was now the chief administrative judge for the Eighth Judicial Circuit, and it was up to him to appoint lawyers for Elmore. Burnett saw no reason why Geddes Anderson and John Beasley shouldn't handle the case again. But Beasley's racial slur about Elmore—the "redheaded nigger"—caught up with him, and he was quietly removed from the case. Burnett replaced him with a young lawyer, Billy J. Garrett Jr., a Greenwood native. After graduating from Lander University, a small liberal arts school on a hundred acres in the center of Greenwood, Garrett had applied to the University of South Carolina law school but was rejected. A dean told him that it was because of affirmative action—the school was under pressure to admit more blacks. Hold your powder, son, he was told. Don't make an issue of it, and you'll be admitted next year. He did and he was.

Garrett, whose father sold insurance and whose mother worked in a textile mill, was more liberal on race issues than most Greenwood residents. In high school he had African American friends and once invited some to his house for dinner and to toss a football; for that, his parents sternly reprimanded him.

Garrett wasn't sure he should accept the Elmore appointment. He was only three years out of law school and had never tried a murder case. But it wasn't his lack of experience that worried him. He believed in the death penalty. He sought the advice of Rauch Wise, the veteran defense lawyer and resident liberal in Greenwood, who was an unwavering opponent of capital punishment. Your personal views on the death penalty don't matter, Wise told him, so long as you do your best to defend Elmore.

He did. Unlike Anderson, unlike just about everyone who had touched the case until that point except Bruck, Garrett believed Elmore when he said he was innocent. He worked tirelessly, searching for witnesses, chasing down leads; he lost twenty-five pounds in the course of a few months of working on the case.

Garrett argued strenuously to Judge Traxler that Anderson be taken off the case. If the court wouldn't allow that, Garrett said he wanted to argue to the jury that Elmore had been poorly represented at his first and second trials; that his lawyers had conducted no investigation, so the juries heard only a one-sided version of the facts.

Townes Jones objected.

"Mr. Geddes Anderson is probably one of the best public defenders I have ever seen in this state," Townes told Judge Traxler, completely serious. He had defended Elmore "with zeal and with competence."

Traxler allowed Anderson to remain as one of Elmore's lawyers, and he would not allow Garrett to introduce evidence about the dismal nature of Anderson's and Beasley's representation at the earlier trials. He did caution Anderson to watch his drinking.

The Greenwood legal community let the young lawyer know his attacks on Anderson were inappropriate. Garrett wasn't deterred. Reflecting his youth—or audaciousness—he now took on William T. Jones.

At both the first and second trials, when Jones had put Gilliam on the stand, he had assured the court that Elmore had confessed to others while in jail awaiting trial, but in the interest of time and expediency, he had said, he would call only Gilliam. Prejudicially to his client, Anderson, in his belief that Elmore was guilty, had accepted that.

Billy Garrett did not. He asked Judge Traxler to order the state to give him the names of these other individuals. Townes Jones objected. His father had never made any representation that there was another person in that jail to whom Elmore had confessed, Jones told Judge Traxler.

Garrett was prepared. He handed Judge Traxler the relevant portions of the transcripts from the first two trials. "I've got the list here," William T. Jones had told Judge Burnett at the first trial, referring to people in the jail to whom Elmore had allegedly confessed. "But just to save time, I'm going to just stop it off with this man," he had continued, referring to Gilliam.

Judge Traxler was convinced. The defendant had a right to the names of people who were in the cell or had knowledge of the alleged statement, he told the younger Jones.

With that, Townes Jones executed an astonishing pirouette. He now said that he was also trying to determine who the other prisoners were. He offered to put his father on the stand to clear up the matter.

William T. Jones III was sworn in. William Townes Jones IV questioned him. He read to his father what he had said at the first trial about there being other persons to whom Elmore had confessed. It was the statement that, moments earlier, Townes had told Judge Traxler his father had never made.

"Would you please tell us who that individual was, if you

know who that individual was?" Townes now asked his father, seeking at least a second name.

The former solicitor said he didn't remember the person's name.

Even Judge Traxler was having difficulty with this. Here was the best prosecutor in the state, a stickler for details, a man with a legendary photographic memory, and he couldn't remember? "You don't know the name of the individual that you were referring to?" Traxler said, barely suppressing his disbelief.

"I do not," Jones said.

With the self-assurance that comes from years of not being challenged, William T. Jones proceeded to dig himself into a deeper ethical hole. He told Judge Traxler that he had not given Anderson the name of a second person to whom Elmore had confessed because, Jones said, he did not know about James Gilliam until after the first trial started. That was untrue.

Jones referred to the letter Gilliam had written to Sergeant Johnson saying that Elmore had confessed to him. "It was written on the sixth and mailed on the eighth, and we didn't know about it until then," Jones told Judge Traxler. That much was true.

When was the trial? Traxler asked.

"The trial commenced earlier that week," Jones said.

"This is a letter you got in the middle of the trial?" Traxler said.

"At the end of it," Jones said.

This was false, which even a quick examination of the record would have revealed. The trial had not begun "earlier that week," which would have been Monday, April 5. It had begun on Monday, April 12. Solicitor Jones had the letter and had talked to Gilliam on Friday, April 9. Jones himself had told the court that at Elmore's first trial.

Jones was either lying to Judge Traxler now or he had lied in the two other trials about the existence of at least a second person. Lying to judges is serious, a cause for an inquiry by the state bar, possibly even disbarment. But nothing happened.

The preliminary motions were out of the way; it was time to pick the jury. It took two days. There were forty-one on the panel, only four of them black. Townes Jones used his peremptory challenges to remove only two prospective jurors—both were African American. He allowed one black to serve on the jury. This was a constitutional maneuver, executed by Jones on the advice of a man sitting next to him, a lanky lawyer from the state attorney general's office, Donald Zelenka. He was head of the criminal division and handled death penalty appeals, all the way to the United States Supreme Court. Jones didn't want to make an error that might result in another reversal by an appellate court and had asked Zelenka to come over from Columbia to aid him.

By allowing one black juror, Zelenka and Jones were reacting to a recent decision by the United States Supreme Court. In *Batson v. Kentucky*, the court had ruled that if a prosecutor used his peremptory challenges to strike black panelists during voir dire, leaving an all-white jury, it was prima facie evidence of discrimination in violation of the Equal Protection Clause of the Fourteenth Amendment. Prosecutors around the country quickly learned how to get around *Batson*, how to severely limit the number of black jurors without running afoul of the Constitution. One tactic was to question a black panelist at length before exercising the preemptory challenge, thus making it look as if he had not been struck from the jury pool because of the color of his skin but because of his answers to the questions. With Zelenka advising him, Jones did exactly this. His questioning of the four black panelists runs fourteen or fifteen transcript pages for each; his questioning of white panelists averaged two pages.

Once the trial began, Townes's witness list in 1987 was his father's from 1982 and 1984—Holloway; Conradi; police officers Johnson and Coursey; SLED agents Parnell, DeFreese, Wells, and Henderson; Elmore's girlfriend; Gilliam.

Garrett felt he didn't have many options. He knew the textbook approach in a case like this, when only the sentence was at issue, was to load up on mitigation evidence, to try to get the jury to feel enough sympathy for Elmore—because he had a limited IQ, had been raised in poverty, and was quiet and respectable—that it would decide his life should be spared. But Garrett didn't see how he could take this approach, the underlying premise of which was, he's guilty but spare his life. Unlike Anderson and Beasley, Garrett believed Elmore when he said he had not killed Mrs. Edwards. When Elmore told Garrett he didn't want to testify, didn't want to go through it again, Garrett understood and didn't force him to.

Garrett knew the odds were against him. "This community was in an uproar," he recalled years after the trial. "This community wanted blood. In the old days, they'd have lynched him."

It took this jury only two hours and twenty minutes to sentence Elmore to death.

"Mr. Elmore, thirty-six jurors from two counties now have heard your case and sentenced you to death," Judge Traxler said. He ordered Elmore to be executed on May 28, 1987, between 4:00 and 6:00 a.m. "May God have mercy on your soul."

Elmore showed no emotion. His sisters sobbed.

The case forever changed Billy Garrett. He was no longer idealistic about the law. "In my heart of hearts and my soul of souls I trusted the system to work," he said. It hadn't. "I know they set him up. Or if they didn't, they broke all the damn rules of fundamental justice that I was taught to believe in to convict him."

Garrett no longer supported the death penalty. He had seen how the system was abused and subject to manipulation. "Not human error, human *manipulation*," he said. If the death penalty could be imposed in a case like this, without a fair trial, "then we don't have the right as a civilized society to pass this judgment."

David Bruck again represented Elmore when the case reached the South Carolina Supreme Court for the third time. He argued that Jones had used his peremptory challenges to keep two panelists off the jury because they were black, in violation of *Batson*. Justice Ernest A. Finney Jr. agreed. Elmore's lawyers had established a prima facie case of discrimination, he said. But Finney, an African American (who was to become the first African American chief justice of the South Carolina Supreme Court), was a minority of one. The court's four other justices ruled that Elmore had not made a prima facie showing of discrimination—Townes Jones could have excluded the jurors because in their answers to his questions they had vacillated about their views on the death penalty, the court said. The trial court's decision was affirmed. The sentence of death was "not arbitrary, excessive, or disproportionate," the court held.

After three trials, three juries, and three appeals, Elmore was back on death row. He had become a living exhibit for proponents of the death penalty, who argue that the appeals process is too long and drags on endlessly, costing the taxpayers money, depriving the victim's family of closure. "It was a mockery of our justice system," said James Walker, the juror from the first trial who was planning to attend the execution. But it wasn't over. The muscle of the State of South Carolina was about to collide with the grit of Diana Holt: the desire of a state to execute a man who had had three trials met the resolve of a woman to keep him alive until he had had at least one fair trial. The script could have been written in Hollywood, but there was much in it that law students could learn from.

BOOK TWO

Innocence Is Not Enough

CHAPTER FOUR

Diana

O N A CLEAR MONDAY morning at the end of February
1995, Diana Holt walked into the Greenwood County
Courthouse and took a seat at the heavy wood counsel table in
the spacious, high-ceilinged courtroom. Though thirty-six years
old, she had been a lawyer for less than a hundred days and was
working at the South Carolina Death Penalty Resource Center. She was in court representing Edward Elmore, in the same
courtroom where he was first sentenced to death in 1982. Her
goal was to get him a new trial. To succeed, Holt had to convince the judge that thirty-six men and women—three juries at
three trials—had gotten it wrong. She knew what it was to tilt
against improbable odds.

Diana Lynn Holt, née Nerren, was born in El Paso's Provi-
dence Memorial Hospital on June 10, 1958, with blue eyes, a fair
complexion, and blondish-red hair, her mother recorded in her
baby book. She got her surname from Robert Forrest Nerren Jr.
He and Diana's mother, Carroll Jackson, had married while he
was home on a forty-eight-hour leave from the air force, thanks
to a judge willing to overlook that they were both under the legal
age for marriage. They had grown up in the same neighborhood,
but she wasn't marrying her high school sweetheart. It was a
marriage of convenience. Jackson was sixteen and pregnant. She
needed respectability. He needed a cover. His first consensual
physical relationship had been with the chaplain at Francis E.

Warren Air Force Base, just outside Cheyenne, Wyoming. In Guam, where he was posted after his leave and marriage, he was a communications specialist with a top-secret clearance. There he had an affair with a male lieutenant colonel. They were caught, and both were dismissed from the service with a dishonorable discharge. (Many years later, Nerren's friends in San Antonio, feeling that an injustice had been done, helped him get it changed to a general discharge, which is just below an honorable discharge.)

Back in Houston, Nerren and Carroll both knew their marriage was hopeless. They soon divorced. Carroll was not ready to be a mother, let alone a single mom, and sent Diana to live with her grandmother, Jimmie Quentella Griffin, for lengthy spells. She lived in a small three-bedroom house in Waco, Texas, and Diana remembered the backyard as being a "symphony of colored flowers." Her grandmother had only a ninth-grade education. Her first husband was killed in an auto accident while she was pregnant with Diana's mother, and another daughter was run over by a neighbor in his driveway when she was two. Jimmie worked in a Laundromat and was poor, though it seemed to Diana that she was always helping people who had less. In one of the most racist states in the nation, at a time when schools, drinking fountains, restaurants, and just about every other place was segregated, her grandmother was color-blind. She instilled in Diana the values that would define her, including the strength to overcome adversity, not indulge in self-pity, and never give in.

Diana's mother was attractive and had no trouble meeting men. She didn't have great judgment, however. While working as a receptionist at the tony Rice Hotel, she met Wally Bell, or that was the name he used. She was twenty; he was twice that. His real name was Walter Dwinell Belshaw. Beefy and bespectacled, with thick, brushed-back silver hair, he had a checkered past (and a sordid future ahead of him). He had done a spell in federal prison for fraud. They got married on the morning of December 24, 1965, before a justice of the peace. Diana wore a pretty pink dress. Afterward everyone went to breakfast. It was a rare happy moment for the seven-year-old.

Belshaw did a little bit of everything—sold earth-moving equipment, played piano in bars, had bit roles in commercials, wrote book reviews, played Santa Claus at Christmas (the memory of him holding children on his lap spooked Diana when she thought about it years later). As time went on, Diana came to see him as simply a "slob," a con man. Life seemed to swing between Neiman Marcus and Goodwill, mostly the latter.

Every Sunday morning and Wednesday evening, Diana went to Southmont Methodist Church. She was in the Girl Scouts. A photo taken when she was eight shows her with bangs, shoulder-length hair, sparkling eyes, and a smile.

The picture of cherubic innocence concealed a fetid reality. Diana remembers the first time her stepfather told her, "If you put your mouth on this, you can get some milk." She was three or four, as best she can recall. That went on for several years, sporadically, usually in his room, which was plastered with *Playboy* centerfolds. When Carroll and Wally had a daughter, he came up with the girl's name—Stacey Darling Millicent Quentella Belshaw. If she was ever pulled over by the cops, he said, and was asked her name, she could reply, "Why, Stacey Darling. What's yours?"

Diana found escape, solace, and some peace in a mimosa tree in the backyard of their ranch-style house at 5650 Oakham. She would climb it and sit in it for hours.

At school, Diana didn't distinguish herself. In the third grade at Windsor Village Elementary, she got three Cs, in arithmetic, language, and handwriting, and two Bs, in reading and spelling. Still, her teacher that year, Julie Hodges, called Diana's mother to tell her that Diana was quite smart, far more so than she was showing in class.

Sixth grade was memorable for Diana. She was chosen to read to pupils in the lower grades, an honor she still treasured when her own children were adults. "It might not sound like much, but it was a big deal," she remembered. For her American history class she wrote a report about Thomas Jefferson; it seemed to her that his accomplishments sprang from his being a lawyer. There weren't a lot of women lawyers at the time, not even many women law students, but it never occurred to Diana that her gender might be a bar. Her stepfather, however, laughed at the notion and told her she was worthless, that she would never amount to anything. How do you ever find your way home from school, you're so stupid? he'd say to her. Wally's derision aside, her aspiration did seem rather implausible; her highest mark her first year at Dowling Junior High School was a C in English. She got Ds in math, world history, and homemaking. Academic achievement did not mark Diana, but her tongue did—"Miss Sassy," her friends called her.

As a high school junior, she enrolled at Houston Technical Institute, where she got Cs in English and biology and flunked math but excelled in photography. She was the school Female Photographer of the Year, and one of her teachers wrote that she had the potential to become "an excellent professional photographer." She wouldn't, but the talent would give her a lifeline.

Her academic performance suffered because she was high on drugs much of the time. She took Quaaludes and occasionally smoked marijuana—supplied by her stepfather, who also started her on a cigarette addiction that she wouldn't be able to kick until she was in her thirties. Belshaw also taught her to drive. On back roads, he would put his left arm over her shoulders and fondle her. I'm just preparing you for what boys will do to you, he would say. He took her to swanky hotels in Houston, the Rice and the Warwick, where he would point out the rich men and say they could really take care of her, that she could have a lot of money. "Use that gold mine you're sitting on," he would say.

Belshaw thought she should become a model. One day, he took her and her best friend, Kim Pinson, to the house of his friend Luke Leonard, who was a photographer. He would put together a portfolio of the young teenagers, Wally explained. Belshaw and Leonard gave the girls drugs. Soon their clothes came off. Diana felt horrible. Leonard kept shooting.

Kim had long, dark hair, brown eyes, and a wary look. The four of them often went to a Christian-run club, the Seamans

Center, which had pool tables, a swimming pool, and a running track. After one night of wholesome fun there, Leonard, who was in his fifties, took advantage of Kim, who was fourteen; another night, "Kim and my old man made out," Diana recorded in her diary.

(Kim died, at the age of forty-eight, "all alone and scared, after years of brutality and chaos," Diana wrote in a deeply moving tribute on the Classmates site for Dowling Junior High School. "We tried to shield each other from abuse but were unsuccessful. Because of her and others, I eventually made it to safety. Kim did not. . . . I love you dearly, my friend. Yours was the heart of gold others searched for but couldn't reach. Rest peacefully.")

Diana and Kim ran away, hitchhiking to Galveston, some fifty miles from Houston. They met some boys on the beach— "beach rats," Diana called them. More drugs and unpleasant sex followed. After a few days, a couple of police officers who suspected they were runaways stopped and questioned them. Diana was relieved in a way, for she could now tell someone what had been happening at home. The police returned her to Houston and told her mother she should not take seriously what her daughter was saying, that it was typical for runaway teenage girls to say things like that. Her mother agreed with the police, which added to Diana's resentment. She was convinced her mother knew what Belshaw was doing to her, or if she didn't, was willfully ignorant.

Eventually, after falling in love with Diana's Girl Scout leader (whose dealings with young girls were no better than Belshaw's), Carroll decided she wanted a divorce. Belshaw fought to gain custody of Stacey. The custody hearing was held in a court-house in downtown Houston, on an upper floor, providing a view of the city skyline. Under questioning by her mother's lawyer, Diana recounted in detail the sexual abuse she had endured from Belshaw. Cross-examination was brutal. She was accused of making it all up. She was wild, loose, wasn't she? The lawyer pulled out a photograph from his briefcase. It was of Diana naked. It was one of those taken by Luke Leonard. The lawyer took one photograph after another from the table and showed them to Diana. She went numb.

The court decided that Carroll was as unfit to be a mother as Wally was to be a father, and three-year-old Stacey was put in the care of the Harris County Family Services Department. Diana was left with her mother, for reasons she didn't know, but perhaps because she was nearly seventeen and the authorities didn't think she'd be as vulnerable as her little sister. Carroll blamed her loss of Stacey on Diana because of what she had said at the hearing about her stepfather's conduct.

A few weeks later, Diana informed her mother that she was going to the school prom with Irving Washington. He was black. They weren't dating, and he wasn't her boyfriend; they were just good buddies. If she didn't go with him, he'd have no one to go with, Diana told her mother.

Carroll begged Diana not to go with him. She felt she would never get Stacey back if her daughter was dating a black man. It was no use. Diana was Diana—independent, resolute. Words led to blows. Carroll slapped her several times, leaving bruises on her cheeks and a black eye; Diana popped her on the nose, which turned black-and-blue. Diana went to the prom with Irving. A month later, she ran away to New Orleans with some friends she had met at a Houston club.

IT WAS TWO YEARS before she made it back home. She quickly hooked up with a long-haired former high school sweetheart, Mark Bowers, and they were married. "He was sweet but fucked-up," she says. "We were both really fucked-up." His mother, who worked in a grocery store, helped Diana get a job with Decker Meat Company, a subsidiary of Armour & Co. She started as a receptionist, but the owner recognized her ability and she was promoted to sales. In a company-supplied powder-blue Malibu, she traveled the region southeast of Houston, calling on grocery stores and supermarkets, peddling mostly pork products and arranging displays.

One of her customers was Menotti's Meat Market in Dickinson, a small town midway between Houston and Galveston. Now divorced from Bowers, she began dating the owner, Eddie Long, grew careless about her work, and was fired. She got pregnant and in January 1981 gave birth to her first child, a son whom she named Jeffrey Alexander. She was unemployed and on food stamps. She and Long married, had a second son, Justin, and moved to San Marcos. Long owned several quarter horses, and Diana spent much time in the barn, grooming and feeding them. There is a picture of Diana, in a down jacket, her blond hair wildly curly, Janis Joplin–style, with Mark Me First, a quarter horse, after it won a three-hundred-yard race at Manor Downs, Texas's oldest pari-mutuel horse-racing track, on a cold, wet, and windy Sunday, February 7, 1982. (At the same time, far away, Edward Lee Elmore sat in jail awaiting his trial.) Diana, always with an excess of energy and drive, now opened a tanning salon in the San Marcos shopping center. She was proud. "Only two tables—but it was mine," she said later. She called it Totally Tanned.

Like her mother, Diana didn't have great judgment when it came to men. She was becoming more liberal but was attracted to redneck conservatives. Long was an angry Vietnam vet. The third time he hit her, she moved out, saying she was going to get a divorce. A few days later, she went by the house to pick up her remaining possessions. Never one who could hold her tongue, she taunted Long: "Oh, by the way, asshole, I got a lawyer." He jumped out of a chair, slammed her against the wall, pulled her hair, kicked and punched her. "Fuck you," she said, "I'm not afraid of you." He grabbed a Titan .25-caliber automatic pistol—with three rounds in the magazine and one in the chamber—jammed it in her stomach, and pulled the trigger. She heard a click. But no bullet fired. She ran out of the house, jumped into her car, and roared through the broad streets of San Marcos to her tanning studio. She ran down the hallway and into her office, picked up the phone, and called the police. Long was right behind her. "As soon as I get out, cuz they can't hold me forever, I will kill your ugly ass," he shouted at her. A few minutes later, the police arrived. "He has a gun!" she screamed, crying and shaking. The police officers drew their weapons and ordered Long to put his hands on his head. They handcuffed him and took him away. Diana left in a separate car. At the station, a police officer showed her the bullet that he had taken from Long's gun. He pointed to a small indentation where the firing pin had struck it. The gun had jammed.

Long was charged with aggravated assault with a deadly weapon. The case dragged on for nearly a year, with Diana unaware of what, if anything, the district attorney was doing until she received a subpoena to appear in court. She arrived early, demure in a loose-fitting lavender skirt, and waited for the case to be called. She waited and waited. At the end of the day, the case still had not been called, and she asked the clerk what was going on. The charges were dismissed, the clerk said; it was just your word against his.

It was a turning point. "I really felt fucked over," she recalled. That sixth-grade dream had never died, and she began to think seriously about becoming a lawyer. Her grandmother encouraged her. She sold Totally Tanned and moved to Waco to live with her grandmother again. She started at McLennan Community College, then transferred to North Harris Community College. After four semesters of straight As, she enrolled at Southwest Texas State University, LBJ's alma mater (since renamed Texas State University–San Marcos). Again she got all As—in algebra, world history, biology, zoology, Spanish, even Golf I. She got pregnant and married the baby's father, Gordon Holt, who worked for a wholesale electrical supply company; they had met through friends. While raising three small boys, she was on the dean's list every semester and graduated summa cum laude, with a major in English and a minor in political science.

She sent off her law school applications, including to Harvard. Hell, why not go for it? she thought. She wasn't surprised when she didn't get in. Given her past, she was amazed when the University of Texas admitted her. In response to the question, Why do you want to practice law? she had written: "I want to practice law because I want to help other people—people who have not been afforded much help in their lives." Holt entered law school thinking she would eventually work in the field of juvenile justice.

Then she encountered Jordan Steiker. He taught property, which is formulaic, all metes and bounds, primogeniture, how to pass on your wealth. Somehow, he managed to work in his passionate opposition to the death penalty. Before coming to Texas, he had clerked for Justice Thurgood Marshall, for whom capital punishment was "morally unacceptable," as Marshall wrote in *Furman*. During the first week of class, Steiker invited his students to join him at a popular beer and burger joint in Austin. He talked about the death penalty. He told them how Justice Marshall instructed his law clerks that whenever an application for a stay of execution came into the court, he was to be notified immediately. Once, Steiker called Justice Marshall around midnight to tell him a stay request had come in. "How are you going to vote?" Steiker asked respectfully. "I can't believe you called me," Justice Marshall boomed back. "You know how I'm going to vote."

The first death penalty case Holt remembers following was that of Charles Brooks, in 1982. It was only the sixth in the country and the first in Texas since the Supreme Court had reinstated the death penalty, and so was major news. Brooks, from a well-off Fort Worth family, and an accomplice, Woody Loudres, had been sentenced to die for the kidnapping and murder of a twenty-six-year-old auto mechanic, whom they bound and gagged and shot once in the head. They had been tried separately. Loudres's conviction was overturned on appeal, and in a subsequent plea bargain he was sentenced to forty years in prison. Brooks's lawyers then sought to have his death sentence set aside: it did not seem right that Loudres should live and Brooks be executed when they were guilty of the same murder. Besides, only one shot had been fired, and it was not clear who had pulled the trigger. The Supreme Court turned down his appeal, 6–3.

When Brooks was strapped to a gurney and wheeled into the death chamber at the state prison in Huntsville, Texas, on

December 7, 1982, he became the first person to be executed by lethal injection. This so-called humane way of death touched off a fierce debate. Opponents of capital punishment feared that juries might find it easier to impose "humane" execution. Some death penalty advocates were against it as well. "It's too lenient," said a young man who had joined a gathering outside the Huntsville death chamber for Brooks's execution. "They've got to go painfully."

Lethal injection as a method of execution had first been proposed in the nineteenth century by a New York doctor as cheaper than hanging, but was not adopted. Britain rejected it in the early 1950s because of opposition by the British Medical Association. Oklahoma was the first state to use it, in 1977, and eventually all capital punishment states followed. The condemned is strapped onto a gurney and wheeled into the execution chamber. Witnesses are on the other side of a window, looking in. The man's arms are swabbed with alcohol, and two intravenous tubes are inserted, one in each arm. From another room, unseen by the condemned man or the witnesses, the executioner first releases a general anesthestic into the tubes. (In surgery, 100 to 150 milligrams is used; for executions, as much as 5,000 milligrams.) This is followed by a muscle relaxant, which paralyzes the diaphragm and lungs, thus making it impossible for the condemned man to breathe. Finally, potassium chloride may be injected, causing death by cardiac arrest.

Death penalty lawyers mounted systematic challenges to the method, and numerous state and federal appellate courts granted stays. In 2008, the United States Supreme Court spoke, in the case of Ralph Baze and Thomas Bowling, who had been convicted of double murders in Kentucky. Their lawyers argued that there was a significant risk of the drugs being improperly administered and that therefore lethal injection was "cruel and unusual," in violation of the Eighth Amendment. A range of organizations filed briefs in support of the position, including the ACLU, the Louis Stein Center for Law and Ethics at Fordham University, Human Rights Watch, and the American Association of Jewish Lawyers and Jurists. The Bush administration and sixteen states filed "friend of the court" briefs in support of Kentucky, which was seeking to execute.

The court rejected the argument. Writing for the majority, Chief Justice John Roberts noted that since 1879, when it upheld use of the firing squad, the court had rejected every challenge to the method of execution. "Our society has nonetheless steadily moved to the more humane methods of carrying out capital punishment," he wrote. "The firing squad, hanging, the electric chair, and the gas chamber have each in turn given way to more humane methods, culminating in today's consensus on lethal injection."

Justice John Paul Stevens joined the majority but said he did so only because he felt bound by the court's previous rulings upholding the constitutionality of the death penalty. Stevens, who had voted with the majority when capital punishment was restored in 1976, made it clear that it was time for state legislatures to consider repealing their death penalty laws. "State-sanctioned killing," he wrote, was "becoming more and more anachronistic."

HOLT WAS NOT AGAINST capital punishment as she listened to the radio reports of Brooks's execution, though she was unnerved by the method. It was not until her first year of law school that her opposition to the death penalty began to take shape. She befriended a Mexican woman and her friends who had camped out on the sidewalk in front of the governor's mansion to protest the pending execution of the woman's son. She brought them food, sympathy, and, with her Spanish, someone they could talk to. In the academic cloister, she discussed capital punishment with her contracts professor, Tom Russell. Close in age, he and Diana became good friends, often talking about their children. He was struck by how quiet she was. "The shiest student you could find," Russell said. During three years of law school, "Miss Sassy" barely spoke. She and Russell debated whether he should write on the blackboard the name of every man who was executed in Texas on the day it happened. She encouraged him to do it. But he wasn't tenured and backed off.

When Holt told Russell that she thought she wanted to work as a death penalty lawyer, he had serious doubts that her commitment would survive the three years of law school, which have a way of turning idealists into corporate lawyers.

In her first year, Diana applied for a Texas Law Fellowship, for students interested in careers in public interest law. Diana doubted she had much of a chance—there were only ten fellowships—but she got one, and the $3,000 stipend was a welcome addition to the family budget. On the recommendation of Professor Steiker, she went to work at the Texas Death Penalty Resource center, in Austin. There were twenty similar offices in capital punishment states around the country. Congress had created them in 1987, in an attempt to provide men and women on death row with competent counsel to challenge their convictions, which often were the result of grossly incompetent trial counsel. Resource center lawyers were strikingly successful—half the death penalty cases they handled ended up with the conviction or sentence being reversed—and the centers came under attack from conservatives. "Taxpayer-funded nests of saboteurs who believed it was their mission to grind the system to a halt," as one conservative legal voice, Kent Scheidegger, put it. He was right that they were taxpayer funded, and if keeping a man alive meant grinding to a halt the system that was going to kill him, the lawyers did that—just as any good corporate lawyer would do if it meant protecting his client from paying out millions of dollars in damages in commercial litigation.

Sheidegger's saboteurs were Holt's heroes, role models, and mentors—Rob Owen, Raoul Schonemann, and Eden Harrington, names as unknown to the public at large as they were well-known to death row inmates. They were energetic, idealistic, passionate lawyers. Diana caught their spirit and found her calling. "Poisoned, hooked, there will be nothing else," she said.

The lawyer who had the most influence on Holt that summer was Joe Margulies. Intense, wiry, and bearded, he was slightly older than the others and had already lost some of his idealism about criminal justice. He had grown up in suburban Washington, D.C., the son of a government lawyer, and had been uncertain what he was going to do when he went to college. Searching, he took a leave of absence from Cornell to work as an investigator in the public defender's office in Washington, D.C. After a year and a half, he returned to Cornell, graduated, and went to work with the public defender in Minneapolis. He was jolted by the state misconduct he witnessed. Police and prosecutors would dissemble, conceal and plant evidence, and engage in other unethical conduct in order to gain a conviction. He decided to become a lawyer, graduated from Northwestern University Law School with honors, and naturally migrated to Texas, the most active state in executions.

"I thought a bunch of smart young lawyers who worked really hard could stop the killing machine," he said, looking back more than two decades later. "I really believed that. We were so fucking young and smart and talented. We all went to hot-shit law schools and clerked and had hot-shit résumés. We worked insane hours. Insane. We were nuts. Drank like fish. It took me a long time to get past that, and not before I burned out big-time." When he ceased representing death row inmates, he still raged against injustice and didn't shy away from unpopular causes. He would be one of the first lawyers to defend suspected terrorists held at Guantánamo and in the secret prisons, signing up when the anger about 9/11 was still raw and lawyers who took the cases were labeled un-American and traitors.

Holt found him to be "dynamic, charismatic, brilliant, wacky," and an exacting mentor. "He could peel the skin off," Holt recalled years after studying under his tutelage. "It was effective—you weren't going to make that mistake again." He also instilled confidence. He once sent Diana and another intern to Del Rio, Texas, to interview a cop who had a particularly nasty reputation and had been thrown off the police force for violence. Diana's colleague decided after a few days in Del Rio that it was too dangerous and bowed out. Joe called Diana and asked if she felt in danger. If she did, she should come home. She said no and that she would call him if it became too risky. He trusted her judgment, and her confidence slowly grew.

"Are you a fact lawyer or a law lawyer?" Margulies barked at Holt on one occasion. She stammered that she was both. "Goddamn it, Holt," he shot back, "anybody can take the law and write it out. You have to have the facts."

In criminal defense appellate work, "law lawyers" are ardent students of the Constitution and can dissect the Supreme Court cases interpreting it. They argue when appropriate that their client did not get a fair trial or was denied effective assistance of counsel, that the state failed to turn over exonerating evidence, that blacks were excluded from the jury, that this constitutional provision and that were violated. Fact lawyers investigate vigorously and search for evidence that shows their client did not commit the crime or, if he did, that his life should be spared. Diana was to become a fact lawyer extraordinaire, an investigator's investigator. No matter how deeply the state had sought to bury evidence, she could find it. She had an ability to get folks to open up to her, even confess to murder. "It's amazing what people will tell her," said a colleague. Maybe her diminutive size put people off their guard. There was also a bit of actress about her, and her Texas accent would become noticeably thicker when she was trying to gain someone's confidence.

The second year of law school didn't beat the idealism out of Diana either. Margulies suggested she broaden her experience by working at the South Carolina Death Penalty Resource Center.

WHAT THE HELL am I doing? Holt thought. It was June 1993 and she was driving across the South in her Nissan minivan loaded with clothes, pillows, photographs, everything she thought she would need, want, and miss during a summer in South Carolina. Most of all, she knew she'd miss her boys—Jeffrey was a few months shy of becoming a teenager, Justin was ten, and Christopher was about to turn five. Am I a horrible mother, leaving them for ten weeks? she asked herself. She was scared, heading toward a totally new experience, but at the same time proud that she had the courage to travel halfway across the country by herself.

On Sunday, she pulled up in front of a town house on the outskirts of Columbia. Her roommate, a first-year law student from Georgetown University in Washington, D.C., Marta Kahn, had already arrived. "There are only two things you need to know about me—one, I smoke, but I'll do it outside," Marta said as they introduced themselves. "Two, I would strongly recommend not speaking to me in the morning." Diana grinned. She smoked, too. And morning was most definitely not the time to talk to *her*.

They bonded quickly—"We're like that Thelma and . . . and . . . what's her fucking name?" Diana exclaimed one day—though they were from totally different backgrounds. Marta, whose father was a psychologist and a staunch Republican (until after one presidential term of George W. Bush), had gone to an elite private girls' school in the nation's capital, National Cathedral, followed by Yale, where she graduated magna cum laude. Marta traced her liberalism to an incident at the Capitol when she was fifteen or sixteen: she had watched as a black man was arrested and roughed up by the cops. At Yale, she took a course on the death penalty.

Marta was ten years younger than Diana and Diana became her best friend, part big sister and part mentor. "She took me under her wing," Marta said. "She was my big booster, a cheerleader, gave me confidence." Marta had never met anyone quite like her—fearless, antiestablishment, passionate, and determined. "When she gets her teeth into something, you'd better not try to take it away."

That first Sunday, after unpacking, Diana suggested they drive down to the resource center and check it out. The center is on the second and third floors of a brick building on the corner of Lady and Sumter, around the corner from the South Carolina Supreme Court. The carpet was worn, the file cabinets were battered, the chairs rickety, and papers were tossed into boxes, which were piled up in closets—a garden-variety public-interest law office.

Margulies had told Holt that two brilliant death penalty lawyers ran the center, David Bruck and John Blume. They became her "gods," though they had entirely different personalities—Bruck was serene, Blume explosive. Never one to shy away from difficult men, Diana gravitated to Blume, whom she found brilliant and bold. The first time she heard his voice, booming from his office down the hall, she thought he sounded like Jethro from *The Beverly Hillbillies.*

During Diana's first week as an intern, she and Blume had a conversation about the center's death row clients. "I don't allow myself to believe any of them are innocent," Blume said. For him, guilt or innocence wasn't the issue. The issue was justice—good defense lawyers, ethical prosecutors, in short, a fair trial. "You've been doing this too long," Holt shot back. She realized later hers was an inappropriate remark.

Over six feet tall with shoulder-length hair, John Henry Blume III was intensely competitive, in court and on the playing field; golf clubs and tennis rackets were part of his office decor. His office attire was shorts and tennis shoes in the summer, blue jeans in winter; a suit and tie were on standby in the corner for court appearances.

Blume grew up in a motel in Myrtle Beach, South Carolina, which his parents owned. At fifteen, he was the Junior Men's East Coast Surfing champion. After graduating from the University of North Carolina, he went to Yale for a master's in theology. While a divinity student, he worked for New Haven legal aid, primarily with juvenile offenders. He decided that he could do more good as a lawyer than as a Methodist minister, so he shifted to Yale Law School. After his first year there, he worked as a summer associate in a large Atlanta law firm, generally a step to a well-paying job with the firm postgraduation. But he was still infused with a sense of social justice.

One morning, he read in *The Atlanta Constitution* about what had become known as the Alday murders, which had shocked the state, region, and nation. Three prison escapees had broken into a farmhouse in Seminole County, Georgia, looking for money and guns, and killed Jerry Alday, his father, two brothers, and an uncle. They forced Jerry Alday's wife into a car and brutally raped her before killing her. In separate trials, the three men had been convicted and sentenced to death. Their cases were now on appeal, and Millard Farmer, the prominent civil rights lawyer, was representing one of them. Blume called Farmer and volunteered to work on the case.

The Alday case was the kind of horrific crime that swells the ranks of capital punishment advocates and makes it hard for death penalty agnostics not to become believers. Blume didn't deny the horror of the crime, but to him the trial had been a farce, a legal lynching. Over half the jurors had been to the Alday funerals, but the judge refused to grant a change of venue or to disqualify them. The Georgia lieutenant governor had been brought in as special prosecutor. As an idealistic law student, Blume thought this was a cause worth fighting for. (Years later, the convictions were overturned on the grounds that the pretrial publicity and community uproar had made a fair trial virtually impossible. On retrial, two of the men, Wayne Coleman and George Dungee, were sentenced to life in prison. Carl Isaacs was sentenced to death; he spent thirty years on death row before he was executed in May 2003.)

In representing men on death row, Blume had found his calling, one that "resonated with my religious background and training—all have sinned and fallen short of the glory of God." But the work exacts a toll. It is emotionally draining to watch a person you have fought for, maybe even gotten to know a bit as a human being, be strapped into the chair or onto the gurney. Burnout is high. Blume found release in music. When his wife gave him an acoustic guitar one Christmas, he rounded up a few musically inclined friends and soon they had a band. They called it The Reprieves.

When Blume turned fifty, he was still a death penalty lawyer, one of the most prominent in the country, and was teaching death penalty law at Cornell University in Ithaca, New York. "I can't imagine doing anything else," he said. "If you care about justice, it's hard to find a field in which there's more injustice than the death penalty."

Elmore's case reeked of injustice to Blume. He wasn't sure why he had given the file to Diana when he was handing out cases to the summer interns. Maybe it was just serendipity, he said years later. Blume didn't offer much guidance, beyond telling her to look at everything afresh; he had even less of an idea where such looking might lead.

A few days later, Holt drove out to the Broad River Correctional Institution, on the outskirts of Columbia, announced herself at the gate, and was led by a guard to a common area. Elmore's name was called, and he came out with a big smile. They sat at a picnic table, in the open air, talking. He was so soft-spoken, so docile, so childlike, that for Diana it was almost "innocence at first sight." She didn't see how someone so gentle could commit such a violent crime. Maybe she had been gullible, she thought later. And the more death row inmates she met and represented, the more guarded she was about concluding they were innocent. But her initial belief that Elmore was innocent grew to certitude the more she worked on the case. Diana would never say she favored Elmore over her other clients. But friends and colleagues detected that she had a special place for him in her heart. She spent time with his family, his sisters and brothers, and earned their trust, which wasn't easy. "My people, they not used to lawyers, but they like Diana," Elmore said. "She's family," said his brother Charles.

She came to banter easily with Elmore. "You can go out there and get a tan," she said once during a telephone conversation on a hot summer day. "I think I'm tan enough already," he said, laughing. When he said he did ten sets of fifty sit-ups each day, Diana responded, "We could put you on a video workout for abs." He laughed. He liked the teasing. "It's good to have a sense of humor, because it is so tense, good to have somebody who can break it down and make it a little lighter," he said.

Elmore's home was an eight- by ten-foot cell. It had a stainless steel toilet and basin and a metal bed bolted to the wall; each inmate was given a plastic mat for the bed. There was a window, about six feet high and three inches wide. The door was solid metal, with a covered slot that would slide open for meal trays and a window through which the guards could look when doing the daily count. Elmore was liked and trusted by the guards. His day would begin around 4:30 in the morning, and after breakfast he worked around death row, cleaning the floors and serving meal trays to other men on "the row," as they called it. He also took food that inmates wanted heated in a microwave to one of the two ovens on the floor. For a few years he had a television in his cell, but when it finally gave out, he didn't have the money to buy a new one.

CHAPTER FIVE

The Intern and the Neighbor

A HEAT WAVE HIT COLUMBIA in July 1993. Temperatures exceeded one hundred degrees for seventeen straight days. With the air-conditioning blasting, Diana sat on the floor in the common area of the center's office, which was crowded with busy interns; her legs crossed, she bent over and perused the Elmore record. When she read the testimony of Mrs. Edwards's neighbor Jimmy Holloway, she was dumbfounded. He was on the stand longer than any witness—thirty-three pages of transcript—and Holt had to read his testimony more than once to absorb its full impact.

"Mr. Holloway, if you will, make yourself as comfortable as you can there and pull that up close where His Honor, the judge, and the fourteen jurors can hear and understand what you have to say, along with counsel for the defendant, please, sir," Solicitor Jones began on the fourth day of Elmore's first trial. Answering questions from Jones, Holloway told the jurors where he lived, where Mrs. Edwards lived, how they had met (at the Oregon Hotel), how long had they been neighbors (thirty-six years). Holloway said that he had watched over Mrs. Edwards after her husband died, and that he had a key to her house.

Jones asked Holloway about the events of Monday, January 18, 1982. He said that he had been surprised to see her car in the driveway, because Mrs. Edwards had told him and his wife that she was going out of town on the weekend, to visit her boyfriend. He decided he should check on her, he said. It was about ten minutes after noon. "When I rounded the curve of the carport," Holloway said, "I noticed that the Sunday morning *Greenville News* and the Monday morning *Greenville News* was laying out there. I picked these two up, thinking maybe Mrs. Edwards was sick, which we have found her before that way."

He knocked on the back door. There was no answer.

"Was the door locked?" asked Jones.

"No, sir."

He went in, he said, and saw the broken pieces of the flowerpots, the partial denture, and the needle-nose pliers on the kitchen floor. He said he heard the television blaring. He proceeded down the hall to her bedroom.

"Give us the benefit of what you remember at this time seeing then," Jones said.

"I remember that her alarm clock was on and ringing."

"Was that an electrical alarm clock?"

"Yes, sir," said Holloway.

"Will they keep on running?"

"Yes, sir."

"All right. Go ahead."

"This is a matter of seconds; I did not see her in her bed and—"

Jones started to ask him about the chest of drawers, but Holloway wanted to talk about the bathroom.

"You went to the bathroom?"

"Yes, sir."

"Tell us what you saw in the bathroom."

"I saw a bloody commode and stuff," said Holloway.

"All right, sir," said Jones.

"I realized that something had happened."

He went on: "As I came out of the bathroom, I finally saw the west wall of her bedroom."

"All right, sir," said Jones.

"I looked down and I saw a knife and I saw these things to the left."

"All right, sir. And on the floor was there a considerable amount of blood that you saw?"

"A tremendous amount."

"All right, sir. At this point, I certainly realize that you had to be upset, but what—did you look into the closet? Was the closet door open or closed?"

"The closet door had—was ajar, but I did not open it at this time. I decided that I should have somebody with me."

Holloway told the jurors that he turned around and walked out of the house, retracing his steps, and went over to see Mrs. Clark, who lived next door.

Did you call the police then? Jones asked.

No. Holloway answered that he and Mrs. Clark had gone back to Dorothy's house.

"Now, where did you and Mrs. Clark go in the house?"

"I went to Mrs. Edwards's bedroom where I saw the bloodstains."

"All right, sir. When the two of you got there, what if anything did you do?"

"I took a pair of woolen gloves out of my hip pocket and I used the corner of the door to the closet to let me open the door to see if her body would be there. And it was."

"The door was ajar about how far?"

"Approximately four inches."

"And then you pulled it how many more inches, or feet?" Jones asked.

"Oh, four or six inches. Enough for me to see what I saw."

"And what did you see?"

"I saw the body of Mrs. Dorothy Edwards."

Jones returned to the automatic coffeepot in the kitchen. It was set for six o'clock. Holloway said he had one just like it.

"You cannot set that coffee pot before seven p.m. the night before if you want it to come on at six o'clock the next morning," he said.

"I want to be specific, now," Jones said. "Do I understand you to tell us that if you want to set it for six a.m.—could the night before at six twenty you set it for six a.m. the next morning?"

"If you did, the coffee would come on then."

"Right then."

"Yes, sir."

Holloway said that he had returned to the house the day after the body had been found, Tuesday.

"During the day of Tuesday, did you obtain services of people to clean up the dust in there of the fingerprinting efforts around the house, plus removing the blood-soaked material?" Jones asked.

"Yes, sir," said Holloway.

WHEN HOLT had finished reading Holloway's testimony, she was aghast, dumbfounded. A writer of a cheap crime novel wouldn't have dared to invent the kind of things that took place. The police had let Holloway into the house to clean it less than twenty-four hours after the crime had been discovered, before anyone had been arrested, before even an arrest warrant had been issued. That the policemen Coursey and Johnson had allowed the person who had found the body, and who therefore in Criminal Investigation 101 should have been a prime suspect, to roam through the house unescorted was beyond comprehension. The questions cascaded in Diana's mind. As Holloway walked through the house, why had he left the television blaring, the alarm clock ringing, the coffeepot on? Why had he gone to get Mrs. Clark? And what about the gloves he put on before opening the closet? From that moment on, Holloway was a suspect to Holt, even if he had not been to the police, and the longer she worked on the case, the more her suspicion gave way to near certitude.

JAMES HOLLOWAY SR. MOVED to Greenwood from Macon, Georgia, in 1939, when he was twenty-three years old. He went to work as a meat cutter for Big Star, a chain of self-service supermarkets that was just beginning to open in the South. The war came and Holloway enlisted; he eventually became a second lieutenant in General Patton's army. Discharged in early 1946, he returned to Greenwood, to the house on Melrose Terrace, and to Big Star. When the grocery chain wanted to transfer him to a bigger store, in Spartanburg, he declined and opened his own grocery store in Greenwood, Big Dollar, at the corner of Phoenix and Magnolia, on the edge of the black community. "Black people have green money and buy white Sunbeam bread," he explained to his son.

He was an energetic small-town entrepreneur. After Big Dollar came the Nuway Ice Cream Parlor, on the square, then another grocery store, Jimmie's Supermarket, on South Main; with four checkout stands, it was one of the largest grocery stores in South Carolina. Eventually, he sold out to a national chain, Piggly Wiggly. He later sold the ice cream parlor and Big Dollar and went into the restaurant business. First he opened Be-Bop, on Phoenix Avenue, followed by Seaboard Diner, on the street of the same name. These catered to Negroes. "Sandwich basket" places, they were called, forerunners of fast-food chains. For less than a dollar, you got a deep-fried pork chop between two pieces of white bread, coleslaw or fries, and an orange drink, which Holloway and his son, Jimmy Junior, made, and which was so big you had to hold it in two hands.

Holloway had another restaurant that catered to whites, where you could get a Delmonico steak, a potato, bread, and tea for $2.19. His wife, Frances, made the pies and cakes; Jimmy Junior was the short-order cook and tended to the jukebox. It was called Holloway Inn, and Holloway unabashedly copied the lettering and blinking lights from Holiday Inn. When a Holiday Inn opened in Greenwood in the early sixties, the first modern hotel in Greenwood, Holloway was hired as manager. Frances ran the food services. Jimmy Junior sat on the roof and watched movies at the drive-in on the other side of Route 25.

A couple of years later, Jim Self, a textile magnate, asked Holloway to run the food service at Self Memorial Hospital, which was built largely with his philanthropy. Frances became the hospital's nutritionist. She didn't have much luck with her husband, who was overweight and had a sweet tooth. He retired in 1980, at the age of sixty-four. In good health, he spent time in his woodshop, building a boat, and at his cabin on Lake Green-wood. Dorothy went there often.

HOLT GOT UP from reading Holloway's testimony and ran down the hall to Blume's office. "John, you won't believe this," she shouted. She begged him to let her talk to Holloway. It wasn't the kind of request Blume normally got, to start investigating a case as if it were at the trial stage. As he was to learn, Diana wasn't quite like other law students, interns, or death penalty lawyers.

Holt rented a car and set out for Greenwood. It was summer; the trees along Route 178 were green. She smoked one cigarette after another for ninety nerve-racking minutes.

She parked on the street in front of 207, walked across the lawn, and knocked on the door of the modest redbrick house with a screened porch. Mrs. Holloway came to the door. Holt, conservatively dressed in a summer skirt, introduced herself in her best southern drawl. "I'm a law student at the South Carolina Death Penalty Resource Center. I'm working on the case of Edward Elmore. Could I speak to Mr. Holloway?" Mrs. Holloway showed her to the den. She meekly excused herself and backed out of the room. Holloway was sitting in a big easy chair—a king on his throne, Holt thought to herself. He was wearing slacks and a short-sleeved oxford sport shirt; he looked like he had just come from teaching Sunday school.

Holt had worried that Holloway would cuss at her, tell her never to come back, and slam the door. But he seemed almost eager, excited, to talk about Elmore and the murder. He started off by saying that he had checked up on Elmore with other folks in the neighborhood he had worked for, and the consensus was that he was hardworking, polite, and trustworthy.

She hadn't been there five minutes when Holloway volunteered, "I am the only one who could kill her and get away with it." Before Holt could stammer, "Is that right? Why?" Holloway continued, "The way she trusted me."

Holloway had a reputation in the neighborhood for pushing

his chest out a bit, trying to seem more important than he was, and now he gave Holt the impression that he enjoyed telling her what he knew. She said very little, just kept writing in her spiral notebook. The neighbors thought he and Dorothy were having an affair, Holloway told Holt. He didn't deny it categorically. She was too polite, or bashful, to ask. He went on and on, without much prompting. It struck Diana that he showed no remorse or sadness that his dear friend and neighbor for nearly four decades had been murdered; he never choked up, didn't shed a tear. "She was born with a silver spoon in her mouth," he said. "She insisted on the finer things. She would buy anything she wanted. She always wore expensive suits." Dorothy and his wife, Frances, were about the same size, he said, and Dorothy often gave her old suits to Frances.

To this stranger, this law student he had never met, Holloway spoke with crude intimacy and in a demeaning way about his neighbor. "I don't see how she wanted any man," he told Holt. "The coroner's report showed that her ovaries were messed up. Sex would have been painful." Why would Elmore have wanted to have sex with her? Holloway asked. "It's not like she had beautiful breasts or anything."

He talked about the murder in detail. The killer had gotten in because Mrs. Edwards trusted him, Holloway said. She had opened the door, and the killer had stuck his foot in it, to block her from shutting it. During the ensuing struggle, Holloway claimed she had grabbed a pair of tongs from a kitchen drawer, only to have the killer take them away from her. "That's what did most of the damage," Holloway told Holt. "He used the ice tongs on her repeatedly." Her death had been slow and painful, he said. "It took twenty-five to thirty minutes for her to die."

Holloway said the police might have suspected him at first, since he'd found the body, and the neighbors had said he and Dorothy had been having an affair. "I told them about Elmore," Holloway now told Holt. "I have no guilty conscience about this whatsoever," he said.

Holt could scarcely believe what she was hearing. When

she had finished, she politely thanked him and said good-bye to Mrs. Holloway. She kept calm as she walked to the car. But as soon as she was behind the wheel, she lit a cigarette and then raced back to Columbia. She couldn't wait to tell Marta what had transpired. Goddamn, how does she do it! Marta thought. She was convinced Elmore would be freed.

Holt, ever bold, went back to see Holloway two more times that summer. He cleared up the mystery of how in the course of their investigation the police had known to look in Mrs. Edwards's checkbook.

"I told them to get me her checkbook and I can pick out the boy who did the chores," Holloway told Holt. "I looked in the book, found Elmore's name, and said, 'This is the man right here.'"

That left another question: How had he known that she paid Elmore with a check? Holt didn't ask him.

At the end of Holt's last visit, Holloway seemed to understand where she was headed. "You're going to try to frame this on me, aren't you?" he asked her. "Well, we're ready for you if you do." Holt wasn't sure what he meant. (Holloway died in 1994.)

Holt's suspicions about Holloway grew a few weeks later. She went to Pensacola, Florida, to interview Mrs. Edwards's daughter, Carolyn Lee. Carolyn received Diana graciously. Turning to her mother's murder, Carolyn recalled for Diana the telephone call she had received from Holloway.

"Hey, Carolyn, this is Jimmy. Are you sitting down?"

"Hi, Jimmy. Yeah, I am."

"I hate to tell you, but your mother's dead."

Carolyn told Diana she found it cold—and strange.

Upon receiving the news, Carolyn had gone to Greenwood, straight to Holloway's house. Together they walked over to her mother's. While there, the phone rang. Carolyn was surprised when Holloway answered it.

"Dorothy's not here; she's dead. Good-bye," Holloway told the caller. It was Dorothy's boyfriend, Lonnie.

Carolyn told Diana that her mother and Lonnie had planned

to marry. When she went through her mother's things at the house the day after the body was discovered, Carolyn said, she had found a negligee in a suitcase. She believed her mother had packed it for her trip to North Carolina to visit him.

For Holt, everything was falling into place now. "Motive uncovered," she thought to herself while interviewing Carolyn. In a word, jealousy.

This was Holt's scenario: Holloway was jealous that Dorothy was going to meet Lonnie. He had gone to her house on Sunday morning before she was to leave. A lovers' quarrel ensued. He lost control. He began jabbing her with the paring knife, as if to say, Here, take this; here, take that—which explained why the wounds were so shallow. Then he set about cleaning up the house, which took him all of Sunday. That night, he set the coffee machine and alarm clock, and opened the *TV Guide* to make it appear she had been murdered Saturday evening. Holt couldn't explain everything, though: Why, for example, had he put the tongs in the drawer to be sure they'd be found?

Elmore may have had three trials, and thirty-six men and women may have found him guilty, but, in Holt's view, the jurors were not told the truth about Holloway. "They did not know that there was reason to suspect him," she would argue on one occasion in trying to get Elmore a new trial. "Those thirty-six people did not know Holloway was the one who could kill Mrs. Edwards and get away with it, the way she trusted him so." Holt's imagination seemed to get the best of her. "Mr. Holloway had owned a grocery store and was later a director of food services. No one pointed out that all the things used to harm Mrs. Edwards were implements from the kitchen, all associated with food. No one pointed out how arranged the kitchen looked after Mrs. Edwards's killer left. Someone returned the tongs, used to do ghastly things to her corpse, to the kitchen drawer. Someone closed the drawer, careful that the tongs were still visible to whoever searched the kitchen."

Holt hadn't come to this seemingly bizarre hypothesis on her own. A retired New York City cop, Vincent Scalise, whom Holt had interviewed as part of her investigation, suggested it to her.

It was suspicious in and of itself that Mrs. Edwards's body had been secreted in the closet, Scalise said. He had been a consultant in the investigations into the John F. Kennedy and Martin Luther King Jr. assassinations, and in his view, Mrs. Edwards's murder was not a random act of violence but had been carefully planned. It was, in his words, "an organized crime that was made to look like a disorganized crime." Elmore didn't have the mental capacity for that, he said.

Holt may have suspected Holloway, but no one else had. Not even Billy Garrett, the one lawyer who believed Elmore was innocent. "I had no inkling that he might be guilty," Garrett said years later. "He was a pillar of the community." Jim Coursey, one of the principal police investigators, was aware of the rumors that Holloway and Edwards were having an affair, and he even thought they might be true, but he just shrugged; the police didn't ask any of the neighbors about the relationship. Roy Raborn, who lived next door to Holloway, wasn't sure what he would have told them. "I still believe Mr. Holloway was 'hooty pooty' around a little bit with her, but I don't believe he would go that far," he said. "As for playing around, yeah, but a lot of men do that and they don't kill."

BLUME WAS IMPRESSED with Holt. When her summer internship was over, he suggested that she move to South Carolina and finish law school there. She kept telling him there was something about her past that he needed to know. He dismissed her, figuring it was about drug use, and that didn't bother him. She was flattered by Blume's offer, but she wasn't about to trade a law degree from the University of Texas, one of the top twenty law schools in the country—where her trial advocacy seminar was taught by the legendary Michael Tigar, a brilliant legal mind and liberal activist, and Dick DeGuerin, a preeminent criminal defense lawyer—for one from the University of South Carolina, which barely ranked in the nation's top hundred. After she returned to Texas, Blume paid for her to fly back to Columbia every other weekend to work on the Elmore case. Finally, in December 1993, she pulled up stakes in her native Texas and moved to South Carolina, after the University of Texas said she could finish at the law school there if a professor agreed to hold her to UT standards. She was now divorced from Gordon Holt, after six years and one son. He had scoffed at her desire to work as a death penalty lawyer, said she wasn't going to be able to make a difference. She had been hearing that all her life, and accepting it, but she was slowly acquiring a sense of self-worth. She had also come to believe that the law was a powerful instrument for doing good.

Holt was hooked on the Elmore case. "You couldn't pry my hands off it," she said. She was convinced he was innocent, a conviction that would grow stronger as she investigated further and discovered more. She became equally convinced that Holloway was the perpetrator. But however guilty Holt might think Holloway was, she had no venue to try him. She wasn't a prosecutor. She couldn't convene a grand jury. The best she could hope for was a new trial for Elmore.

207 Melrose Terrace, home of Dorothy Ely Edwards, a seventy-six-year-old widow who was found murdered in her bedroom closet in Greenwood, South Carolina, in January 1982 *(Greenwood Police Department)*

A newspaper photo of investigators at 207 Melrose Terrace the day Mrs. Edwards's body was found (The Index-Journal)

A damaged family photo of Edward Lee Elmore, circa 1979

James Holloway Sr., Mrs. Edwards's next-door neighbor and close friend, as he appeared in a contemporary local newspaper. Holloway found Mrs. Edwards's bloodied body and called the police. His actions and later statements to Elmore's lawyer Diana Holt raised questions. (The Index-Journal)

Mrs. Edwards's bed. This is the only picture the police investigators took of the bed where the state claimed she was sexually assaulted. The potentially contaminating camera equipment on the bed belongs to the police investigators. (*Greenwood Police Department*)

A police photo of the kitchen where the state claimed the perpetrator had forced his way into the house and beaten Mrs. Edwards. A partial denture was found on the floor, and a pair of tongs, which was used on the victim, was sticking out of a drawer. (*Greenwood Police Department*)

The war memorial in downtown Greenwood on which the local men who died in World Wars I and II are listed by race—"White" and "Colored." *(C. Rauch Wise)*

The Greenwood County Courthouse, where Edward Lee Elmore was tried, convicted, and sentenced to death in 1982 *(C. Rauch Wise)*

After thirty-two years as the county prosecutor, William T. Jones III, who prosecuted Elmore at his first and second trials, hands off the office to his son Townes, who prosecuted Elmore in his third trial. Judge James Moore, the judge in Elmore's second trial, is in the background of this newspaper photo. (*The Index-Journal*)

Billy J. Garrett Jr., only recently out of law school, was assigned to represent Elmore at his third trial. Garrett was convinced that Elmore was innocent, and the unfairness of the trial in his eyes caused him to switch from being a believer in the death penalty to a staunch opponent. (*Courtesy of Billy Garrett*)

Diana Holt would become the lawyer most committed to getting Elmore a fair trial. She'd had an extremely hard early life and legal problems of her own. Here she is at seventeen in Baton Rouge, Louisiana.

Elmore's appellate legal team (left to right): John Blume, Diana Holt, Christopher Jensen, and David Bruck, on the steps of the South Carolina Supreme Court after a hearing in the case (*Kevin Bell*)

Edward Lee Elmore being led into the Greenwood County courtroom for a hearing in December 2000. His lawyers were seeking a new trial after finding evidence that the state claimed had been lost since January 1982. (*WSPA*)

Earl Wells, the state forensic chemist who had examined evidence and then claimed to have lost it. He found it sixteen years later in his office desk, where it had been all along. He's listening to testimony at the hearing when Elmore's lawyers accused him of perjury. (*Associated Press / Mary Ann Chastain*)

Diana Holt, Edward Lee Elmore, and John Blume at the hearing
(Associated Press / Mary Ann Chastain)

Donald Zelenka, head of the capital litigation unit at the South Carolina attorney general's office, who vigorously opposed a new trial for Elmore *(WSPA)*

Judge J. Ernest Kinard Jr. presiding over the hearing. He ruled against Elmore's request for a new trial, adopting the state's argument wholesale. *(WSPA)*

Edward Lee Elmore's family waving to him as he was driven back to prison after the hearing *(Associated Press / Mary Ann Chastain)*

Judge J. Mark Hayes II, who ruled on Elmore's request that he not be executed because he was mentally retarded *(Bob Dalton / Spartanburg Herald-Journal)*

CHAPTER SIX

Innocence Is Not Enough

H OLT WAS WORKING fourteen, fifteen, up to eighteen hours a day on the case, every day. It was February 1995, some twenty months after she had first heard of Edward Lee Elmore. Since then, she had graduated from law school and been admitted to practice in South Carolina, and was in an unlikely relationship with a civil litigator, Kevin Bell (who would become husband number four).

On February 28, Holt, with Elmore seated next to her, was in the Greenwood courthouse where he had first been convicted and sentenced to death thirteen years earlier. It was the first day of Elmore's post-conviction relief hearing, or PCR, the venue for a convicted defendant to argue that there are material facts the trial court failed to consider that justify a new trial. It is much like a civil trial before a judge. The convicted defendant may present new evidence and witnesses, who are examined and cross-examined. Holt's cocounsel, and at this point the lead lawyer, was a high-priced corporate litigator from New York, J. Christopher Jensen. He was forty-seven years old, sported a bushy mustache, wore eyeglasses, and was representing Elmore pro bono. Their goal was to get Elmore a new trial. Although the record showed that Elmore had had three trials, "we don't think he's had his first trial yet," Jensen told J. Ernest Kinard Jr., who was presiding over the hearing and would decide if

Elmore deserved a new trial. "In thinking about this last night, it occurred to me that this was like a loosely knit sweater—the whole case, a very loosely knit sweater—and if you tug on any strand, the whole sweater comes unraveled," Jensen went on in his opening statement to Judge Kinard, a fifty-five-year-old jurist who had grown up in nearby Newberry. Unravel it is just what Holt and Jensen were about to do, and when they finished, the sweater would bear little resemblance to the one that Jones, father and son, had woven for the juries.

J. Christopher Jensen was a partner with a prestigious New York City law firm, Cowan, Liebowitz & Latman, specializing in intellectual and property disputes. His office in a high-rise on Avenue of the Americas, between Forty-Third and Forty-Fourth Streets, had a view of Bryant Park and the New York Public Library. Like many corporate lawyers, Jensen felt a need to do something more meaningful than help rich people get richer. He signed up with a program the American Bar Association had launched in 1986 to recruit lawyers to handle the appeals of death row inmates. For a condemned man to get one of these lawyers was like winning the lottery. Jensen had been linked up with the South Carolina Death Penalty Resource Center. John Blume asked him if he'd take the Elmore case, even before Holt had appeared as a summer intern. Jensen wasn't quite sure why he had said yes. He was partly motivated by the legal challenges of the case and, he admitted, by the ego gratification that comes if you are successful.

Jensen had grown up a conservative in Idaho, the son of a Walgreens pharmacist, but had moved east and drifted left. At Columbia University during the tumultuous late 1960s, he had demonstrated against the Vietnam War and had avoided the draft as a conscientious objector. But he was not opposed to the death penalty out of any religious or moral beliefs. His misgivings arose out of his years of experience in the courtroom. The adversarial nature of a trial is based on the notion that justice will be done when opposing sides vigorously present their case through competent, motivated lawyers. As cherished and valued as it is, the adversarial system is run by humans, and humans make mistakes. It is one thing for judges and jurors to err in a civil case, for weak and incompetent lawyers to represent the plaintiff or defendant, but quite another matter when a man's life is at stake. It was the way the judicial system had worked in Elmore's case, or more accurately had failed to work, that troubled Jensen.

"I look at his trials—actually three trials—and I can't believe it!" he said. Excluding jury selection, each of Elmore's trials lasted three days. "Three days!" In most cities, a drunk driving case takes longer; even a trial for petty shoplifting might. To Jensen, the representation Geddes Anderson and John Beasley provided Elmore didn't even rise to the level of abysmal. "What's the point in having a lawyer at all?" asked Jensen rhetorically. He was about to display what a really good trial lawyer could do.

The O. J. Simpson trial was in its second month at the time of Elmore's PCR hearing. One day, a teacher at Greenwood High School brought his class to the courthouse. During a break, he introduced himself to Jensen, explaining that his students were fascinated by the Simpson case and he wanted to show them a trial in action. "You want to draw a perfect parallel," says Jensen. "Look at these two trials. Two guys charged with murder. No eyewitnesses. Lots of forensic evidence—blood, fingerprints, hair. Elmore gets a three-day trial, no meaningful defense. Simpson's trial goes on for months. Look what money gets you." Holt bristled when comparisons were made to the O.J. case. There was no doubt in her mind that Elmore was completely innocent; she was not so sure about O.J.

Jensen never asked himself whether Elmore was guilty or innocent. It was not a question he had to address. For Jensen, like many criminal defense lawyers, in defending a criminal suspect he is defending the integrity of the judicial system and the Constitution, as well as the individual. By demanding that a guilty person have a fair trial, defense lawyers are ensuring that an innocent person will as well. Eventually, after looking at the evidence, listening to the witnesses, and consulting experts,

Jensen came to believe as Holt did that Elmore was innocent. He wasn't surprised that Elmore might have said to a couple of cops, "Okay, if you say I did it, but I don't remember." Like everyone who met Elmore, Jensen was struck by his childlike nature; he was always trying to please and never argued. Jensen was wary of being seen as the northern liberal coming down to teach southern rednecks about justice. He knew he had entered a foreign world, however, when he met William T. Jones, who asked, "What's your church?" Jensen was taken aback. In New York, you don't ask someone you have just met about his religion, and Jensen didn't think it was any of Jones's business that he was an atheist, a descendant of Mormon pioneers who had married a Jewish girl from New York. As he spent more time in South Carolina, though, Jensen came to realize the significance of the religious question. In the South, the death penalty is acceptable to many because it is cloaked in religious righteousness.

Jensen wasn't flamboyant, not in the manner of F. Lee Bailey, Gerry Spence, Alan Dershowitz, or Johnnie Cochran. But he'd had the best courtroom training a young lawyer can get—six years in the U.S. attorney's office for the Eastern District of New York (in Brooklyn), rising to chief of the civil division. He and Diana now made a formidable team, he in court, she out of court. Together, they did all the things any good defense counsel would have done at Elmore's trial, so many things that Anderson and Beasley had not. They interviewed witnesses, found their own experts, dug up evidence the state had sought to hide, and exposed inconsistencies, discrepancies, and lies. As they kept at it, they were at times astonished. The state's case against Elmore was more flawed, weaker, and more marred by questionable prosecutorial conduct than they had realized.

But the barricades Holt and Jensen had to get over, around, or through to get Elmore a new trial were more redoubtable than those Anderson and Beasley had faced in seeking to have him acquitted in the first instance. Once a person has been convicted, no matter how shaky the conviction, there is set in motion an almost inexorable process that ends in his execution.

Once a person has been convicted, gone is the presumption of innocence. On appeal, the presumption is that the defendant had a fair trial, that the jury acted reasonably. It is not enough for his appellate lawyers to sow reasonable doubt, even if there was a lot. It was not enough for Holt and Jensen to produce evidence, if they had it, that Holloway was the probable perpetrator. It was not enough to show that Anderson and Beasley were lazy, or that Anderson was drunk, or that Beasley was a racist. It was not even enough to present a persuasive case that Elmore was innocent. Innocence alone does not entitle a defendant to a new trial.

The Supreme Court had articulated this two years earlier in *Herrera v. Collins.* "Due process does not require that every conceivable step be taken, at whatever cost, to eliminate the possibility of convicting an innocent person," Chief Justice William Rehnquist wrote for the majority. "To conclude otherwise would all but paralyze our system for enforcement of the criminal law." Which is to say, the need for finality in legal proceedings sometimes trumps what might be seen as fundamental fairness. Leonel Torres Herrera, a drug dealer, was on death row in connection with the murder of two Texas police officers. Ten years after Herrera had been convicted, his brother Raul told his lawyer that he had killed the officers, who, he said, were involved with them in a drug-running operation. Raul's oldest son also swore that he had seen his father kill the officers. Based on these confessions, Herrera sought a new trial.

The court ruled that Herrera was not entitled to one. Federal courts "sit to insure that individuals are not imprisoned in violation of the Constitution—not to correct errors of fact," Rehnquist explained. After a defendant has had a fair trial, "the presumption of innocence disappears," he noted. In order to get a new trial, a convicted person has to establish that one of his constitutional rights was violated.

Justice Blackmun dissented. "I believe it contrary to any standard of decency to execute someone who is actually innocent," he said. He underscored his feelings by reading his opinion aloud from the bench. "The execution of a person who can show that he is innocent comes perilously close to simple murder." Justices John Paul Stevens and David Souter joined Blackmun.

Justice Antonin Scalia scoffed. The justices were letting their personal opinions override sound legal reasoning, he said. If the majority decision offended their consciences, he went on, "perhaps they should doubt the calibration of their consciences or, better still, the usefulness of 'conscience shocking' as a legal test." Justice Clarence Thomas agreed.

Four months after the court had spoken, Herrera was strapped to the gurney. His last words: "I am innocent, innocent, innocent. Make no mistake about this. I owe society nothing. I am an innocent man and something very wrong is taking place tonight." The needles were inserted.

The Herrera case was not a good one to test whether a claim of innocence warrants a new trial. The evidence "overwhelmingly demonstrates" that Herrera killed the two policemen, Justice Sandra Day O'Connor noted in a concurring opinion; the affidavits submitted a decade later are "bereft of credibility."

Lawyers and activists seeking to use the courts for fundamental social change, whether conservative or liberal, look for cases that present compelling facts; the legal issues are wrapped around those. For opponents of capital punishment seeking to have the courts allow a new trial on the basis of new evidence, it would have been better to have a case in which the claim of innocence was strong, a case like Elmore's for example. But Herrera's lawyers had an ethical obligation to their client to pursue every appeal. *Herrera* was also one of those cases that bolster the argument of law-and-order conservatives, and the belief of many Americans, that death row lawyers file frivolous claims. But when you're fighting to keep a man alive, who is to say that a claim is frivolous?

The day *Herrera v. Collins* was decided, the flags in the capital were at half-mast. Justice Thurgood Marshall had passed away the day before at the age of eighty-four. People waited for hours in a long weaving line to pass his coffin, which lay in state at the Supreme Court. The National Cathedral was filled and millions watched on television. It was the passing of a legend, a man who had grown up in the segregated South, been turned away at hotels, and argued *Brown v. Board of Education,* and the only member of the court to have defended a murder case. The court had lost an unwavering voice against the death penalty, but the previously uncertain voice of Justice Blackmun had acquired a new tone.

In *Furman,* Justice Blackmun had dissented from the views of Marshall and Brennan that capital punishment was unconstitutional, and he was consequently in the majority that upheld the constitutionality of the death penalty in *Gregg.* Two decades later, studying the appeals from death row inmates that had come before the court, he concluded that "the death penalty remains fraught with arbitrariness, discrimination, caprice, and mistake." His observation came in the case of an African American, Bruce Callins, who had been convicted and sentenced to death for the murder of a white man during the robbery of a topless bar. With his execution imminent, his lawyers filed for a writ of certiorari, the formal name for what is essentially a request for review. Under the Supreme Court's rules, four justices must agree before a case is accepted for full argument, a rule necessary to winnow the hundreds of appeals the court receives to a manageable number. The justices rarely issue opinions when deciding whether or not to accept a case, but simply note in one paragraph whether the writ was granted or denied. But Blackmun had something to say about capital punishment and his own evolution. In a highly personal seven-thousand-word, twenty-two page opinion, Justice Blackmun made reference to all the wrongs that he had seen over the years, from bad lawyers to prosecutorial-inclined judges to overly zealous prosecutors.

"For more than 20 years, I have endeavored—indeed, I have struggled—along with a majority of this Court, to develop procedural and substantive rules that would lend more than the mere appearance of fairness to the death penalty endeavor," Blackmun wrote. "Rather than continue to coddle the Court's delusion that the desired level of fairness has been achieved and the need for regulation eviscerated, I feel morally and intellectually obligated simply to concede that the death penalty experiment has failed."

He concluded: "From this day forward, I no longer shall tinker with the machinery of death." It became one of the best-known utterances of his long and illustrious judicial career, says his biographer Linda Greenhouse.

Justice Scalia mocked his fellow justice. Convictions in opposition to the death penalty are often passionate and deeply held, he said, but that is "no excuse for reading them into a Constitution that does not contain them." Reflecting the depth of the emotion on both sides of the capital punishment debate, how deeply divided the country, Scalia went on:

> Much less is there any excuse for using that course to thrust a minority's views upon the people. Justice Blackmun begins his statement by describing with poignancy the death of a convicted murderer by lethal injection. He chooses, as the case in which to make that statement, one of the less brutal of the murders that regularly come before us—the murder of a man ripped by a bullet suddenly and unexpectedly, with no opportunity to prepare himself and his affairs, and left to bleed to death on the floor of a tavern. The death-by-injection which Justice Blackmun describes looks pretty desirable next to that. It looks even better next to some of the other cases currently before us which Justice Blackmun did not select as the vehicle for his announcement that the death penalty is always unconstitutional—for example, the case of the 11-year-old girl raped by four men and then killed by stuffing her panties down her throat. How enviable a quiet death by lethal injection compared with that! If the people conclude that such more brutal deaths may be deterred by capital punishment; indeed, if they merely conclude that justice requires such brutal deaths to be avenged by capital punishment; the creation of false, untextual and unhistorical contradictions within the Court's Eighth Amendment jurisprudence should not prevent them.

Justice Blackmun was the lone voice for review, and on Texas death row, awaiting his execution, Callins wrote the justice a short letter thanking him. "I hope you are at peace within yourself for doing as you did," he wrote. Callins was strapped to the gurney on May 21, 1997.

The Supreme Court in *Herrera,* however, left open the possibility that a defendant's claim of innocence might entitle him to a new trial. But it would require "a truly persuasive demonstration" of actual innocence, and the threshold for making the claim was "extraordinarily high," the court said. Maybe impossibly high. Not even contradictory statements by prosecutors about who committed a murder were enough.

Jesse Dewayne Jacobs was arrested for killing Etta Urdiales, the wife of his sister's boyfriend, who had been abducted, taken to the woods, placed on a sleeping bag, and shot in the head with a .38. Jacobs confessed to the police. But at trial, he said that in fact his sister Bobbie Hogan had killed Urdiales. The jury found Jacobs guilty and sentenced him to death. Several months later, the State of Texas charged Hogan with the murder. Now the prosecutor, the same man who had prosecuted Jacobs, told the jury that the state had been wrong in saying Jacobs had killed Urdiales. After further investigation, he said, he had concluded that Hogan had in fact committed the crime. The jury convicted Hogan of involuntary manslaughter.

Jacobs sought a new trial, arguing that the state was now saying he had not killed Urdiales, that it had, in effect, disavowed the evidence on which it had convicted him. The U.S. Supreme Court declined to take the case, 6–3. "I find this course of events deeply troubling," said Justice Stevens, who voted to hear the case. "It would be fundamentally unfair to execute a person on the basis of a factual determination that the state has formally disavowed." Jacobs was executed on January 4, 1995.

The Jacobs case is not unique. In Texas, James Lee Beathard was executed, in 1999, for the murder of Gene Hathorn Sr., his wife, and their fourteen-year-old son while they were watching television in their mobile home in East Texas. No physical evidence connected Beathard to the crime—no fingerprints, no footprints, no blood. He was convicted largely on the testimony of an accomplice, Gene Hathorn Jr., who harbored a deep hatred of his father and thought he would inherit under his father's will. "Hathorn might be a cold-blooded killer, but there hasn't been any evidence in this courtroom that he is a liar," the prosecutor, Joe L. Price, said during his closing argument at Beathard's trial. Several months later, the prosecutor tried Hathorn, who again pinned the blame on Beathard. Now, in his closing argument to the jurors, Price said that if they believed Hathorn, "I'm a one-eyed hunting dog." Hathorn was also sentenced to die. (His conviction was eventually reversed by the Texas Court of Criminal Appeals, and in a plea agreement, he was sentenced to life in prison.)

It is easier for a camel to pass through the eye of a needle than for a condemned man claiming innocence to get a new trial.

In Missouri, Joseph Amrine, in jail for robbery, was convicted and sentenced to die for killing an inmate. There was no physical evidence linking Amrine to the murder, but three prisoners testified that he had told them that he had killed the man. All three later recanted, and a prison guard said that the real killer was one of the inmates who had fingered Amrine.

The state refused to give Amrine a new trial. He'd had his day in court. "I tend to defer to the twelve people who sat in the jury box and looked at the witnesses in the eye," said Missouri attorney general Jay Nixon (who later became the state's Democratic governor). "This case has been reviewed by many good judges." That was the state's mantra in death penalty cases: the jury has decided; judges have reviewed it; how can there be any question that the man is guilty? In Elmore's case, state officials argued it was *three* judges and *three* juries who had decided.

When Amrine's case reached the Missouri Supreme Court, Nixon's office argued that a claim of innocence did not justify a new trial. This is what the Supreme Court had said in *Herrera*. During oral argument, Justice Laura Denvir Stith was judicially incredulous.

"Are you suggesting if we don't find there's a constitutional violation and if even we find that Mr. Amrine is actually innocent, he should be executed?" she asked the state's lawyer.

"That's correct, Your Honor," he answered.

Another justice, Michael Wolff, was equally disbelieving.

"To make sure we are clear on this, if we find in a particular case DNA absolutely excludes somebody as the murderer, then we must execute them anyway, if we can't find an underlying constitutional violation at their trial?"

"Yes, Your Honor."

The justices of the Missouri Supreme Court could not accept that. "It is difficult to imagine a more manifestly unjust and unconstitutional result than permitting the execution of an innocent person," the court said. Relying on Missouri law, not the U.S. Constitution, it overturned Mr. Amrine's conviction and ordered a new trial.

Missouri prosecutors were not ready to give up. They wanted to perform DNA tests of the blood on Amrine's clothes to see if it was the victim's. Earlier, Amrine's lawyer, Sean O'Brien, a passionate and effective advocate for death row inmates, had asked the state for the clothes so that they could do just that. The state said that the clothes had been destroyed. Now, miraculously, they were found. Ultimately, the state realized it didn't have a case, and Amrine walked out of prison after serving eighteen years for a crime he didn't commit. Elmore's case looked a lot like Amrine's.

HOLT AND JENSEN knew that they were facing the *Herrera* barrier: To get a new trial for Elmore, they had to do more than present evidence that he was innocent. They had to establish that his constitutional rights had been violated.

One of their arguments continued to be that Anderson and Beasley had represented Elmore so incompetently that he had been denied his right to counsel as guaranteed by the Sixth Amendment. It is an argument frequently advanced by lawyers representing death row inmates in their appeals. It is a difficult argument to win. "Judicial scrutiny of counsel's performance must be highly deferential," the Supreme Court declared in 1984, in *Strickland v. Washington.* There is "a strong presumption that counsel's conduct falls within the wide range of reasonable professional assistance," it went on.

It doesn't take much for judges to find that the *Strickland* standard has been met, that the representation has been adequate. "The Constitution, as interpreted by the courts, does not require that the accused, even in a capital case, be represented by able or effective counsel," a Fifth Circuit Court of Appeals judge declared in one case. "Consequently, accused persons who are represented by not-legally-ineffective lawyers may be condemned to die when the same accused, if represented by effective counsel, would receive at least the clemency of a life sentence." A Texas court trial judge went further: "The Constitution doesn't say the lawyer has to be awake." Or sober.

In North Carolina, Thomas Portwood relieved the pressure of handling capital cases with a fifth of 80-proof rum most nights, even during trial. He swore it didn't affect his performance. One of his clients, Ronald Frye, was convicted and sentenced to death for stabbing his landlord with a pair of scissors. As with most capital cases, there was no question of Frye's guilt; the issue was whether he should be executed. The story of Frye's life was numbingly similar to the stories of a great many men on death row—poverty, child abuse, alcoholic parents, limited mental abilities. When he was a small child, his mother gave him and his brother to a couple she met at a gas station. The man was an alcoholic; he bullwhipped the boys regularly and forced them to whip each other as he watched. When Frye was taken from the couple's custody, at age eleven, he went to live with his biological father and his second wife. His father forced him to watch as he beat his wife. As a teenager, Ron Frye was heavily into crack and alcohol, and he suffered migraine headaches and delusions. Portwood presented none of this to the jury.

On appeal, Frye's lawyers argued that he had been denied effective assistance of counsel because Portwood had been drunk. A federal district court disagreed. There was no indication that "Portwood's performance was impaired by his addiction," the judge wrote. The U.S. Supreme Court turned down Frye's appeal.

Frye was strapped to a gurney. "I'm sorry," he said to the nephews of the man he had killed, who came to witness the execution. "Forgive me."

IN ELMORE'S CASE, South Carolina vigorously defended the representation that Anderson and Beasley had provided. "It revealed a quality of justice which I think is appropriate in this state, a hard-driving defense," the state's lawyer, Donald Zelenka, told Judge Kinard during Elmore's PCR. Beyond that, he went on, "we submit that this case will stand for the proposition that we in South Carolina do have a system of justice that we can stand behind. We do have quality representation by members of the bar." He defended the prosecutors as well. "We do have honest and ethical and justice-seeking decisions by the prosecutors of this state, particularly William Jones and Townes Jones." Holt kept a lawyerly poker face.

Zelenka couldn't resist a barb at the lawyer from New York and at Holt, who had lived in South Carolina only a year or so. "I regret that sometimes people from outside the state don't understand or really recognize all the communities in which we live in this state and the ability of attorneys who practice law in this state, the prosecutors who have been involved in this state to separate and seek justice, not just seek somebody to be convicted."

Holt, sitting only a few feet away, felt like saying, Excuse me, Mr. Zelenka, aren't you from Ohio?

Yes, indeed. Donald John Zelenka was born and raised in Akron; his father was a mechanical engineer with Ohio Edison. After Firestone High School, where he'd worn his blond hair fashionably collar length, in the early 1970s, he studied economics at Ohio State, where he was a member of the Interfraternity Council and played trombone in the marching band. He moved to South Carolina for law school, impressed by USC's faculty and clinical programs as well as "the big-time USC sports with

Frank McGuire's basketball and Paul Dietzel's football teams." But in his heart he remained an Ohioan, as much as Holt did a Texan. He returned each year for the Ohio State–Michigan football game and played slide trombone in the alumni band. Decades after moving to South Carolina, his favorite football teams were still the Ohio State Buckeyes and the Cleveland Browns; the Cleveland Orchestra (along with Bruce Springsteen and Cat Stevens) made his favorite music.

During law school, labor relations and employment law were the courses he enjoyed the most. He finished in the top third of his class and went to work for the federal court in Richmond, Virginia, doing computerized research, a relatively new phenomenon. Persuaded by friends, he returned to Columbia and went to work in the attorney general's office; he was twenty-seven, with his hair still long but thinning. He had found his calling, and by the time of Elmore's post-conviction review, he was in charge of the capital litigation unit—and balding.

He appeared several times before the United States Supreme Court, arguing on behalf of the state that a man's conviction and death sentence be upheld. He became an unexpected footnote in history due to one case, *Holmes v. South Carolina*. Bobby Lee Holmes was convicted of the rape, robbery, and murder of an eighty-six-year-old woman. The trial lasted four days. The prosecution introduced Holmes's palm print, which had been found at the scene; fibers from his sweatshirt were found on the victim's bed; her DNA turned up in his underwear; her blood on his tank top. Holmes maintained he was innocent, and his attorney, William Nettles, who would become U.S. attorney in South Carolina, sought to introduce evidence that another man had committed the crime. The trial court excluded the evidence of a potential third party's guilt. John Blume represented Holmes before the U.S. Supreme Court. He argued that the trial court's exclusion of the evidence violated the defendant's constitutional right to a fair trial. Zelenka argued that the prosecution's case was overwhelming, and that a defendant's right to introduce evidence was "not unlimited" but was subject to "reasonable restrictions." Near the end of his allotted time for oral argument, Zelenka was interrupted by a question from Justice Thomas, about the standard the court was to apply. It was a notable moment and was to become more so. Justice Thomas did not often speak from the bench, and this question, in 2006, was the last he asked for more than five years, the longest any justice had gone without asking a question for at least forty years. At issue in *Holmes* was an evidence rule under which a defendant may not introduce evidence that another person had committed the crime in question when the court felt that the prosecution had presented a strong case of guilt. States have wide latitude in establishing rules of evidence, but there are limits, the court said. And this rule, Justice Samuel Alito said for a unanimous court, denied the defendant "a meaningful opportunity to present a complete defense," and was therefore unconstitutional. (Following the Supreme Court's decision, Holmes was sentenced to life without parole.)

Zelenka was uncompromising in his support for capital punishment. A woman who had an abortion in the third trimester was guilty of murder and should be executed, he argued in one case. He was disappointed when the Supreme Court ruled in 2005 that executing a person who was under eighteen when he committed the crime he was being punished for was barred by the Eighth Amendment. The decision, in *Roper v. Simmons*, overturned the court's contrary ruling issued only sixteen years earlier. At the age of seventeen, and a junior in high school, Christopher Simmons planned to commit a burglary and murder "in chilling, callous terms," Justice Anthony Kennedy wrote for the five-person majority. Simmons assured two accomplices they would get away with it because they were minors. They broke into Shirley Crook's house at two in the morning, put duct tape over her eyes and mouth, tied her hands, put her in a minivan, and drove her to a state park, where they threw her from a railroad trestle into the Meramec River, in eastern Missouri. However horrific the crime was, the majority held that "the death penalty is a disproportionate punishment for juveniles." Capital punishment must be limited to those whose "extreme culpability makes them the most deserving of execution," the court said, citing an earlier Supreme Court case. A juvenile offender does not fit this category, the court said. For one thing, "as any parent knows," Justice Kennedy wrote, juveniles lack the maturity and sense of responsibility of an adult. Kennedy went on to say that the court, over the many years of ruling on death penalty appeals, had recognized that there were two purposes served by capital punishment: retribution and deterrence. "Whether viewed as an attempt to express the community's moral outrage or as an attempt to right the balance for the wrong to the victim, the case for retribution is not as strong with a minor as with an adult," Kennedy wrote. "Retribution is not proportional if the law's most severe penalty is imposed on one whose culpability or blameworthiness is diminished, to a substantial degree, by reason of youth and immaturity." As for deterrence, "it is unclear whether the death penalty has a significant or even measureable deterrent effect on juveniles," Kennedy wrote.

In reversing its earlier ruling that it was permissible to execute juveniles, the court looked at the "national consensus" and "evolving standards of decency," which were tests for interpreting the Eighth Amendment, the majority said. Thirty states prohibited execution of minors, the court noted: twelve rejected the death penalty altogether, and eighteen states that had the death penalty exempted minors. Finally, the majority noted, "the overwhelming weight of international opinion is against the juvenile death penalty."

Justice Scalia dissented, joined by Chief Justice Rehnquist and Justice Thomas. A "strict constructionist" who looked to the Founding Fathers' "original intent" in deciding cases, Scalia declared that the Constitution hadn't changed from when the court had earlier ruled that the Eighth Amendment did not prohibit the execution of juveniles. He had no use for the concept of interpreting the Constitution by looking at "evolving standards of decency." He was most disdainful, however, of the notion that the United States should consider the views of other nations. "The Court thus proclaims itself sole arbiter of our nation's moral standards—and in the course of discharging that awesome responsibility purports to take guidance from the views of foreign courts and legislatures. Because I do not believe that the meaning of our Eighth Amendment, any more than the meaning of other provisions of our Constitution, should be determined by the subjective views of five Members of this Court and like-minded foreigners, I dissent," Scalia wrote.

IN HIS OPENING STATEMENT at Elmore's PCR, Zelenka reminded Judge Kinard that Elmore had been convicted and sentenced by three juries. "Those jurors, the State of South Carolina, the jurors of Newberry County, candidly are looking to Your Honor to ensure that justice will continue to be done in this case." After law school, Kinard had practiced with a small firm in Camden, some forty-five miles east of Columbia, where he was active in St. Timothy's Lutheran Church, a member of the Camden Country Club, and secretary of the Camden Charity Horse Show. Jensen found Kinard to be gracious and patient, displaying none of the resentment toward the out-of-town lawyer that Jensen had felt in other jurisdictions where he had appeared.

"I recognize the burden on Mr. Elmore and his counsel to convince me that errors occurred which would mandate a new trial," Kinard said after listening attentively to Jensen and then Zelenka. He told the lawyers he had the transcripts from the three trials, which he would read. But for now, at the PCR, he would listen to the evidence offered by Elmore's lawyers "like I was a jury or sitting here from ground zero." That was just what Holt and Jensen wanted.

THE GIRLFRIEND, REVISITED

JENSEN CALLED his first witness, Elmore's ex-girlfriend, Mary Alice Harris. (She had remarried, so her last name had changed.) She was still a clerk at Kmart.

A colleague of Holt's at the Death Penalty Resource Center who had been helping with the appeal, Tony Miles, conducted the questioning. A twenty-seven-year-old African American, Miles was the son of a prominent civil rights activist from the 1950s and '60s, Elijah Walter Miles. After graduating from Boalt Hall law school at the University of California, Berkeley, Tony had joined the resource center in Columbia. (He left the center a few months after the hearing, moving to Washington, D.C., to work in the federal public defender's office.) Miles directed Harris to the evening of January 16, 1982, the night the state said Mrs. Edwards had been murdered, the night that Elmore had shown up at Mary's apartment, where he wasn't wanted, and, in anger, had ripped off his shirt, which she then threw away. Her testimony was the same as it had been at Elmore's trials.

But Miles asked the question that no one had asked at those trials—not the prosecutors, certainly, and not Elmore's lawyers.

"Did you notice if there was any blood on his shirt that night?" Miles asked.

"I didn't notice anything on his shirt that night," she answered. "He was close enough so that I could see him. I didn't see anything."

"If there was any blood on his shirt that night, are you confident you would have noticed it?"

"Yes, I would have."

"And why is that?" Miles asked.

"Because he was only three feet away from me at all times. I could have saw it. He was talking to me."

On cross-examination, Zelenka sought to undermine her testimony by suggesting she had rehearsed it with Elmore's lawyers, maybe even been told what to say. It is a conventional, and somewhat weak, cross-examination technique. Good trial lawyers interview their witnesses before putting them on the stand and know what they are going to say (which isn't the same as telling them what to say).

"How often have you discussed this matter with anybody that's currently representing Mr. Elmore prior to your testimony here today?" Zelenka asked.

"I haven't discussed it with anybody."

Zelenka didn't believe her. Had she never talked to Elmore's lawyers about the shirt he was wearing, about whether there was blood on it?

Nope.

Zelenka wasn't doing well.

Then he asked: Did you ever talk to Anderson or Beasley?

No. Never.

That was a bad question for Zelenka to ask. How could the state argue that Elmore had been competently represented if Anderson and Beasley had not interviewed his girlfriend, the woman he was with on the night Mrs. Edwards was supposedly murdered?

Zelenka wisely dropped the issue.

He returned to questions about the shirt and forgot a basic rule for trial lawyers: Don't ask a question to which you don't know the answer.

Why had she thrown the shirt away? he asked.

"I threw it away because I didn't want his clothes in my apartment."

It wasn't going well for the state. Zelenka stopped asking questions.

Harris stepped down.

THE JAILHOUSE INFORMANT, REVISITED

"At this time, Your Honor," Chris Jensen said to Judge Kinard, "we would like to call Mr. James Gilliam to the stand for examination by Diana Holt from the resource center." Gilliam stood, walked to the witness box, was sworn in, and took his seat. Holt thought he was Hollywood handsome. He was fidgeting, all six foot seven of him. It was hard to know who was more nervous, Gilliam or Holt, who had never examined a witness before. Indeed, she had never made a court appearance as a lawyer.

Holt had always scoffed at Gilliam's testimony. On its face, it was risible. Could anyone take seriously that someone would ask, "If you have sex with a woman and you wash up, would it show any signs that you've had sex?" Or that a common murderer, or a rapist, would wipe down an entire house to eliminate his fingerprints—and then clean up the kitchen and carefully arrange things on the victim's bureau?

Gilliam had testified for the state and against Elmore at all three trials. Then he had an attack of conscience. First, he told his wife that he had lied. She told him he had better see their pastor, Rev. Emmanuel Spearman. Spearman had known the Gilliam family for years—James's grandmother, his mother, and the woman he married. "We all grew up in the church together," Spearman said.

Spearman lived in an expandable mobile home, permanently parked on a piece of land with evergreens and broad-leaved trees in Hodges, a few miles north of Greenwood. Spearman and Gilliam are both big men, and they seemed to consume the entire living room, furnished with artificial flowers, a piano, a grandfather clock. Spearman sat on a white sofa, Gilliam across from him, next to an artificial tree.

Gilliam told his pastor that he had lied and that he had decided to come clean because he did not want Elmore's death on his hands. "Edward never confessed to me," Gilliam told his pastor. The guards in the jail had told him what to say in the letter, and later, Jones, in his office, told him what to say at trial. In exchange for his testimony, Jones told Gilliam that his jail time would be reduced. He had been facing eighteen months in the state penitentiary; three days after his appearance on the stand, Jones kept his promise, and Gilliam was allowed to serve his time on work release in Aiken, where his family lived.

Spearman wasn't surprised Gilliam had lied; that was consistent with his reputation. "I felt like he was lying from the beginning, because why would Elmore confess to a stranger he didn't even know, while all along he had been telling everyone he didn't do it?" Spearman told Gilliam he needed to talk to Elmore's lawyers.

Not long after, Gilliam, in trouble again for failing to make child support payments, ran into Rauch Wise in the hallway outside the family courtroom. Wise had represented Gilliam a few years earlier, on a charge of receiving stolen goods. Gilliam told Wise he wanted to see Billy Garrett. "You know, you're not on Billy's list of favorite people," Wise responded, referring to the fact that he had testified against Elmore. "Yeah, but I lied," Gilliam said. The whole thing had been staged, even down to the writing of the letter, Gilliam told Wise.

Given Gilliam's reputation, and the fact that he was claiming to have lied under oath three times, the obvious question was, Why believe him now? Wise decided it was necessary to give him a polygraph and arranged for an expert to come over from Augusta, Georgia. He asked Gilliam a series of questions.

"Did you lie in court when you testified against Elmore?"

"Yes."

"Was the story you told about Elmore a complete and absolute lie?"

"Yes."

Question 9: "Did Al Johnson furnish you the story you told in court?"

Gilliam said yes.

He was lying. But when that question was removed from those he was asked, Gilliam was found to be telling the truth.

Wise alerted David Bruck. But there wasn't anything that could be done at that point, no way that Gilliam's lies and recantation could be put before a court, and Bruck put a note in the file.

Eight years later, as she was preparing for the PCR, Holt desperately began trying to locate Gilliam. He was hard to find, of course, hiding from police, lawyers, and child support payments. She called Gilliam's mother, his sister, his wife. She told them James was needed at Elmore's hearing. Could they pass a message to him, have him call her? She heard nothing.

A few days before the hearing, the line buzzed in Rauch Wise's law office, on the ground floor of a two-story redbrick building on Main Street. Along with the various diplomas and bar accreditations hanging on the walls, the office is appointed with what Wise calls "prison art," pieces done by prisoners, including a very handsome three-mast schooner. James Gilliam is on the line, the receptionist said. He was calling from a Western

Union office in New York, off Times Square—collect, of course. Wise accepted it. It was vintage Gilliam, Wise thought: he wanted to borrow some money.

Don't hang up, Wise said. He pressed the hold button and punched in Holt's number in Columbia. Wise told Holt who was on his other line. Stunned, she put Wise on hold and punched in Jensen's number in New York. You're not going to believe this, she said. Our star witness is in New York City. Back and forth, it went—Jensen, Holt, Wise, Gilliam. Through Wise, Holt told Gilliam that the hearing was to begin in a few days. Would Gilliam be willing to testify about his lie? Gilliam said he would.

The challenge was to get him back to South Carolina, and quickly. No one wanted to give him money; they knew he'd disappear with it. Jensen came up with a plan, which he explained to Holt, who relayed it to Wise, who told Gilliam, Don't move; stay right where you are; look for a woman in a red dress. The woman in the red dress was Jensen's secretary, who quickly walked the few blocks to Times Square; she bought a bus ticket to South Carolina and gave it to Gilliam.

A few days later, Gilliam showed up in Columbia. Holt had him given a polygraph. There were three relevant questions:

Was your testimony at Edward Elmore's trials completely true?

Was your testimony about what Edward Elmore told you about the murder of Dorothy Edwards true?

Was your testimony that Edward Elmore confessed to you in the Greenwood County jail true?

Gilliam answered no to all.

"There was no deception indicated in any of Mr. Gilliam's responses," concluded the examiner, L. Stan Fulmer.

The night before the hearing, Gilliam stayed at his mother's home in Greenwood. A police car pulled up and remained out front all night. It wasn't to protect Gilliam but to intimidate him, and Holt was still uncertain whether Gilliam would take the stand. Next morning, when Gilliam walked up to the courthouse to testify, Townes Jones spotted him. The prosecutor was surprised and hurried over to talk to him. When Holt saw

Jones talking to her star witness, she quickly inserted herself between them; she wasn't sure how much damage Jones had already done. Jensen confronted Jones. What the hell was that all about? Just protecting the witness, Jones answered, with what Jensen took to be a smirk.

In the courtroom, Gilliam put his hand on the Bible and swore to tell the truth, the whole truth, and nothing but the truth, just as he had three times before in Elmore's case. Then he took the witness box, the same place he had sat in 1982 and 1984. He was wearing a three-piece dove-gray suit, which one of Holt's colleagues had managed to get cleaned over the weekend.

State your name, please, Holt began.

Kinard interrupted.

Was this the witness who was going to recant? Zelenka had alerted him.

Holt, examining a witness for the first time, was so nervous she could only nod.

Kinard addressed Gilliam. "Mr. Gilliam, of course, you just swore to tell the truth and the whole truth. You understand that?"

Yes, Gilliam said.

Kinard swiveled in his chair and reached for a volume of the South Carolina criminal code on the bookshelves behind him. He opened to the page marked by his clerk. He read the South Carolina law on perjury to Gilliam: "It is unlawful for any person to willfully give false, misleading, or incomplete testimony under oath in any court or regulatory proceeding in this state." And anyone who violates that law, that is, who gives false testimony, can be sent to jail for five years, he read to Gilliam. Gilliam said he understood.

Holt tried to go on. Her knees were shaking; she felt like she was going to wet her pants.

"Mr. Gilliam, are you prepared to tell the truth today?"

"I want to tell the truth, but I don't want to be impeached," he said, misusing a word he had just been hearing from Jones about what might happen if he testified.

"Are you afraid?"

"Sure, I'm afraid, but I don't want to go to jail."

"But you're prepared to tell the truth?"

"What about this perjury thing?"

Holt nervously tried to get into the substance of his recantation. "Mr. Gilliam, do you remember where you were . . . ?"

Gilliam wasn't quite ready.

"No, no, no," he said, turning to Judge Kinard. "What about the perjury? I want to talk about the perjury."

Kinard advised him that he might want to get a lawyer and reminded him that he could be guilty of perjury. (Was Kinard trying to protect Gilliam or the state's case? Holt wondered.)

"Mr. Gilliam, will you tell the truth today?" she asked.

"I want to tell the truth, but I don't want to go to jail for no five years. I mean, it sounds strange. I came in here, and I told a lie. Now I come back to tell the truth, and now you're going to lock me up because I want to tell the truth."

Oh, shit, we've lost him, Jensen said to himself. No way he is going to tell the truth now. The courtroom was full of police. It was hard to miss the message.

Holt was flustered, uncertain what to do.

"All right. I'll testify," Gilliam said.

Holt wasn't quite sure she had heard him correctly.

"Sir?"

"I'll go ahead and testify."

When she realized what he had said, she told him softly, "I think you're brave."

Under questioning by Holt, Gilliam said one of the senior police officers at the Greenwood County jail had asked him "to help out with Mr. Elmore" and had put the two men in the same cell. But all Elmore had told him was that he had not killed Mrs. Edwards.

"Did Mr. Elmore say, 'If you have sex with a woman and wash it off, can they tell'?" she asked.

"No, he didn't."

"Did Mr. Elmore say, 'They won't find any fingerprints, because I wiped them down'?"

"No, he didn't."

"Did Mr. Elmore say, 'I didn't mean to kill her, but she started screaming, so I had to'?"

"No, he didn't," said Gilliam.

"Did you testify in 1982 and 1984 and 1987 that he did?"

"Yes, I did."

"But today you're telling this court that's not true?"

"I'm telling this court the whole truth."

Gilliam asked to address the judge: "I'd just like to apologize to the court, to my mother, and to myself. That's it. If they're going to lock me up for telling the truth, I'm ready to go."

And go he might well. Don Zelenka stood up and began his cross-examination. In answer to Zelenka's first questions, Gilliam repeated what he had just told Holt: a senior official at the jail had said to him, "You help me out on the Elmore thing, and we'll look out for you." But Elmore had never talked to him, Gilliam now testified.

But hadn't Gilliam written a letter to Sergeant Johnson shortly before Elmore's first trial saying that he wanted to talk to him about the Elmore case? Zelenka now asked.

"Yes, I told a lie," Gilliam answered.

"Well, you did write the letter to Mr. Johnson?" Zelenka asked.

"I did write the letter, but it was a lie," Gilliam said.

"And did you talk to Mr. Johnson"?

"Yes, to try to benefit myself," Gilliam answered. "That's the only reason I did it."

Gilliam said that neither Sergeant Johnson nor Solicitor Jones had told him what to say. (Wise wasn't surprised at this. He knew Gilliam had enough street smarts, and enough experience with the criminal justice system as a defendant, to figure out what the state wanted to hear.)

Zelenka asked Gilliam about each of his prior statements, under oath, at the three trials. Had they been lies? Each time, Gilliam repeated that they had been.

"Like you said, I testified to that all four times; but I am here today to tell you the testimony was a lie. There ain't nothing that you can get out of this, sir." (Holt didn't know why Gilliam said four times. Maybe he was referring to the letter to Johnson, but it didn't really matter.)

Gilliam was firm, sat erect, head held high. Holt knew that Gilliam was streetwise, slick, and very self-interested. Coming back to tell the truth about Elmore was probably the most decent thing he'd ever done. Watching him hold his own with Zelenka, his resolve tangible, she thought he was the picture of a man speaking truth to power. Steeled, unblinking, he didn't slouch but instead seemed to lean into Zelenka when he answered.

ZELENKA: Why was it a lie in 1987?
GILLIAM: It's a lie now. It was a lie then. It's a lie now. That's all I'm concerned about it. Nothing you can get out of here.
ZELENKA: Why was it a lie in 1987?
GILLIAM: I'm telling you the truth.
ZELENKA: Why didn't you testify truthfully in 1987?
GILLIAM: Well, at that time I was trying to get out of jail. I was still living in Greenwood County.
ZELENKA: In 1987? At the last trial?
GILLIAM: Yes. I still lived in Greenwood County.
ZELENKA: Still living in Greenwood County?
GILLIAM: Still living in Greenwood County, and you ain't going to tread on no water, my friend.
ZELENKA: Same thing in 1984?
GILLIAM: '84.
ZELENKA: In '82?
GILLIAM: '82.

Wasn't Gilliam just trying to save Elmore from the electric chair? He asked, You don't believe in the death penalty, do you? No, not really, said Gilliam.

ZELENKA: And you don't want Mr. Elmore to die in the electric chair?
GILLIAM: No.
ZELENKA: Even if he did these crimes?

GILLIAM: This is my opinion. If you did it, and you know, really know, they did it, he should die in the electric chair. If he didn't do it, I don't think nobody should die in the electric chair.

ZELENKA: So you really think he should die in the electric chair?

GILLIAM: If he's guilty.

ZELENKA: But you deny that he had any discussions with you in jail?

GILLIAM: Yes. Now, that's the truth. Only thing that Elmore told me was that he didn't do it. All the other stuff, I made up.

Jensen had harbored doubts about Gilliam, wondered, as would most, why his recantation should be believed. But after listening to his testimony in that environment, with perjury charges hanging over him, when he had everything to lose and nothing to gain, when he could have stepped off the stand and been tossed in jail, Jensen changed his mind. "At that moment I was certain, to a moral certainty, that he was telling the truth."

"It was on my conscience. I went back and cleaned it up," Gilliam said years later. "I made peace with myself, and I told the truth."

As the first day of the PCR ended, Jensen and Tony Miles picked up their briefcases and started to go, leaving Diana to carry boxes of their files. "I'm not your f'ing file girl, and you're going to move the f'ing boxes, or the f'ing boxes aren't moving," she said. It wasn't uttered in anger. The men shrugged and helped carry the boxes.

DUELING PATHOLOGISTS

THE TONE OF the hearing changed dramatically on the second day, from hard rock concert to classical symphony performance. After Harris and Gilliam, Jensen called Dr. Jonathan Arden, a pathologist, to the stand. His list of degrees and credentials was nearly as long as Gilliam's rap sheet. He had studied at Johns

Hopkins University, graduated from the University of Michigan with distinction, then gone on to earn a medical degree there; spent three years as a resident in anatomic pathology at New York University Medical Center; and became deputy medical examiner–pathologist in Suffolk County, New York, before joining the Office of Chief Medical Examiner in New York City, where he was then employed. On the side, he took consulting work, without any juridical bias it seemed. In criminal cases, he testified for the state and for the defendant; in civil cases, for plaintiffs and defendants. He would acquire international renown a few years later when, as the chief medical examiner in Washington, D.C., he performed the autopsy on Chandra Levy, the congressional intern whose disappearance and murder in the summer of 2001 became front-page news after it was revealed that she had been having an affair with her congressman, Gary Condit. (A decade later, another man was convicted of the crime.)

Arden was one of the two medical examiners John Blume had recommended to Holt when she was searching for experts to help Elmore. The other was from North Carolina, and she would have preferred him because he lived nearby, didn't charge as much, and was a southerner. When he wasn't available, she contacted Arden. Over the phone, she briefly summarized the case. He asked her to send him Dr. Conradi's autopsy report, her testimony at the three trials, and the photographs the police had taken of Mrs. Edwards's body. Studying them, Arden reached a conclusion that no one else had, including Holt and Jensen.

Arden, with a black beard, neatly trimmed hair, and rimless glasses, was on the witness stand longer than anyone else during the PCR. He spoke rapidly, uttering full paragraphs in a single breath like a true New Yorker. Jensen kept trying to slow him down to Judge Kinard's southern rhythms, just as he had done himself.

Arden knew Dr. Conradi from various professional organizations and medical conventions, and he was uncomfortable criticizing her (just as lawyers are reluctant to testify against lawyers, and engineers against engineers). But he had to say that Dr. Conradi's report reminded him of something that might be written by one of his first-year interns (he was a clinical assistant professor of pathology at the State University of New York Health Sciences Center in Brooklyn). For starters, Dr. Conradi had confused lacerations with stab wounds, Arden told Judge Kinard. A laceration is caused by a blunt blow, which splits soft tissue. With a bit of dry humor, he added, "The so-called cut that a boxer receives of course is never a cut—assuming they don't allow knives in the boxing ring—but the cut that a boxer receives is a perfect example of a laceration."

It might seem academic—stab versus laceration—but Arden made clear it was serious. "Obviously, the implication of what the injury means is different and this is the underlying reason that I am so adamant about this point and why maybe I'm getting too worked up about this point."

As put forward by the police and the prosecution, aided by newspaper reporting, the public perception was that Mrs. Edwards had been slashed with a butcher knife, à la Hitchcock's *Psycho*. That was not what happened. A blunt instrument, such as the ashtray or bottle tongs, and not a knife, had caused most of Dorothy Edwards's injuries, Arden explained for Judge Kinard's benefit. This suggested an entirely different kind of perpetrator and crime. Why would a robber or a rapist bash Mrs. Edwards with an ashtray *and* take bottle tongs to her? And though murderers usually stab their victims violently, the knife wounds on Mrs. Edwards were shallow, all less than an inch deep, suggesting the perpetrator had jabbed her repeatedly, but not in a frenzy.

Next, Arden dealt another blow to the state's case.

"No sexual assault was perpetrated upon her live body," he testified.

But Mrs. Edwards had suffered injuries to her vagina. What explained those? Jensen asked

Probably the bottle tongs, Arden said. He also said these injuries were inflicted "postmortem."

After she died?

Yes. Apologizing for the "the long-winded introduction," he

explained how he had reached that conclusion. There were no bruises of the vagina. "And of course you need to be alive in order to have a bruise, because a bruise simply represents the escape of blood from the blood vessels that are damaged by the trauma. So in the strictest sense, dead bodies do not bruise."

Jensen handed Dr. Arden two photographs that Dr. Conradi had taken while conducting her autopsy. One was of Mrs. Edwards's torso, with the bottle tongs next to it. Dr. Conradi had placed them there and then taken the picture, to demonstrate that the tongs had caused the injuries.

Arden agreed with Dr. Conradi that the "short, superficial, pink and yellow injuries" were caused by the bottle tongs. But, he added, they had been inflicted "postmortem or at best perimortem." Perimortem, Arden patiently explained, means at or near the time of death.

Why a robber or rapist would take the bottle tongs to Mrs. Edwards after she had died wasn't for Arden to answer.

Arden had been on the stand for over an hour and was now about to deliver an even greater shock to the state's case. It had become a given that Dorothy Edwards was murdered on Saturday evening. No one had challenged it. The foundation had been laid at the first trial when Dr. Conradi, in answer to Jones's questions, testified that Mrs. Edwards had been murdered from twelve hours to three days before she received the body for the autopsy, and that her best estimate was sixty-five hours before she examined the body.

Sloppy, at best, Arden said about her parameters. Yes, he said, determining the time of death is not an exact science, and medical examiners should couch their conclusion in ranges. But twelve hours before examining the body as one boundary? How could that even be theoretically possible? Dr. Conradi performed the autopsy at 11:00 a.m. on Tuesday. Twelve hours before that would have meant that Mrs. Edwards was murdered Monday evening. That was several hours *after* Holloway and the police found her body.

Well, if it had not been twelve hours before, when was she murdered? Jensen asked.

Arden explained that medical examiners use several factors to determine time of death: the state of decomposition of the body; the presence of soft, or "mushy," tissue; fly eggs, or body maggots; green discoloration; a foul odor. All of these generally begin to appear a couple of days after death. Yet Dr. Conradi mentioned none of these in her autopsy report. That would mean Mrs. Edwards had been dead less than two days when Dr. Conradi performed the autopsy at midday Tuesday.

The principal medical factor in estimating time of death is rigor mortis, or the degree of stiffness in the body. Dr. Arden now delivered a medical primer.

"To begin with, the nice textbook generalizations of rigor mortis tell you that it begins—well, the process begins right after death, but it is not clinically—it is not apparent." Within five to six hours, it is visible. It reaches its maximum in the neighborhood of twelve to possibly eighteen hours. It then begins falling off and is gone within forty-eight hours. Those are the general parameters. But various factors affect rigor mortis—age, level of fitness, and physical exertion prior to death hasten the passing of rigor mortis—and Mrs. Edwards, a few weeks shy of seventy-six and fit, had been in a hell of a fight with her attacker, from all the indications.

Judge Kinard interrupted. How much longer was this going to take? he asked.

Jensen said he was nearly finished. "I know the reporter has indicated she's fatigued and the witness speaks very rapidly. It's difficult testimony to take." Perhaps a break would be appropriate.

The court reporter said she could go on.

Jensen resumed his questioning. In light of everything—the temperature in the house, the degree of rigor mortis, the state of decomposition of the body—did Dr. Arden have an opinion based on a reasonable degree of medical certainty as to the time of death of Mrs. Edwards?

Arden's answer was, of course, lengthy.

"I can tell you that having considered all of those factors, and I will not reiterate them here at this point, my initial impression was that she had died approximately twenty-four hours prior to the time she was discovered," he began.

That would be Sunday afternoon. She was most likely murdered between two and three o'clock on Sunday afternoon, though it could have been as early as 10:00 a.m., he said.

Could Mrs. Edwards have been killed on Saturday evening? Jensen asked.

No. That was the short answer, but Arden didn't give short answers. "In my opinion, and I hold this opinion and every other one that I have expressed to a reasonable medical certainty, that is extraordinarily unlikely and improbable really in the extreme. It would be unfair and unreasonable for me to say that that is physically impossible. But it is so incredibly unlikely that I cannot believe that that was the case. I strongly hold the opinion that Mrs. Edwards was not killed Saturday night as claimed."

Jensen pushed him. Would Arden say the possibility she was murdered on Saturday night was 20 percent? Ten percent?

"If you forced me to assign a number to something that is really not numerical, I cannot imagine going as far or any farther than one percent possibility," Arden responded. Then he added, "I think one percent may be overestimating."

"I have no further questions," Jensen announced.

It was four o'clock and everyone was tired, but Judge Kinard wanted to keep going. After a fifteen-minute break, Arden retook the stand.

The burden of trying to salvage something from the damage wrought by Arden's testimony fell to Salley Elliott, an associate of Don Zelenka's in the attorney general's office. Elliott was at least one person who could claim not to be an outsider. She was born, raised, and educated in South Carolina. Now forty-two years old, she had started working in the attorney general's office in 1982, the year of Elmore's first trial. Diana liked her.

"Mr. Arden, you testified—" Elliott began her cross-examination.

He corrected her. "It's *Dr.* Arden."

Elliott had to address the matter of what caused the injuries to the vagina. The state's theory was that Elmore had raped

Mrs. Edwards. In his summation to the jury at Elmore's trial, Solicitor Jones had asserted, graphically, "When he put his part of his body into the part of her privates, it was so repulsive to the lady that she, then, grabbed down there for the first time and came out with forty-something of his pubic hairs." Yet Dr. Conradi had found no sperm, nor an increased acid phosphate level, both generally present in instances of rape or sexual intercourse.

Elliott asked Arden, "We don't always have sperm present when there has been penile penetration, do we?"

Correct, he said.

"We don't always have acid phosphate present when we have sexual intercourse, do we?" She quickly corrected herself. There was no evidence of intercourse. "Penile penetration," she said.

That is correct, Arden said, but he reiterated that a blunt instrument, the bottle tongs, had most likely caused the injuries to the vagina.

"You would agree with me, would you not, that a penis is a blunt object that can cause an abrasion?" Elliott asked.

"In the general sense, an erect penis is a blunt object which can cause some sorts of abrasions," Arden agreed, deadpan.

Elliott left this topic and turned to the time of death, which was a far more serious issue for the state. Once again, Elliott wanted to remind the court that the witness was an outsider, not one of them. Arden had just testified that a body dead for more than two days would show evidence of eggs, maggots, and decomposition. "At what point in time after death would you expect to find in South Carolina fly eggs when the body is inside the home?" Elliott asked him. Arden had to concede that he was "not intimately familiar with the flies of South Carolina."

That little exchange aside, Elliott asked Dr. Arden if his disagreement with Dr. Conradi about the time of death was significant. Wasn't this a customary difference among pathologists?

No, Arden said, most pathologists agree on time of death, at least the ranges. "I cannot recall with certainty any other case where another forensic pathologist has testified and disagreed with me on a time of death estimate." In fact, this was the first time he had ever reached an opinion about the time of death that varied from that of the doctor who conducted the autopsy.

Had Dr. Arden discussed with Dr. Conradi her findings about the time of death? Elliott asked.

No, he had not.

"You did not ask her what she meant by sixty-five hours?" In her autopsy report, Dr. Conradi had estimated the time of death at sixty-five hours before she examined the body.

"I think I understand the concept of sixty-five hours without clarification," Arden responded drily.

Maybe Dr. Arden and Dr. Conradi disagreed about rigor mortis, but in estimating the time of death, Dr. Conradi relied on more than just the condition of the body, Elliott noted. Hadn't she also relied on the so-called historical information—the fact that Mrs. Edwards was supposed to leave on a trip on Sunday, the ringing alarm clock, the turned-on coffeepot, the *TV Guide* open to Saturday night?

Yes, but that did not change his opinion.

Elliott finished.

Now it was Jensen's turn again, and he picked up on the matter of this "historical information," which Dr. Conradi testified she had relied on when setting the time of death. Yes, Arden said, he was aware of testimony that the alarm clock was ringing, that the coffeepot was on, that newspapers were found in the driveway. Those were interesting bits of information, not to be dismissed lightly. "But most of those conflict, seriously conflict, with the information provided by the body. I cannot explain away her rigor mortis. I cannot explain away her postmortem condition. I cannot explain away what the body is telling me because the *TV Guide* was open to a certain page."

After Jensen was finished and Arden stepped down, Jensen said to Judge Kinard, "Your Honor, it's been a long day." He had been on his feet more than two hours with Arden. He was losing his voice. He wanted to recess for the day. Kinard, however, was possessed with the same desire as the judges at Elmore's trials, to get it over with quickly. He had expected the hearing to last three days, wrapping up by Wednesday. It was Tuesday, Jensen still had several more witnesses, and then Zelenka would be calling his.

"I don't want to punish anyone," Kinard said, but it was only five thirty, and perhaps they should take one more witness, then quit for the day. "But if you are physically drained and your perspicacity is slowly leaving, we can delay until in the morning," he told Jensen. "Whatever. Your call on that."

"I have to confess to being a little tired," Jensen said. He leaned over to confer with Holt.

"All right, if you don't feel up to it, we can easily be out of here and cranked back up in the morning," Kinard said. "Seven fifteen, quarter to eight."

Jensen blanched. "Well, I like to—"

"No, I was kidding," Kinard said. Tomorrow morning, 9:15.

HOLT AND JENSEN walked in the dark back to the Inn on the Square, where they were staying. The inn's motto was "Southern Elegance at Its Best," but "Functional, Comfortable, and Clean" was more like it. At $50 a night, the inn was to be their home and office during the PCR. The receptionist and staff would often ask Jensen about the hearing. One day Jensen had a question for them. He had noticed not a word about the hearing in *The Index-Journal*. Why was that? Jensen asked. Willy T. has given the order, someone said. Jensen didn't know if it was true or not, but it was a reflection of how much power Solicitor Jones, even retired, exercised in Greenwood. And it was a reflection of the town's attitude. The newspaper had covered the three trials when the state presented damning evidence against Elmore; most of the stories were on the front page. Now, when Jensen and Holt were presenting evidence favorable to Elmore, the newspaper was silent.

At the hotel, Elmore's legal team would change into more comfortable clothes and then meet in their hotel "war room," which housed boxes with the records from Elmore's trials and the exhibits. They would go over what had transpired in court that day and look forward to the next. Holt would frequently call John Blume for advice, and she would coach Jensen on the next day's witness. She had put together the structure of the case and had practically memorized the trial transcript. In the morning, after Jensen ate breakfast—hominy grits and scrambled eggs—and Holt gulped coffee, they would head back to the courtroom. Jensen was terrified, given that Elmore's life was at stake.

The battle of the pathologists was suspended while Jensen and Holt called other witnesses and then Zelenka began calling witnesses for the state. It resumed on the fourth day of the hearing when Zelenka put Dr. Conradi on the stand. She, too, was a native New Yorker, but any traces of her origin were largely gone. She was raised in upstate New York and attended nearby St. Lawrence University and the University of Rochester before being admitted to the University of Cincinnati College of Medicine, followed by an internship and four years of residency at Cincinnati General Hospital. After that, she and her husband, Edward Conradi—they met in medical school—went to Germany, where he fulfilled his military obligation. After the army, he got a job in South Carolina, and she began working as a forensic pathologist for the state. She later became a professor of pathology at the Medical University of South Carolina, in Charleston.

Conradi was sworn in, and Elliott asked her to review her autopsy findings. Conradi asked if she could illustrate with slides she had taken of the body. The court agreed. Conradi stepped down from the witness stand to a slide projector that had been set up. She clicked through sixteen slides and explained the injuries each showed, including abrasions on the vagina; cuts and bruises on the face; stab wounds on the right side of the back and neck, "probably produced by a knife"; and stab wounds behind the right ear. When she finished, she took her seat in the witness box again.

Elliott turned to the question of whether the tongs or a penis had caused the injuries to Mrs. Edwards's vagina. It wasn't out of prurient interest. Solicitor Jones had portrayed Elmore as having raped Mrs. Edwards, or at least having stuck his penis inside her, which is when she was said to have ripped out his pubic hairs. He even had Gilliam testify that Elmore had told him he had washed afterward in order to eliminate any semen.

"Were those injuries consistent with penetration by an erect penis?" Elliott asked.

Conradi would only say that they "could have been caused by an erect penis, yes."

"Had the tongs been utilized, what might you have expected to see?" Elliott asked.

Again, Conradi did not give the answer the state wanted. The tongs may have been used, she said. "I can't rule them out completely, but if the tongs were used forcefully, I wouldn't have been surprised to see linear lacerations in the vagina, and we did not see that." Still, she repeated, she couldn't "rule out the tongs completely."

Nor could she be certain about the time of death, and that was a far more serious problem for the state. If Mrs. Edwards had not been murdered on Saturday evening but on Sunday, as Dr. Arden testified, Elmore should walk out a free man, because on Sunday, he was at his mother's, watching television and drinking beer; the state hadn't disputed that.

It was time for another seminar on rigor mortis. Dr. Conradi's rule of thumb was that it begins at four hours after death in muscles of the fingers and jaw; at twenty-eight hours, it is starting to leave; and by forty-eight hours, it is ordinarily gone. In her autopsy, Dr. Conradi had found partial rigor of the left knee and hip, and full rigor of the left ankle. Given that she examined the body on Tuesday, this would mean that Mrs. Edwards had been murdered sometime on Sunday, which was what Dr. Arden concluded.

Dr. Conradi could not explain the stiffness. "Her left ankle was stiff, and I can't explain that," she said in answer to a question from Elliott. "I don't know if she had arthritis in that ankle or if the ankle just remained stiff over this period of time from the time of death."

Jensen and Holt looked at each other, contemplating the

absurdity of Dr. Conradi's claim that arthritis was the cause of the stiffness in Mrs. Edwards's body, not rigor mortis. Judge Kinard smiled, bemused.

Elliott pushed on. Again, she asked Conradi for her estimate of the time of death. Conradi stuck with what she had said at the three trials. "Probably the evening of the sixteenth. Based on everything." That "everything" was the historical, as opposed to medical, information—the information the police had given her. Pathologists generally determine the time of death largely based on what the police tell them. In this case, however, the police, unbeknownst to Conradi, were relying on what Holloway had told them. He was the only one who told the police that Mrs. Edwards was planning to go out of town on Sunday. He was the one who said that the alarm clock was ringing when he walked in and he'd left it on, that the coffeepot was on and he had not turned it off. He was the only one who testified to seeing the Sunday and Monday editions of *The Greenville News* in the driveway on Monday morning. He said he picked them up and put them inside. No one else testified to seeing those newspapers, not in three trials.

When Elliott finished her questioning of Dr. Conradi, Jensen stood. He stayed on the subject of rigor mortis. In her autopsy report, Dr. Conradi gave the time of death as sixty-five hours before the autopsy. "I'm having a little difficulty understanding this," Jensen said. "If rigor begins to pass off at twenty-eight hours and is fully gone at forty-eight hours, then how could you have a body at eleven a.m. on the nineteenth that still had indications of full rigor in some joints and partial rigor in others and then say that the time of death was sixty-five hours earlier, which was well beyond the forty-eight-hour range that you indicated?"

She repeated that she had settled on Saturday night because that was when the police had determined Mrs. Edwards was murdered.

"Just to clarify a few things," she said. "The only joint that she had full rigor in was the left ankle joint. She may have had arthritis in that joint. I don't know."

Jensen couldn't believe it.

"Dr. Conradi, are you telling me you can't tell the difference between rigor and rheumatism in this woman?"

"No, I really can't."

Jensen might have said, "QED."

Something else about Conradi's testimony upset Jensen and Holt. Those slides Dr. Conradi had just shown the court, where had they come from? A few weeks prior to the hearing, Holt and Jensen had gone to Charleston, to the medical school where Conradi taught, to interview her. They asked her for all the photographs and slides she had, whether taken by SLED agents or by herself during the autopsy. She did not give them anything.

Now she had produced slides. What else did she have? Jensen wanted to know.

What about the original photographs taken by the police and turned over to her? Did she have those? Jensen asked.

"Yes, I have them with me."

"You do?" Jensen said, surprised.

"I do have them with me," she said nonchalantly.

"May we see them?" he asked, nonplussed.

Conradi reached into a bag she had brought with her and pulled out several photographs.

Holt and Jensen began looking at them.

Conradi interrupted: "I'm sorry. Here are some additional photographs." She pulled more out of her bag. Sergeant Owen had given them to her when he brought the body.

Jensen, Holt, Elliott, and Zelenka were all baffled.

"Would this be a good time for a break?" Judge Kinard asked.

The court recessed at 3:45. Proceedings resumed at 4:00.

Jensen could barely contain his anger. There were fifteen photographs neither he nor Diana had seen before. In one, SLED agent Parnell had worked himself into the closet and pointed his lens down at Mrs. Edwards's body. The photo shows her torso and legs, bloody and bruised. Her robe is pulled up. Her knees are bent. A low-heeled dress boot is threaded between Mrs. Edwards's legs.

Holt stared. She had seen other pictures of the body, but

they were not as clear as these. The boot had been blurred in the other photos. It seemed to her that the only way that boot could have gotten there was for the killer to have carefully placed it. The boot was a crucial piece of evidence, covered with blood, and presumably it had the fingerprints of the person who put it there.

Were you ever given that shoe to examine? Jensen asked Conradi.

No, sir, she answered.

Nor was anyone else.

BLOOD, BLUE JEANS, FOOTPRINTS, AND FINGERPRINTS

ANOTHER PHOTOGRAPH puzzled Holt. It showed a large pool of blood on the carpet outside the closet door. But Holt noticed that there was no blood on the wood strip between the closet and the bedroom carpet. How was that possible? It takes about twenty-five minutes for a person who has been stabbed or shot to bleed out, which means the strip should have been soaked in blood.

Hayward Starling, a former state investigator from North Carolina, cleared up the mystery when he was called as a witness for Elmore. He was seventy-two years old, his hair white, and he didn't project the authority or confidence that Arden had. But he wasn't a northerner and was likely to have some added credibility by virtue of having worked for North Carolina's State Bureau of Investigation, the equivalent of SLED, for thirty-eight years.

Looking at those photographs, did Starling have an opinion as to how the victim ended up in the closet? Jensen asked after Starling was sworn in.

"My opinion is that she was moved to that location. She was carried to that location."

In other words, Jensen went on, to be sure it was clear, "someone would have to have physically picked her up after she had lain on that carpet bleeding for a substantial period of time and dragged her or moved her into that closet, is that correct?"

"In my opinion, that's probably what happened, yes," said Starling.

The answers to Jensen's next questions were self-evident, but the lawyer was being careful to build the record.

"Now, do you have any opinion based on those observations of the crime scene, the pooling of blood on the carpet, and the blood on the wall and evidence that you have testified to about how the victim was moved, as to whether or not the person or persons who did this would have blood on their clothing?"

"I do," Starling said.

"What is your opinion?"

"It's my opinion that the person would have blood on his clothing."

At Elmore's trial, the SLED serologist testified that he had found only five tiny spots of blood on the blue jeans that had been taken from Elmore's mother's house.

"Would you expect to see a larger quantity of blood than what was evident on Mr. Elmore's jeans?" Jensen asked Starling.

"I would expect to see more blood, yes, sir."

Holt glanced at Zelenka. He was shaking his head, seemingly in disbelief, as he studied the photographs himself and listened to Starling. This changed the nature of the case. Dorothy Edwards had bled to death on her bedroom floor. Her body had then been picked up, and while she was being lowered to the floor in the closet, her blood-soaked hair left streaks down the bureau. The perpetrator had then carefully placed a boot between her knees. Finished, he had closed the closet door. That's not the way enraged homicidal maniacs normally treat their victims. They are more likely to leave the body and flee.

Zelenka couldn't challenge the fact that there was so little blood on the jeans. So he devised a novel theory to explain why. He raised it during his cross-examination of Starling. "And if he did not have his pants on," Zelenka began a lengthy question, wouldn't that explain why there was so little blood on the jeans?

Starling didn't grasp what the state's lawyer was suggesting. He gave the same answer as before—there should have been more blood on Elmore's clothes if he was the perpetrator, if he had moved her body into the closet.

Zelenka stuck with his naked perpetrator theory. "But that assumes that he would have had the clothes on at that particular time, is that correct?"

"That's correct," Starling said. "If he'd had them either on or his trousers pulled down, yes."

Starling wasn't the only one who seemed to find it hard to believe that Zelenka was suggesting that Elmore had taken off his jeans before sexually assaulting Mrs. Edwards. Someone in the courtroom surreptitiously slipped Zelenka a brief handwritten note offering what he thought was a more plausible explanation for the lack of blood. "She was found upside down in closet—probably was picked up <u>by the ankles</u>—avoiding a great deal of blood on clothes." Even Zelenka found that hypothesis too fanciful, and he didn't advance it to Judge Kinard. The note was not signed. (Many years later, Geddes Anderson admitted he'd written the note. He realized that it might raise questions about the quality of his representation of Elmore if he was giving the state a theory that would help keep his former client on death row. Quickly after admitting authorship, he insisted, as he had before, that he had vigorously defended Elmore. He added, again, that he thought he was guilty.)

Other questions about the blood on the blue jeans were wanting for answers. For starters, whose blood was it? At trial, the SLED serologist had testified that the blood on the jeans was type A and that Mrs. Edwards had type A and Elmore type B.

On the third day of the PCR, Jensen called Elmore's brother Charles to the stand. Anderson and Beasley hadn't bothered to interview Charles, and he had never been called to testify at any of his brother's trials. Jensen examined most of the witnesses, but Holt handled Charles, just as she had Gilliam. They were comfortable with her. She wasn't just another white lawyer; she was one of them.

"Please state your name for the record," she began.

Charles Elmore.

"Are you any relation to Mr. Eddie Elmore?"

"Yes, ma'am. That is my brother." He was thirty-two years old now, four years younger than Edward.

"Did you share clothes with your brother?" Holt asked, gently.

"Yes, ma'am, I did."

Those jeans that the police had collected from Abbeville, whose were those?

"They was mine."

How about those shoes taken off Eddie's feet when he was arrested, had Charles worn those? Holt asked.

"Yes, ma'am, I had. I had them. I had since I got them."

Did Eddie and Charles often wear each other's clothes, switch off every couple of days?

"Yes, ma'am."

Did Charles have a washing machine?

"No, ma'am, at the time, no."

How long had it been since the jeans had been washed? she asked.

About a week, maybe, was the response.

She asked what kind of work Charles did. Did he handle razor blades in his work? Might he have bled on those blue jeans?

"Well, you know I could have, ma'am, to be honest with you now. I remember, you know, I was going to—I used to hang up the bathroom, you know, wallpaper the bathroom, you know, and probably about some of the best things I can use was a razor blade, and if I ain't too mistaken, I believe I cut a little old, you know, line on my finger, if I ain't too mistaken."

Zelenka then had a few questions. Did Charles know his blood type?

He was nervous, and at first, he said, no, he didn't. Then, "I take that back. If I ain't too mistaken, you know, I believe it's A." So, the blood could have been Charles's just as easily as it could have been Mrs. Edwards's.

The blood spots had been tested by SLED serologist John Barron. He had testified at Elmore's trials, and now at the PCR he was called as a witness for the State. Zelenka asked him about the blood tests he had performed. Jensen had less routine matters to probe.

Were the jeans in a bag or container when they arrived in your lab? Jensen asked Barron.

Barron said he couldn't remember.

Were they sealed with evidence tape? Jensen asked.

Barron said he couldn't recall that either.

Did SLED have any policy to seal exhibits with evidence tape so they couldn't be removed from the package? Jensen asked.

No.

Did Barron seal the package after he received it?

There was no record that he had, answered Barron.

"So we have no way of knowing how many times that garment was taken out of the bag and put back into the bag?" Jensen asked.

"No."

Jensen was improvising, reacting to answers to ask more questions, trying to build a narrative. It was a bit like writing a novel in which the author isn't sure where the plot and characters will take the story. But this was not fiction, and disbelief was being stacked on top of incredulity—evidence not sealed, no record of how often it was in and out of the bag. There was also the question of where the blue jeans had been after they arrived at SLED.

While Jensen was questioning witnesses, Holt would often be looking through filing boxes they had brought to court, which contained a mishmash of documents, including those that the state had turned over to them prior to the PCR, as it was required to do. When Barron was on the stand, Holt came upon a document they hadn't noticed before—four pages long and handwritten. It was a list of the state's exhibits, ninety-eight items altogether. To the right of each item was a series of initials of the police officer or SLED agent who'd had possession of the item. This was the "chain of custody" prepared by Solicitor Jones, who knew that he would have to be able to account for where every item of evidence had been from the time it was taken by the police until it was introduced at trial. The state must do this to rebut any suggestion that the evidence has been planted or tampered with—innocently, negligently, or intentionally. A judge may exclude evidence if he is not satisfied with the chain of custody.

Item 86 on the list was Elmore's coat; item 87, his pants. To the right of each item were names and initials: *Van, Earl, J.B., Tom, JTC, Dickenson, Earl, J.B.*

Translation: Detective Vanlerberghe, who had taken the jeans from Elmore's mother's house on the day he was arrested, had delivered them to Earl Wells, head of the forensics department at SLED, who had given them to John Barron for testing. From Barron they had gone to SLED agent Tom Henderson, who had given them to Greenwood police captain James Coursey, who had given them to Greenwood police detective Perry Dickenson, who had given them back to Earl Wells, who had returned them to Barron.

What the hell is this? Holt said to herself. Why had the jeans passed through so many hands, and who had done what with them? One name in that chain leaped out: Tom Henderson. He was the SLED agent who had volunteered to work on the case, who had concluded within a day or two of the murder that Elmore was guilty, who had claimed that Elmore had said to him, "If I did it, I don't remember." Henderson, as much as any single individual, had sent Elmore to death row.

SLED records showed that Henderson had taken the shoes, blue jeans, and coat out of the lab on February 3, and there is no record of how long he had them, or of why he gave them to Coursey instead of back to the SLED lab, or of why he had them in the first place. When Henderson took the jeans from the lab, he was no longer involved in the case, had no role in any of the forensic analysis. Of the ninety-eight items on the list, Henderson had taken only Elmore's blue jeans, coat, and shoes.

When Holt realized what she had found, she whispered excitedly to Chris. By this time, Judge Kinard was used to Holt whispering to Jensen, though he didn't know that she was usually telling him what question to ask next. The judge waited patiently while the two lawyers conferred.

Jensen picked up the questioning: "And why would these garments be given to Mr. Henderson?" he asked Barron.

"I don't know."

Barron said he had completed the tests on the blood spots on February 19, which was sixteen days after Henderson had taken them.

How was that possible? Jensen wanted to know.

Barron said he had cut out the spots of blood on the jeans before he had given them to Henderson.

How could he be sure of that? "Is there any record anywhere as to when you removed the stains?" Jensen asked.

"Not in writing, no," Barron said.

Inexplicably, Jensen and Holt did not call Henderson as a witness. It was many years before they realized the seriousness of their lapse.

DAN DEFREESE WAS the next SLED agent forced to sit uncomfortably in the witness chair, dodging as best he could the questions Jensen aimed at him. He was the fingerprint expert who had testified at Elmore's trial that he had found only six prints in the house: one was Elmore's (found by the back door), and two belonged to Mrs. Edwards. The other three, he wrote in his report and testified at Elmore's trial, had "insufficient ridge detail for comparison," which meant they could not be matched to known prints.

Jensen was about to give Holt a course in the art of cross-examination. It is like building a corral, each question making it harder for the witness to escape. There is also a bit of stealth; the first questions are easy, to relax the witness, to not let him know what is coming.

"You testified at your earlier trials that in your experience as a fingerprint identification expert, that you considered that you could make an identification if you had ten points of comparison; is that correct?" Jensen asked.

"Yes, I think I said that ten was about my minimum number."

Jensen showed DeFreese blowups of two prints that De-Freese had lifted from the back door.

"Now, in looking at those two enlargements, can you tell me whether or not you see in those two pictures at least ten points of possible identification?"

"In one, yes, sir, I do."

But hadn't he written in his report that these prints were insufficient for analysis?

DeFreese hedged. "I believe that's correct, yes, sir."

Only "believe"? Jensen picked up a copy of DeFreese's report from the heavy counsel table and read from it: "*Latent impressions were found to contain insufficient ridge detail for comparison.*"

"What does it mean when you say 'insufficient ridge detail'?" Jensen asked.

"That would mean that it did not contain sufficiently clear or sufficiently numerous details within the latent impression for analysis."

"Would you now agree with me that that observation that you made in your report was not accurate?" ("Not accurate" was Jensen's decorous lawyerly way of saying "false.")

"With regard to one of those, yes, sir, I would."

Jensen tacked. "Is it your testimony that there's less than ten points of detail here that could be used for comparison purposes?"

"No, sir, I think I just said that there are at least that many."

"Then why would you say that this was insufficient ridge detail for comparison purposes?"

"I don't know. Evidently I was incorrect."

DeFreese, who had joined SLED in 1967 while a sophomore at the University of South Carolina, wasn't doing well.

Jensen turned to the prints DeFreese had lifted in the bathroom. At Elmore's trial, DeFreese testified that one found on the underside of the toilet seat had insufficient ridge detail for comparison purposes. Jensen showed DeFreese a photographic blowup of that lifted print. "What do you see there?" he asked. "What kinds of prints are those?"

DeFreese didn't answer, as if by waiting he could make Jensen go away.

"I'm just asking if they're palm prints or fingerprints," Jensen said.

"They are most likely fingerprints."

"Would it be fair to say that they most likely are the tips of the fingers?"

"They certainly could be, yes, sir."

"And in that picture in at least one of those fingertips, do you see ten points of possible comparison?"

Again, DeFreese wanted to avoid having to answer. He'd just had to admit to one "incorrect" report. He knew what was coming. Jensen waited. Finally, DeFreese said, "Only by using the greatest amount of imagination. I don't see in either one of these ten really good points. If you wanted to imagine some things being there, I suppose you could get ten."

Jensen continued tightening the circle around DeFreese. The print that had been found outside on the door, which DeFreese now admitted had enough points for identification, and the one on the underside of the toilet seat, which he acknowledged might have—had DeFreese compared these two with Elmore's?

Yes.

"Well, if you had compared these prints with Mr. Elmore's prints and found that they matched, would you have recorded that in your report?"

"I would have."

So they weren't Elmore's. Why hadn't he put that in his report?

"Either it was improperly recorded by me or someone else, or as is the case with the superimposed print, I could not absolutely eliminate the possibility that Mr. Elmore may have contributed to it."

It was becoming clear to Holt why on Tuesday, January 19, 1982, Sergeant Owen had not taken Mrs. Edwards's body from the autopsy to the mortuary, which is the customary routine, but rather had delivered it to SLED. They needed to get Mrs. Edwards's fingerprints to determine if the ones found by the back door and in the bathroom were hers, since they weren't Elmore's.

Jensen now asked DeFreese, if the prints found on the outside door and the underside of the toilet seat had matched Mrs. Edwards's, would he have recorded that?

Yes, said DeFreese.

Holt was barely able to contain her disbelief or control her exhilaration: a back-door print that didn't belong to Elmore or Edwards, a print on the underside of the toilet seat that didn't belong to either of them.

When Jensen finished with the SLED agent, Zelenka had some questions for him. He appeared to be as incredulous as Jensen, as well as being unprepared for DeFreese's answers.

"You didn't find that these prints matched?" Zelenka asked.

That is what DeFreese had just testified. But he was so shaken that he told Zelenka he didn't understand the question. "I'm sorry, sir?"

"You didn't find that the prints matched the victim or the defendant that you have been discussing, is that correct?"

Again, DeFreese said, "I'm not sure I follow your question."

The prints he had just testified about, the one by the back door, the one on the underside of the toilet seat, the ones he said were not the defendant's or the victim's, Zelenka explained.

"Right, I did not find that they matched the defendant or the victim, no, sir."

When Zelenka finished with DeFreese, Jensen had another opportunity, and he wanted to drive the point home, to be sure it had registered with Judge Kinard.

"Is there any doubt in your mind at all that these are not Mr. Elmore's prints?" he asked DeFreese.

The SLED agent couldn't bring himself to say no, so he put it obliquely: "If I had found Mr. Elmore's prints there, I would have said so."

How could they lose now? Holt thought. A state investigator had admitted to submitting an "inaccurate" report—false or fraudulent, in Holt's view, it didn't matter—and having "improperly recorded" another finding. Wasn't this prosecutorial misconduct? Furthermore, the prosecution is required under the Constitution, as interpreted by the Supreme Court in *Brady v. Maryland,* to turn over all potentially exonerating evidence to the defendant. Wasn't it a violation of *Brady* for the state not to have told Elmore that a fingerprint on the toilet in the victim's bathroom wasn't his or the victim's? The state had not only failed to turn over the evidence, it had, Holt now realized, essentially dissembled in order to hide it when DeFreese claimed there were not enough details for comparison when in fact there were.

Somewhat mischievously, when discussing the case with friends, Holt would ask: When men urinate, how do they lift up the toilet seat? Who had been in Dorothy's private bathroom? She had a pretty strong suspicion.

It is elementary criminal investigation procedure to compare fingerprints found at the scene to those of individuals known to have been in the house legitimately, in order to eliminate those individuals as the source of the prints. Given that DeFreese had found at least two prints that didn't match Elmore's or Edwards's, had he taken prints of anyone else, asked Jensen, such as Mr. Holloway, to eliminate him as the source of the prints?

"No, sir, I didn't, and none were submitted," said DeFreese.

Holt and Jensen were disassembling the state's case, bit by bit, exposing incompetence, negligence, or worse. What happened to that footprint at the back door, the one the first officer on the scene, Charles Holtzclaw, had noticed immediately and had pointed out to the next officer, who had covered it to protect it? There was no evidence that the police matched it to Elmore's shoes. Was it Holloway's? Since the police never suspected him, they didn't try to match it to his shoes. A potentially critical piece of evidence vanished from the police investigation. Likewise, the bloody shoe print on the blue carpet in the dining room, the one Sergeants Owen and Johnson had recorded seeing, hadn't been cut out and taken for testing.

But it was the sherry bottle on the kitchen countertop that obsessed Holt. She knew it had been dusted for fingerprints—

she could see the fingerprint powder on it in the SLED photographs—but it had vanished. It was not on SLED's list of examined items. It was never mentioned at any of Elmore's trials. That made Holt very suspicious. She was confident that if Elmore's fingerprints had been found on the bottle, the state would have screamed the results. Again, she had a pretty good idea of whose fingerprints were on that bottle, and again, there was no forum for her to vent that suspicion.

HAIR ON THE BED, REVISITED

IN THE HANDS of SLED agents, potentially exonerating evidence seemed to have inexplicably been lost. Damning evidence, on the other hand, miraculously was found.

At Elmore's trials, SLED agent Ira Byrd Parnell testified that he had collected hairs from Mrs. Edwards's bed, spread over an area of about thirty inches by eighteen inches. Wells testified that they were Elmore's. In his closing argument, Solicitor Jones was graphic: *"When he put his part of his body into the part of her privates, it was so repulsive to the lady that she, then, grabbed down there for the first time and came out with forty-something of his pubic hairs."*

"It was the most convincing element in the whole trial," said Ganza Bryant, a twenty-eight year old alternate juror in the first trial and an African American who had been in the first class to integrate Greenwood High. "How does my pubic hair get there unless you've been there? I may do work for her, but for my pubic hairs to get there I had to have slept with her or done something."

"That's what convicted him," said a juror from the second trial.

Holt ridiculed Solicitor Jones's version of what happened. It was preposterous to believe that Mrs. Edwards, exhibiting "superhuman strength for a battered and bloodied woman of advanced years," managed to reach up "and pull with enough force and grip to rip out over forty hairs from her assailant's pubic region, without getting any of the hair particles under her fingernails," Holt said, "or anywhere on her sticky, bloody body, or on her sticky, bloody robe."

As Jensen and Holt drew out the contradictions, inconsistencies, and impossibilities in the state's "hair-on-the-bed" evidence, it was the legal equivalent of watching people climb out of a phone booth—they just kept coming and coming. The number of hairs alone that the state claimed to have found made Holt suspicious. *Forty-some* hairs at a rape scene? If true, it belonged in the Guinness book of world records. Preposterous, said Hayward Starling, the veteran North Carolina investigator. He usually found only two or three at a rape scene, he said. "Most I've ever found, as I recall, were six or eight, and I considered it a field day."

The testimony of the state's own critical witnesses belied anything having happened on the bed. "The bedcovers were folded down as if somebody was folding the cover down to get ready to go to bed," Johnson testified at Elmore's trial. "The bed had been used and folded—it looked like put back together, or made ready for bed again," Jimmy Holloway testified. He hadn't noticed any wrinkles or indentations, he said, answering a question from Solicitor Jones. Jones didn't like what he was hearing from his witness. "You're not saying that there were no wrinkles or indentations in the bed covers, just that you don't now recall having seen such?" Holloway was clear. "I have a photographic memory of what I saw there."

Holt laughed when she thought about the state's theory: after sexually assaulting Mrs. Edwards, Elmore murdered her, dragged her into the closet, then came back and made the bed (as well as spending several hours cleaning the house, washing the dishes, and putting the tongs in the drawer).

Jensen poured more doubt on the state's hair-on-the-bed evidence through his cross-examination of SLED agents DeFreese, Parnell, and Wells, who couldn't keep their stories straight.

DeFreese and Parnell had photographed the crime scene. Four rolls of film—three Kodacolor II, one Plus-X—each twenty-four exposures, ninety-six pictures in all. They photographed the kitchen, where there was evidence of a struggle, and the den, where the state said Mrs. Edwards had been watching television when her murderer forced his way into the house. They even took photographs of the guest bedroom—including the bed—where nothing had happened, where nothing had been disturbed, where no evidence was found.

But neither agent took a picture of the victim's bed, where the violent sexual assault was said to have occurred. There is a photograph in which the bed is visible, but only the bottom two-thirds. And there is camera gear on it. On this supposedly prime piece of evidence, the SLED agents had dumped their camera bodies, lenses, and bags.

Thirteen years after the first trial, the state realized that the absence of any photographs of the bed was a problem and that Elmore's lawyers would exploit this. In the manner of all good trial lawyers, Zelenka sought to mitigate the damage by getting the information out himself, as if there were nothing to hide. Why didn't Parnell take a picture of the bed and of the hairs he said he'd found on it? Zelenka asked him at the PCR.

"It was an oversight on my part," Parnell said.

Did you take the sheets as evidence? Zelenka asked.

No.

Why not?

"There were no obvious blood or other stains present," Parnell said. "Nothing of evidentiary value on them."

When it was Jensen's turn to cross-examine Parnell, he wanted to underscore that the SLED agents had not taken the sheets, which, unless they were grossly incompetent, cast serious doubts on whether anything had happened to Dorothy Edwards on that bed.

"You testified that after inspecting these sheets, that you decided there was nothing of evidential value on the sheets, so you didn't collect them?" he asked Parnell.

"That's correct."

"Is it conceivable that a microscopic or chemical examination might have revealed something on the sheets that you didn't see?"

Parnell was categorical: "I saw nothing else that could have been examined."

Jensen kept asking the question in varying ways. Parnell kept saying there was no reason to take the sheets because there was nothing on them. "We examined the sheets visually. We did not see any stains of any kind."

No blood on a bed where a violent rape had occurred? The explanation must be, Holt would say mockingly, what Solicitor Jones had said in his closing argument to the jury: "*She could have been swallowing the blood.*"

Parnell insisted he had found hairs on the bed, put them in a plastic baggie, and written on it.

Jensen turned to that. When they went through the house gathering evidence, Parnell and DeFreese had placed each item they collected into a bag and affixed a SLED label:

SOUTH CAROLINA LAW ENFORCEMENT DIVISION
Firearms Laboratory
Victim: Dorothy E. Edwards
Offense: Murder
Date: Jan. 18-82
County: Greenwood P.D.   Time: _____
Article: _____

Where Found: _____
Collected By:

_____

This tag was on every piece of SLED evidence the state introduced at Elmore's trials—including pliers, dentures, *TV Guide,* calendar, checkbook—except for the bag with the hair Parnell said he'd found on the bed. There was no label on that bag. Instead, on the baggie in which Parnell said he had put the hairs he found on the bed he had written directly:

1-18-82 Greenwood, S.C.
209 Melrose Terrace
Dorothy E. Edwards res.
Hairs removed from bed by this examiner.

Why didn't he use a label on this bag? Jensen asked Parnell. First, in a non sequitur, he said that he hadn't affixed a label because he had been the one who had found the hairs and put them in the bag. Jensen pointed out that Parnell had put labels on other pieces of evidence he had found. Parnell responded with another non sequitur: "There's also one in there that Mr. DeFreese did, that I didn't do."

Jensen kept at it. Why was it that this one particular exhibit, the ziplock bag of hair, didn't have one of those labels on it?

"Are you talking about the physical label itself?" Parnell answered.

"Yes, it didn't have a label like the other exhibits. It just had some handwriting on the outside of the plastic bag?" Jensen noted.

"It was something I could write on, as opposed to writing on something else that would possibly mess up a fingerprint or whatever might have been on it," said Parnell.

That didn't work either. All the exhibits were in plastic bags, so Parnell could have written directly on any of them.

"So is there any particular reason why this exhibit wasn't treated the same way, that you can recall?"

"None that I recall."

That was as good as Jensen was going to get.

He turned to another question.

"And this particular bag, was it ever sealed to your knowledge?"

"Not while I had it," said Parnell. "It was my intention to take it straight to our hair and fibers examiner at the time. I did not seal it with tape."

Jensen could not believe what he was hearing. "Knocked me off my chair," he would say later. Evidence not sealed? In New

York, in most courts throughout the land, a judge would not have allowed the baggie into evidence, or if he had, the defense lawyer could argue that it should be treated with great doubt. Anyone could have put hair into that bag.

Jensen had still another question for Parnell. To whom had he given the unsealed baggie with the hairs? "To Lieutenant Earl Wells with our chemistry department at the time," Parnell said. "It was midmorning on the nineteenth."

Earl Wells was later called as a witness for the state at the PCR. Answering questions from Zelenka, he said that Parnell had given him the hairs. That was not what he had testified, under oath, at Elmore's first trial. DeFreese had given him the hairs, Wells had testified. And at the trial, DeFreese also testified that he had given them to Wells.

Jensen asked Wells what had happened to the hairs that had been yanked from Elmore. How were they delivered to him?

Wells didn't remember. He assumed they were in a container of some kind.

Do you have those containers today? Jensen asked.

No, sir.

"Would it surprise you if I told you that there were no containers of the suspect's hair?" Jensen asked.

"Would it surprise me? Conceivably. I don't know."

The state agents were entangling themselves in a thorny thicket. They couldn't agree on what the hairs had been put into, who had given them to Earl Wells, or when. They didn't even know how many hairs were supposedly found on the bed and examined.

At Elmore's first trial, Jones, in his opening statement said "there were found fifty-three hairs." When Earl Wells was on the stand, Jones showed him State Exhibit 58 and asked if it contained "fifty-three hairs gathered from the bed of the deceased, Dorothy Edwards." Wells corrected him: there were only forty-nine hairs in the bag when he received it. He went on to say that there were only forty-two left, because he had taken seven out and mounted them on slides for microscopic examination. And Wells wasn't sure how many slides he had used.

"There could have been two, three, four, five, multiple hairs, single hairs mounted," he told Jensen at the PCR. "I'm not sure."

"Do those slides exist?" Jensen asked Wells.

"They existed at one time, yes, sir."

Jensen pointed out to Wells, and Judge Kinard, that no slides were introduced into evidence at Elmore's trials.

The state's case was beginning to resemble Pinocchio's nose. And it was about to grow in length. Parnell had testified that he dropped off the hairs to Wells "midmorning on the nineteenth."

That is not what Wells testified.

It was "one or two in the morning" of the nineteenth when he examined the evidence, he said in answer to a question from Jensen. He'd been at home when he got a call asking him to go down to SLED headquarters, he explained. He was met there by Parnell, who was on his way from Greenwood to Charleston with the victim's body, according to Wells. He said, he had a clear recollection. "The body was in a body bag," he said, brought "into the laboratory on a gurney." At that time, Wells said, he was given a baggie with a "quantity of hair," which he said he was told had come from the bed of Mrs. Edwards. "I examined the questioned hair under a microscope to determine, number one, possible racial origin."

"Did you reach any conclusions at that time from your examination?" Jensen asked.

"I identified the hair as being of a Negroid race origin."

Wells continued. The hairs had a reddish tint to them, he said, and he had immediately called the Greenwood Police Department and told the person he spoke to that the hairs were "from a Negroid individual with reddish-black hair." The policeman replied that he knew someone in Greenwood County who had those characteristics, Wells testified.

But it was not possible for Wells to have seen the body at one or two in the morning. Mrs. Edwards's body was in the cooler at Self Memorial Hospital then, secured by evidence tape, Sgt. John Owen recorded in his four-page police report prepared at the time.

He had removed it at 6:15 a.m. on the morning of the nineteenth, Owen wrote, and then he and two other officers drove the body to the medical university in Charleston, 196 miles across the state. They arrived there at 10:15. Owen had a reputation on the force for being a stickler for detail, for taking his job very seriously, too seriously in the view of some officers. He'd even give his mother a speeding ticket, they said.

At 4:09 p.m., Owen and the others left Charleston with the body and the evidence Dr. Conradi had gathered during her autopsy, Owen went on. They arrived at SLED headquarters just before seven. "I met Lt. Wells in the Chemistry Dept.," Owen wrote. "This evidence was surrendered to him at 6:59 p.m. on January 19th, 1982."

This was some sixteen hours *after* Wells claimed to have examined it.

Undercutting Wells's testimony and bolstering the conclusion that no hairs were found on the bed are the police reports and court proceedings prior to trial. In none of them is there any mention of any hairs of any color on Mrs. Edwards's bed.

Sergeant Johnson, who was initially in charge of the investigation at the crime scene, said in his report that evidence gathered in the house had been turned over to Owen. In his report, Owen wrote: "This evidence consisted of: one pair of needle nose pliers, One case pairing knife, One cake knife, or spatchler marked Gitie's Blade, One upper denture, One fragment dentures, One fragments ashtray, One bottle tongs, One pill bottle, and color Photographs of the position of the body." Nothing about any hairs on the bed.

A few days after the crime, after Elmore had been arrested, the Greenwood deputy coroner, Grady Hill, prepared a one-page report summarizing developments. It was neatly written in longhand.

Capt. Coursey called for Sled crime scene investigators.

Lt. Dan DeFreese found a handprint of the defendant at the scene. He gathered much other evidence at the scene also.

*Got defendants bloody clothes from home of his mother
in Abbeville.*

Got shoes off his feet (blood on shoes).

Got head hair and pubic hair samples (combed & pulled).

Got saliva & blood samples.

*Don't have an autopsy report yet, but the Dr. said there
were many injuries and evidence of sexual assault.*

*A cancelled check was found in her latest statement from
the bank which was made out to the defendant. That along
with a print that was found at the scene is how we got started
looking for the defendant.*

In all this detail, there is no mention of any hairs being
found on Mrs. Edwards's bed, nothing about Earl Wells alerting
the police to look for someone with reddish-black hair, which
would have been a more persuasive reason to arrest Elmore than
a canceled check and fingerprint, which had innocent explana-
tions.

A few weeks after that, there was a preliminary hearing in
Magistrate's Court. Anderson and Beasley questioned whether
there had been probable cause to arrest Elmore. Lt. Lee Moore,
liaison officer between the department and the court, was sworn
in. In answer to questions, he testified about how Coursey and
the SLED agents had gone to the scene, 209 Melrose Terrace,
and gathered evidence. They had found evidence of the check
to Elmore and the fingerprint by the back door. Elmore's fingerprints were on file at the police department because of his
earlier arrests on domestic violence charges; they were sent to
SLED, which said the one found by the back door matched his.
This was the basis for arresting Elmore, Lieutenant Moore said.

"I would like to ask you right now, what else do you have
other than what you've said?" Beasley had asked.

"I don't know anything other than what I've given you,"
Moore replied. "But I think that's probable cause, because of
the check and because of his prints found there because the
matchup was positive."

After Elmore had been arrested, the police had taken pubic and head hairs from him, Moore explained.

"Do you know if any were found there at the house?" Beasley asked.

"No, sir, not to my knowledge."

It was hard to be more definitive than that. That was March 25.

Three weeks later, at Elmore's trial, the hairs made their first appearance, when Parnell testified he'd picked them off the bed and Wells testified that he'd examined them and they matched Elmore's.

Earl Wells was the last witness at the PCR. Now Holt went to work marshaling the testimony into a legal brief.

AT THE CONCLUSION of the PCR, Holt and Jensen were convinced that no hair had ever been found on the bed. In a word, it had been planted. The hairs supposedly found on the bed were those that Greenwood police captain Coursey had yanked from Elmore the morning he was arrested. Elmore's lawyers now thought they had a broader picture of what had happened. By the afternoon of January 19, the state realized it didn't have much of a case against Elmore. It had only one fingerprint from the scene that was Elmore's, and that could have been put there when he was cleaning Mrs. Edwards's gutters and windows. There were three fingerprints that weren't his, and after Mrs. Edwards's body had been brought to SLED, the state knew that those fingerprints weren't hers either. Thus, the state had to come up with evidence to implicate Elmore, and, Holt concluded, this was why Coursey had pulled out so many hairs.

SUMMING UP

"MISCOUNTED, mishandled, mischaracterized, and misrepresented"—that is how Holt sought to discredit the state's hair-on-the-bed evidence.

The language was contained in the "Applicant's Post-Hearing

Memorandum of Law in Support of the Amended Application for Post-Conviction Relief." Amid the 241 pages of legal arguments, bolstered by case citations and footnotes, Holt stirred in some spicy scorn and sarcasm.

"To accept the state's version of events, one has to suspend logic and reason, and believe the least likely explanation for virtually every piece of evidence," she wrote. "Edward Elmore, 5'7" tall, weighing 145 pounds, killed Mrs. Edwards, who bled to death, picked up her 130-pound bloody, slippery body and secreted her body in a closet with a boot between her knees. He put the tongs back in the kitchen drawer, stepped one foot in the pool of blood then hopped on the other foot all the way through the house, out the back door and down the steps, before finally stepping down with his bloody shoe, then hopped some more, all without leaving any of his blood or fingerprints inside her home and without getting any of her blood on his shirt or jacket, but getting small spots of both her blood and his own blood on his jeans." (Holt used the weight for Dorothy Edwards that the medical examiner, Dr. Conradi, had recorded on her autopsy report; Mrs. Edwards weighed twenty pounds less.)

Holt was angry and realized later that she had probably been a bit too wiseass, not lawyerly enough.

"Mr. Elmore told the jurors the truth. He told them he did not kill Mrs. Edwards. He told them he was innocent. The problem was the thirty-six jurors could not hear Mr. Elmore because the lies, misrepresentations and omissions of James Gilliam, Earl Wells, Dan DeFreese, and Dr. Conradi drowned out Mr. Elmore's voice of truth." She was not shy about naming Holloway. "The jurors were not told the truth about Mr. Holloway. They did not know that there was reason to suspect him," she wrote.

Holt, Miles, and Jensen filed their brief in October 1995. The state's reply was due thirty days later, but because of other pressing cases, Zelenka requested and was granted repeated extensions; it was five months before he submitted the state's reply brief (demonstrating that delays in carrying out an execution are not always because of maneuvers by defense lawyers).

He had to concede that Agent DeFreese had testified improperly at Elmore's trials when he swore that there was not enough ridge detail on one of the fingerprints found at the house to identify it. That was "regrettable," he wrote. But that did not deprive Elmore of a fair trial, Zelenka argued. Zelenka conceded as well that maybe there was another fingerprint that didn't belong to either Elmore or Mrs. Edwards, the one on the underside of the toilet seat. But that didn't mean Elmore was entitled to a new trial. "It was not constitutional error," he argued.

It was "unfortunate," Zelenka wrote, that the SLED agents had not taken any pictures of the bed. He dismissed it as an "oversight." There was no reason the investigators should have taken the bedsheets as evidence, since there were no stains or blood on them, Zelenka argued. Again, this was not a constitutional error.

With the briefs in, Holt and Jensen waited for Kinard's ruling.

Elmore and death row inmates around the country were dealt a setback in April 1996 when President Clinton signed the Antiterrorism and Effective Death Penalty Act, or AEDPA. It cut off funding for the death penalty resource centers, such as the one where Holt worked. The new law also restricted defendants to filing only one habeas corpus petition in federal court. A writ of habeas corpus, which has its roots in English common law, is the legal process through which a defendant argues that he is being held in prison in violation of his constitutional rights. It is a particularly valuable right in capital cases. State judges, who have to worry about being reelected, either in popular votes or by the legislature, are often uneasy about reversing the conviction of a murderer on some constitutional ground that the public may not understand; federal judges have life tenure and are more immune to popular anger. The "antiterrorism" part of the new law was a response to the bombing by Timothy McVeigh of the federal building in Oklahoma City that killed nearly two hundred people. What "effective" meant in the Antiterrorism and Effective Death Penalty Act was that executions would be swifter.

"After three decades of Republican dominance of the issue, President Clinton has scrapped his party's traditional approach to crime and criminal justice, embracing a series of punitive measures that have given him conservative credentials and threatened the Republicans' lock on law and order," *The New York Times* wrote.

Conservatives and prosecutors rejoiced. In 1977, the average time that a condemned man spent on death row before his sentence was finally carried out was slightly more than four years; by 1996, it was more than eleven. In California, the average time was thirteen years; in Arizona, eight. "Never has the grim reaper been denied so unjustly for so long," said an Arizona prosecutor. Elmore might have been exhibit A: he was first sentenced to die when Ronald Reagan was in the second year of his presidency, he survived George H. W. Bush's tenure, and he was still alive at the end of Clinton's second term.

Eight days after President Clinton signed the new federal death penalty law, the Court of Appeals for the Eleventh Circuit denied a Georgia death row inmate, Ellis Wayne Felker, the right to file a second habeas petition. Felker, who had been convicted in 1982 for the rape and murder of a nineteen-year-old college student, immediately filed a petition for review with the Supreme Court. For the court's conservatives, it was an opportunity to do something about what they considered endless appeals. Five justices voted to hear the case and set oral argument for June, even though the regular season for oral arguments had ended. It was the fastest the court had acted since 1971, when the government tried to block *The New York Times* from publishing the Pentagon Papers. Justices John Paul Stevens, David Souter, Ruth Bader Ginsburg, and Stephen Breyer argued against taking the case, saying it was "unnecessary and profoundly unwise" to move so quickly; they urged the court to act "with the utmost deliberation, rather than unseemly haste." After the case was fully briefed and argued, the dissenting justices joined with the majority and a unanimous court upheld the constitutionality of the new law. It wasn't for the court to decide on the wisdom of the law, only on its constitutionality, the justices said, and Congress had the constitutional authority to limit an inmate's right to appeal.

The consequences of the ruling were predictable, and just what the law's proponents wanted. Executions accelerated. Felker was electrocuted at 7:30 p.m. on November 15, 1996. In 1997, seventy-four men were put to death in seventeen states; Texas, under Governor George W. Bush, was the runaway leader with thirty-eight. It was an all-time high since the Supreme Court had reinstated the death penalty in 1976. The toll kept climbing—to ninety-eight in 1999.

As a result of the new law, the South Carolina Death Penalty Resource Center became the South Carolina Post-Conviction Community Defender Organization, an unwieldy mouthful still headed by John Blume, with interns and lawyers still working out of the same offices on Sumter. Court-approved fees largely funded it now.

Holt and Jensen went back to Greenwood in July 1996 for oral arguments on Elmore's request for a new trial. "Edward Lee Elmore, who's seated here next to me, has never had a fair trial, anything reasonably approximating a fair trial," Chris Jensen told Judge Kinard. "Let him have one now."

"...MAY WELL NOT BE GUILTY"

SIX MONTHS LATER, in December 1996, Judge Kinard issued his ruling. When Jensen read it, he was stunned. He knew it was unlikely he would win, but Kinard had adopted the state's argument wholesale. Judges often ask the parties to submit a proposed findings of fact and conclusions of law. But the judge is expected to apply his own thinking before issuing the court order. The United States Supreme Court has "criticized courts for their verbatim adoption of findings of fact prepared by prevailing parties," Justice White noted for a unanimous court in *Ander-*

son v. Bessemer City. Following *Bessemer,* the Supreme Court of Alabama reversed the conviction of a defendant in a capital case, Robert Shawn Ingram, when a judge ruling on the defendant's post-conviction petition adopted wholesale the state's draft order dismissing the petition. "It is axiomatic that an order granting or denying relief . . . must be an order of the trial court," a unanimous Alabama supreme court said. "It must be a manifestation of the finding and conclusions of the court." By embracing the state's proposed order indiscriminately, the judge puts in question whether the findings and conclusions are in fact his, the Alabama justices said.

In light of *Bessemer,* Judge Kinard's conduct was even more judiciously egregious. It wasn't a proposed order that he adopted verbatim. He took the state's "Memorandum of Law in Opposition to the Application for Post-Conviction Relief" and made it his "Order Denying Application for Post-Conviction Relief in Its Entirety." He didn't modify a paragraph, a word, a comma. He didn't even clean up the typos.

When discussing the fingerprint evidence, Judge Kinard's order reads: "The Applicant also contends that counsel should have acquired fingerprint experts to challenge the state's findings. This issue is thoroughly addressed in Section 4 of this Brief which is incorporated herein by reference." But this wasn't a brief. Lawyers write briefs. Judges, and courts, issue orders.

Addressing Dr. Conradi's testimony and the differences between her and Dr. Arden, Judge Kinard's order reads: "(Respondent would incorporate by reference its argument in Argument 15, pages 145–177, on ineffectiveness of resentencing counsel with respect to the testimony of Dr. Conradi, pp. 158–172.)" This language was verbatim from the state's brief, including the parenthesis. But Judge Kinard was "the Court" not the respondent. Once Elmore had filed for post-conviction relief, the state was the respondent.

Since he had copied the state's brief verbatim, Judge Kinard found it "regrettable" that SLED agent DeFreese had improperly testified about one of the fingerprints, and "unfortunate" that SLED agents had neglected to photograph the bed where

Elmore's pubic hairs were allegedly found. He wasn't troubled by the blue jeans having been given to Henderson, and the inability of the SLED agents to account for where they had been. "Proof of chain of custody need not negate all possibility of tampering, but must establish a complete chain of evidence as far as practicable," Zelenka/Kinard wrote. He dismissed Gilliam. "James Gilliam did not testify falsely at the three trials—the post conviction relief recantations are the matters not worthy of belief." He rejected out of hand that Anderson had been drunk during trial or that Beasley was a racist. "The claim that the attorney was acting in an alcoholic haze, or that his co-counsel was unable to zealously perform in Elmore's behalf due to alleged racist attitudes, is without merit and not supported by fact." Again, this language was lifted directly from Zelenka's brief.

Kinard sent the order to the lawyers and accompanied it with a three-paragraph letter. The last sentence reads: "Edward Lee Elmore may well not be guilty and I appreciate the effort put forth by defense counsel and perhaps an appellate court may agree with one of your positions and grant relief."

When Holt read that, she stormed down the hall to Blume's office, hysterical. "What the hell's the matter with you?" he said. "Elmore," she replied, and threw the letter on the floor.

In all his years representing men on death row, Blume had never seen anything like it. The judge had concluded that Elmore might well not be guilty, but he wouldn't give him a new trial. It seemed as if he didn't have the courage.

It was a defining moment for Holt. Until now, she thought Elmore would get a new trial, that eventually justice would prevail, that he wouldn't be executed for a crime he didn't commit. "If he can say 'he might be innocent,' but then sign that order, all hope is lost," she said. Holt enlarged the sentence and taped it on a wall in her spartan office. Kinard's remark further deepened her commitment, not that it ever wavered. This was not to be her last disappointment.

ON THE PERSONAL FRONT, however, Diana had cause for joy. Five months after Kinard's order, at eleven a.m. on Saturday,

May 31, 1997, Holt, about to turn thirty-nine, walked down the aisle of Washington Street United Methodist Church and said her vows with Kevin Bell. When John Blume saw her, he had to suppress a giggle. This woman, whom he was used to seeing in blue jeans, was dressed in a cream-colored bridal gown. Holt and Bell had met during her first summer in Columbia, and she moved into his house the following summer while studying for the South Carolina bar exam. At some point, she told him there was something he needed to know about her if their relationship was going to continue. They sat on a knoll behind his house on the cul-de-sac, and she said what she had to say. He shrugged. This time Diana wouldn't take her husband's name, but this marriage, her fourth, would last.

CHAPTER SEVEN

The Search for Item T

B ECAUSE ELMORE had been denied a new trial by Judge Kinard, his next stop was the South Carolina Supreme Court. But before the justices ruled—indeed, even before Elmore's lawyers had appeared in front of them to make their arguments—a bureaucratic action jolted the case. Holt and Jensen wanted certain of the Elmore exhibits brought to Columbia to be available for examination by the high court justices should they wish to view them in light of the arguments advanced. Holt drafted a proposed order and sent it to the court. On July 2, 1998, the court issued a routine "transportation order" to the Greenwood County clerk. It commanded him to send the listed exhibits. Ten weeks later, the Greenwood sheriff delivered only some of the items. Certain exhibits couldn't be located, the Greenwood clerk informed the supreme court. Among the missing articles was what was identified as "Item T."

Item T was innocuous enough on its face. It consisted of four glass slides on which several hairs had been mounted. These were not the hairs that Parnell claimed to have picked off the bed. These were hairs that Dr. Conradi had found on Mrs. Edwards's body during the autopsy. "Examination of the chest and abdomen reveals occasional dark colored tightly curled apparent pubic hair," she wrote in her autopsy report. Sergeant Owen had given these hairs, along with other evidence, to Earl Wells when delivering the body to SLED. Wells mounted them on slides and examined them. He placed a T on each slide and put all four into a padded cardboard slide holder, about three inches by five inches. On the front, in red block letters, was stamped MEDICAL SPECIMEN. Above that, Wells wrote the case number, 82–297. He marked the holder with a T. It was never given to Elmore's lawyers. When Jensen read the trial transcript, he was "immensely curious" and deeply suspicious. This was the evidence that Jones told Judge Burnett had justified Elmore's arrest, and it hadn't been given to the defense.

In a criminal trial, the state is required to give the defense a list of the evidence it intends to introduce and the names of witnesses it plans to call. Above all, the prosecutor is obligated to turn over anything that the police or investigators have uncovered during their investigation that might be beneficial to the defendant. The Supreme Court established this rule in 1963 in a landmark case, *Brady v. Maryland*. John Brady and his partner, Charles Boblit, had lain in wait for a businessman to return home in order to steal his car and money. They hit him over the head, stuffed him back into his car, and drove him into the nearby woods, where he was strangled to death. The abductors split the $250 they found in the victim's wallet. Brady and Boblit were tried separately. Both were convicted of first-degree murder and sentenced to death. Several years later, in the course of Brady's appeals, his lawyers discovered a statement Boblit had given to the police in which Boblit said he had strangled the victim. The prosecutor had not given the statement to Brady's lawyers. On appeal, Brady's lawyers argued that the prosecution's failure to give the defense Boblit's statement had deprived Brady of a fair trial. The Supreme Court agreed. "The suppression by the prosecution of evidence favorable to an accused upon request violates due process where the evidence is material either to guilt or to punishment, irrespective of the good faith or bad faith of the prosecution," Justice Douglas wrote.

Underlying the Supreme Court's decision was a bedrock principle of the American judicial system: the duty of the prosecution is not to obtain a conviction but to do justice. Or, as

Justice Douglas put it, "Society wins not only when the guilty are convicted but when criminal trials are fair; our system of the administration of justice suffers when any accused is treated unfairly."

This tenet is so integral to American justice that the Supreme Court has said the prosecutor has more than just an obligation to turn over any exculpatory evidence of which he is aware. He must go further and search for such evidence that any officer of the state might have. "The individual prosecutor has a duty to learn of any favorable evidence known to the others acting on the government's behalf in the case, including the police," Justice Souter wrote in *Kyles v. Whitley.*

After examining the four Item T slides, Earl Wells wrote in his report that he had found only "blue fibers." In other words, he was saying that Dr. Conradi had been wrong: there were no hairs on the body. A decade on, Holt and Jensen mounted a tireless search, not just for the missing Item T but for all the evidence and exhibits in the Elmore case, whether they had been introduced at trial or not.

In June 1994, Jensen wrote Zelenka: "I would also like to know whether you have been able to locate the SLED exhibits that were not introduced into evidence at any of the trials. These exhibits include several items of physical evidence that were either collected at the crime scene or taken from the body of the victim by Dr. Conradi and delivered to SLED."

Zelenka sent a fax to SLED in which he asked if they had anything from the Elmore case there. "No physical evidence remains at SLED regarding this case," Lt. Michael J. Brown, supervisory special agent, wrote back.

Jensen was frustrated, and at the PCR in 1995 he told Judge Kinard, "I want to make it clear for the record that we have attempted to obtain those exhibits and that the exhibits are simply not there. I don't want to be surprised at a later date when these other SLED exhibits suddenly appear."

Zelenka assured Kinard that the state was not holding back. "We've been doing diligent searches both of the records of the Greenwood County Sheriff's Department and we've made request of the Greenwood City Police Department on at least three occasions to search all their records for the existence of any further evidence." Everything that was found had been turned over to Elmore's lawyers, he assured the court.

During the PCR, Jensen asked Wells if he had any slides or other items he had examined in the case. Wells assured him that he did not. He reiterated that "my microscopic examination revealed that the only thing present in that item was blue fibers; no hair."

Holt and Jensen were stymied. Then they got an unexpected break from unexpected quarters. When not all the exhibits requested in the South Carolina Supreme Court's transportation order had been brought to Columbia, the court clerk called the attorney general's office and asked him to look for the missing items.

Zelenka again called Wells. Look for evidence in the Elmore case, he told him.

A few days later, during a conversation on another case, Wells told Zelenka, "I've got some news for you." He had found evidence from the Elmore case: Item T. Wells said he had found it at the back of a file drawer in his twin-pedestal government-issue metal desk.

Zelenka was not happy, and he subsequently concluded that Wells had had Item T in his desk all along, for more than sixteen years—the entire time that SLED had been telling Zelenka, and Zelenka had been making representations to the court, that no further evidence could be found; the entire time that Wells had sworn under oath that he did not have Item T.

A day or two later, Holt happened to call Zelenka on another matter. During their conversation, he told her that Wells had found this material. She was staggered. "What? What are you saying?" Her white cordless phone to her ear, she paced from her office, through the den, into the living room, back and around. "You say you found what?"

At this point, Zelenka wasn't about to look at the evidence without Holt being present, and Holt wasn't about to allow him to. The lawyers agreed to meet at Wells's office on a given date. When they arrived, Wells had another bombshell. He had looked at the slides again, he said, and there weren't only blue fibers. There were hairs, too. Holt realized Wells had known this from the outset, back in 1982 when he examined the slides. With the naked eye, you can tell a fiber from a hair. Further, under a microscope, it is easy to determine the race of a hair, whether it is Caucasian or Negroid, and whether it is a pubic hair or a head hair.

Zelenka was reeling. How could he argue that, under *Brady* and *Kyles,* Item T should not have been turned over to Elmore's lawyers at trial? It was clearly time for yet another search for the evidence in the case. Holt and Zelenka drove to Greenwood, separately. They met in the parking lot behind the courthouse. Inside, they told the clerk that they were looking for the exhibits in the Elmore case. "Hasn't that boy been executed yet?" the clerk asked. He's had three trials, that's enough, the clerk said. Holt was enraged. "Good thing he hasn't been, since you people have been withholding evidence," she snapped. The clerk told them the exhibits weren't there, that they were at the police station.

Leaving the courthouse, Holt rounded on Zelenka. How the hell did he think Elmore got a fair trial when the court that was supposed to be neutral had that attitude?

She didn't expect to fare much better at the police station. She had gone there with Sergeant Johnson prior to the PCR, and he had assured her there was no evidence from the case to be found. Zelenka and Holt walked into the station. Zelenka identified himself to the duty officer, Wayne Hughes, and introduced Holt. He told Hughes they were looking for the exhibits in the Elmore case.

Hughes got up, went through a door off to the right, and returned pushing a cart piled with exhibits. Holt and Zelenka examined them, then sat talking about the exhibits that still hadn't been located. Hughes interrupted. Excuse me for listening, he said. But if you want me to do a quick look I will. He left again.

Zelenka was growing increasingly uneasy. If Hughes brought

out anything more, he might have to go home and quit his job, if he wasn't fired, he said to Holt.

He had barely spoken when Hughes returned with two large boxes and a mailing tube. Written on their sides, in large, bold letters: EDWARD LEE ELMORE. Holt gaped. This was the very material she and Jensen had been trying to get. Zelenka was dismayed. This was the material Zelenka had assured Judge Kinard didn't exist.

The boxes were packed with potentially explosive evidence: a piece of bedroom carpet, a piece of gum found in the backyard, the robe Mrs. Edwards was wearing on the night she was murdered. If she had pulled out forty-some pubic hairs while being assaulted, presumably there'd be one or two on her robe. Holt had the robe examined. There were no Negroid hairs on it. Elmore must have undressed her, raped her, had her put her robe back on, and then killed her, Holt would say scathingly.

Still, the top prize was Item T. Not only had it been found, but Wells now admitted that it was hair. But whose hair was it? Was it Negroid or Caucasian?

Holt sought, and received, the court's permission to have Item T examined by an analytical microscopist in Chicago, Skip Palenik. Fifty years old, Palenik liked to say his career began when he started looking through a microscope as an eight-year-old. He had worked on numerous high-profile cases, including the bombing of the federal building in Oklahoma. About 80 percent of the time he worked for the prosecution. Holt flew to O'Hare, rented a car, and drove thirty miles west to Palenik's office in a medical building in suburban Elgin, Illinois. She had Item T in her hand. She wasn't about to let it out of her sight. She spent the night in Chicago, flying home the next day.

Holt spent most of the day with Palenik as he examined each slide with a stereomicroscope and a polarizing microscope. He further examined slides 1 and 4 with a comparison microscope.

His findings:

Slide 1: A single pubic hair, Caucasian. He compared it with hairs from Mrs. Edwards. No match.

Slide 2: Three hairs, which may or may not have been human.

One brown Caucasian hair fragment. There were also tiny bits of "blue dyed kemp wool fiber," probably from a carpet.

Slide 3: A hair badly mounted, so hard to be certain, but appeared to be "a light brown Caucasian head hair." Unlike most head hairs from the victim, which were white, he noted.

Slide 4: A white Caucasian head hair with some dried blood on it. Could be the victim's, "but there is a finite likelihood that it could originate from another white haired person."

He concluded, "None of these hairs are microscopically similar to Mr. Elmore's head or pubic hair."

Palenik sent Holt a letter with his results. It was June 1999, six years to the month since she had started working on the Elmore case. She called Zelenka. Surely he'd agree to a new trial now, she told him. His obligation, she reminded him, was to do justice.

In a manual for government appellate lawyers, Zelenka contrasted their role with that of defense lawyers. The latter, he wrote, were bound by the Constitution to provide a vigorous defense. "Our role as prosecutors, however, is much higher—to be a minister of justice," he wrote. That is the noble legal theory. The reality is too often far removed, as Zelenka demonstrated.

If there is a flaw in the adversarial system of justice that has developed in America, it is that the adversarial nature of it outweighs justice. Prosecutors want to win at trial. Appellate lawyers want to win on appeal. Justice often gets lost. Moreover, for an attorney general's office to say that new evidence supports the inmate's claim of innocence, or that his trial was constitutionally flawed, is an admission of error by the state. In Elmore's case, it would mean admitting that such errors had been committed three times. In fighting Elmore's lawyers at every turn, Don Zelenka and the attorney general's office were behaving like counterparts around the country.

AT THE TIME ZELENKA was resisting Elmore's appeals, in Arizona the state's lawyers were exhibiting a concomitant determination to have Ramón Martínez-Villareal executed. He and a friend had broken into a house in Tumacacori, Arizona, hard on the Mexican border, and made off with several high-caliber rifles and ammunition. On their way to Mexico, they came upon two men grading a road. The men were killed. It was not clear who pulled the trigger, Martínez-Villareal or his partner. The police never found the other man. Martínez-Villareal was arrested in Mexico and kicked around a bit before being turned over to the Arizona authorities. He was charged with felony murder (murder during the commission of a felony), convicted, and sentenced to death.

Martínez-Villareal, four foot nine, 130 pounds, was severely mentally retarded, with an IQ between 50 and 64, and suffered from schizophrenia, depression, and brain damage. During his trial, he didn't know the difference between the spectators and the jurors. His biggest concern was his new boots, which had been taken from him when he was arrested. He kept asking his lawyer when he would get them back. When the judge pronounced the death sentence, Martínez-Villareal asked his lawyer when he would get his boots.

None of the lawyers in the small town of Santa Cruz had wanted to touch the case, certainly not at $30 a hour, which is what the state paid, so the court had appointed the last man on the list, William Rothstein, only four years out of law school. He had never tried a murder case. Rothstein presented no evidence of his client's mental retardation. On appeal, Martínez-Villareal's new lawyers argued that he had been denied effective assistance of counsel.

For several years, the case bounced back and forth between the state and federal courts, including the Supreme Court. In 1997, the case took an astonishing turn. "Had we been made aware of any prior mental history, it would have been my recommendation that we not proceed with a death penalty request," the district attorney who prosecuted Martínez-Villareal, Bruce Stirling, told a parole board considering Martínez-Villareal's application for a commutation. "One of the primary functions of the county attorney's office and all prosecutors is to seek justice," he said.

The trial judge who had sentenced Martínez-Villareal to death also said that he had been wrong. There was "no question" that Martínez-Villareal had not been adequately represented at trial, said Judge Roberto Monteil.

"And under these circumstances, do you think it's fair to execute Mr. Martínez?" a board member asked.

"No," said the judge.

In the annals of death penalty jurisprudence, it was unlikely there was another case in which both the prosecutor and the judge said that they had been wrong in seeking the death penalty. Nevertheless, the parole board voted 5–1 against clemency. The lawyers won another stay and made another trip to the U.S. Supreme Court. Now they argued Martínez-Villareal was insane and therefore could not be executed under *Ford v. Wainwright,* a 1986 Supreme Court decision barring the execution of an insane person. The court agreed, and the case was returned to the Arizona state courts. The state won the next round and set another execution date. Then the Arizona legislature passed a law banning the execution of the mentally retarded. Still, the attorney general didn't give up. He argued that the law wasn't retroactive. Finally, in June 2002, in *Atkins v. Virginia,* the Supreme Court held that it violated the Constitution to execute an individual who was mentally retarded, which is generally defined as someone with an IQ under 70. The state of Arizona finally gave up trying to execute Martínez-Villareal, grudgingly.

Zelenka was as resolute as his Arizona counterparts. Even after Item T had been located and Palenik said the hairs were only Caucasian, Zelenka didn't think that a new trial for Elmore was justified. Earl Wells should look at the slides again, he proposed. Holt was incredulous. Despite their disagreements, until then she had considered him a civil servant simply doing his job, albeit with a different value system than hers. Now she saw him as a prosecutor driven by a determination to win, not by the pursuit of truth or justice. The relationship continued to sour.

With Zelenka refusing to agree to a new trial, Holt and Jensen returned to court. "It is our view that at this stage there is really only one course open to the court, which is to grant relief on this petition and allow us to have a new criminal trial for Mr. Elmore," Jensen told Judge Kinard. It was now clear that Item T had been "misdescribed," Jensen said, again using a restrained euphemism. "Whether that was done deliberately in order to conceal the evidence or it was just done as a result of negligent, faulty law enforcement efforts by SLED, is irrelevant." The fact was that for nearly seventeen years, SLED had said it could not find Item T, when it was in SLED's possession all the time. And Earl Wells had sworn under oath that it was blue fiber on those slides, not hair. Jensen invited Judge Kinard to look at the slides. "You can tell by looking with the naked eye that there is not just blue fiber on those slides, that there is hair on those slides."

Jensen pleaded, "Let Mr. Elmore have the trial that he never got. Let Mr. Elmore have due process. Let Mr. Elmore be represented by effective counsel who will look at this evidence in a serious way and who will present his case for his innocence and allow the jury to decide that case."

Zelenka wouldn't budge. Item T needed to be examined further, he argued to Judge Kinard, proposing, as he had to Holt, that Wells look at the slides again. It will only take him a few hours, he assured Judge Kinard.

Holt was beside herself. She didn't often speak in the court. As bold, gutsy, and intrepid as she was on some levels, she was also basically shy and insecure. Now she could not hold back. She related to Judge Kinard her conversation with Zelenka. "I told him that I considered it absolutely of no value to this court to have Mr. Wells look at the hair again. In fact, I didn't understand why Mr. Zelenka would want Mr. Wells to look at the hair considering that Mr. Wells has had the hair in his possession for seventeen years; that Mr. Wells is the person who received this hair evidence from Sandra Conradi who mounted it on slides, who examined it under a microscope and then wrote down the result of his analysis as blue fiber. Mr. Wells at this point has maybe more interest in the outcome of this analysis of that hair evidence than Mr. Elmore does. So I don't think that Mr. Wells is the appropriate person to examine the hair."

Judge Kinard interrupted: "And you are getting frustrated?" he asked with an avuncular smile.

Holt apologized.

But Kinard, too, was disturbed by the suggestion that Wells should examine the slides. He ordered an independent analysis, allowing the state to select the examiner. The state chose a retired FBI forensic scientist whose specialty was hair and fibers, Myron Scholberg.

On the morning of August 10, 1999, Holt flew up to Richmond, Virginia, rented a car, and then drove to Scholberg's home in Williamsburg. She was carrying the four glass slides that were Item T. In order to rebut any suggestion that she might tamper with the slides, she had them copied at Wells's SLED office on the day they were found. Salley Elliott, who had driven up with her family for a vacation that would follow, met her there. The three engaged in a stream of social banter in Scholberg's office, a small, long, narrow room in his house, talking about their kids and other unrelated matters; they could have been at a luncheon, Holt thought. Scholberg was at a desk, peering into his microscope. Holt stood so close that she could practically see into the microscope herself. She scribbled notes while Scholberg muttered. "I didn't know SLED was this bad," he said at one point, raising Holt's spirits. He mumbled that he couldn't understand how Wells could possibly have looked at the slides and not seen hair. When he finished, he returned the slides to Holt, who wasn't sure what he had concluded.

Later that day, Scholberg sat at his typewriter and wrote Don Zelenka a report. It was only two pages long, but it allowed for no equivocation.

Slide 1: A single pubic hair "of Caucasian origin that is microscopically like those of the victim."

Slide 2: Three animal hair fragments and a woolen fragment; in addition, a Caucasian hair fragment.

Slide 3: A single Caucasian head hair, which could have come from the victim.

Slide 4: A single Caucasian head hair "microscopically like those of the victim."

"No hairs of Negroid origin were observed on any of the slides," he wrote.

In light of Scholberg's report, Holt was now beginning to put the pieces of the puzzle together. Wells had known as soon as he looked at the hairs that they were Caucasian, not Negroid. This was Tuesday afternoon, the day after the body was found, and before Elmore had been arrested. At the same time, having taken Mrs. Edwards's fingerprints, SLED knew there were fingerprints in the house that were neither hers nor Elmore's. In light of these two findings, the state had almost no case against Elmore, or only a very weak one at best. Thus, Holt's theory went, Coursey had yanked the inordinate number of pubic hairs from Elmore, and these were the ones the state said were found on Mrs. Edwards's bed.

Holt contemplated her next move: DNA testing. She needed to know if it was Mrs. Edwards's hair. If it wasn't, that would be prima facie evidence that a white person had murdered Mrs. Edwards, and would also suggest that the police had lied and planted evidence.

Around the country, DNA testing was giving hope to prisoners who claimed they were innocent. Some cases looked a lot like Elmore's.

One month after Mrs. Edwards was murdered, in Nampa, Idaho, nine-year-old Daralyn Johnson was found in a ditch on the edge of the Snake River, brutally raped. The police found three pubic hairs on her small body—one on her sock, two on her underpants. For seven months, the police were stymied. Then they focused on Charles Fain, a Vietnam vet and heavy drinker who bounced between Oregon and Idaho, working at whatever odd jobs he could find. He had recently moved back to Idaho and was living with a woman a block away from Daralyn. That and the fact that he had light brown hair were the only reasons the police had for questioning him. He said he had been 360 miles away at his parents' in Redmond, Oregon, at the time Daralyn was killed. The police asked him to take a polygraph test, and he agreed to it. When he denied that he had raped and murdered Daralyn Johnson, the examiner concluded he was telling the truth.

Still, the state, under pressure from the community to solve the heinous crime, charged him. Siding with the prosecution, the judge did not allow the polygraph into evidence. An FBI agent testified that the hair found on Daralyn matched Fain's. And as in Elmore's case, the state produced a jailhouse informant, actually two, who had shared a cell with Fain while he was awaiting his trial. They testified in lurid detail about what they said Fain had told them about the crime, much as Gilliam had about Elmore. Fain was convicted after an eight-day trial, and the judge sentenced him to death. Fain's conviction was upheld by state and federal courts.

Fain had been on death row sixteen years when his appellate lawyers persuaded a court to order DNA tests on the hairs found on Daralyn. It was August 1999, the same month that Myron Scholberg was examining Item T. The results showed that the hair on Daralyn's sock and panties were not Fain's. The state decided not to prosecute him again, and on August 23, 2001, Fain, who had entered death row when he was thirty-five, walked to freedom, eleven days shy of his fifty-third birthday.

The state's decision was not widely applauded.

"It doesn't really change my opinion that much that Fain's guilty," said the prosecutor, Richard Harris.

The trial judge, James Doolittle, agreed: "In my opinion, he's guilty." The DNA results did not sway him.

Holt was nervous about DNA testing. While DNA exonerations of death row inmates often made the headlines, she knew there were many convictions as the result of DNA tests. And if the Greenwood police had lied or planted evidence, which she was increasingly convinced they had, the DNA tested would come back positive. Or what, just what, if Elmore was guilty? She didn't believe it, but with the consequences potentially lethal, she could not take any chances. She called Elmore. It was, after all, his life. She put it as simply and bluntly as possible.

"Let me break it down for you, Eddie," she said. "If that hair is yours, when the man looks in that microscope he is going to see Elmore."

"It's not me," Elmore said softly. He told her to go ahead.

CHAPTER EIGHT

Digging Up the Past

H OLT SEEMED TO SPECIALIZE in innocence cases, that is, cases in which the man on death row is factually innocent, not just "technically" or "legally" innocent because of constitutional errors during his trial. There aren't many. Most death row inmates committed the crime, even if they shouldn't be executed.

Opponents of the death penalty make much of the number of death row inmates who have been exonerated. But "exonerated" does not mean "innocent." In most cases in which an appellate court sets aside a death sentence, the "exonerated" person committed the crime, but he cannot be executed for any one of several legal reasons: he was denied the effective assistance of counsel as guaranteed by the Sixth Amendment; blacks were improperly excluded from the jury; he is mentally retarded; the jury was improperly instructed; the judge excluded evidence that might have caused jurors to spare the man's life. These individuals are sometimes said to be "legally innocent." The Elmore case was in a lull in October 1999, awaiting DNA testing, when John Blume handed Diana another seemingly impossible case of a man with a claim of factual innocence.

Richard Charles Johnson was scheduled to be executed in thirty days for the murder of a state trooper. Johnson was a twenty-three-year-old knockabout who had hooked up with a fifty-two-year-old real estate developer from suburban Washington, D.C., Daniel Swanson. Swanson was heading to Florida in his RV when he met Johnson at a restaurant in Morehead City, North Carolina, and invited him along. Inside the RV, Johnson found stacks of X-rated movies and porn magazines. Crossing into South Carolina, they picked up Curtis Harbert, twenty years old and on the run from criminal charges, who was hitchhiking around the country with Connie Sue Hess, a seventeen-year-old from Nebraska who had been institutionalized twice and was into drugs and sex with truckers. The foursome piled into the motor home, and soon Harbert, Hess, and Swanson were in bed, and Swanson was shot in the back of the head with a .357 pistol. The RV continued south, Johnson driving. He was wiped out on drugs and booze, and the RV was weaving all over the road, bouncing off guardrails. Hess was rubbing her breasts on the window at passing truckers. A trucker alerted a state trooper, who turned on his revolving light and siren and pulled them over. When the officer, Bruce Smalls, approached the RV, the door opened and he was shot with a .38-caliber pistol, shoved onto the shoulder of the highway, and shot again. Johnson fled in one direction, Harbert and Hess in another. All were quickly caught.

The state tried only Johnson. The prosecution had no physical evidence implicating Johnson—there was no gunpowder residue on his hands—but Harbert was willing to testify against him. Johnson was convicted and sentenced to death. Three days later, the state dropped all charges against Harbert and Hess. Johnson's conviction was overturned on appeal, the state tried him again and won a conviction, and he was sentenced to death once more.

With Johnson's execution imminent, Holt managed to locate Connie Hess, in Norfolk, Nebraska, at a facility designed to help individuals recovering from mental illness reintegrate into the community. She told Holt about the hitchhiking, the drugs, and the sex in the bed. Harbert had killed Swanson, she told Holt. When Officer Smalls knocked on the RV door, she had grabbed a gun and handed it to Harbert, who shot Smalls. Then Hess had taken the gun from Harbert. Smalls was slouched in the doorway of the RV, and she kicked him to the ground. "There you go, bastard," she had shouted, firing more shots into him. Holt had Hess's statement notarized and headed back to Columbia.

A few days before Johnson was to be executed, Blume asked the South Carolina Supreme Court for a stay, on the basis of Hess's statement to Holt that Johnson had not killed the trooper. The last time the court had issued a stay had been so long ago that no one could remember. Less than twenty-four hours before Johnson was to be strapped to the gurney, the court granted the stay, and it ordered an investigation into the case. The state was not happy. SLED and the attorney general's office set out to destroy Holt.

Holt had an incident in her past that made her vulnerable. Her closest friends didn't know, save her husband and Marta Kahn. Her boys, who were teenagers now, didn't even know.

It had happened back in 1975, when she was seventeen, in the wake of her mother's lurid divorce from Walter Belshaw and her mother's recriminations that followed. Diana was feeling lost, abandoned, and unloved. One night, she and a friend went to Papa Feel Good, a Houston club. They made friends with a threesome—Jennifer Wiley, seventeen; her boyfriend, Richard Morrison, who was in his late twenties; and Harold Brown, nineteen. The next day, the three showed up at Diana's apartment with a cache of jewelry and money. They had broken into somebody's home, they said. The four set off for New Orleans.

After three days of partying, Diana got homesick. Her new friends were not sympathetic. If she wanted money to go home, she would have to get the money somehow. She put on her schoolgirl dress, went to the French Quarter, took a seat at an outside table, and ordered a Tom Collins. An older guy was sitting a few tables away. She began flirting with him. The man introduced himself as Sandy Blades. They walked to his car. Just as he was getting into the driver's seat, Harold Brown came up and pointed a gun at Blades. Blades started to reach under his seat. He was a U.S. marshal and had a .9 mm pistol. Brown reacted quickly, sticking the barrel of his pistol at Blades's temple. Blades surrendered his gun, along with $61. Harold and Diana were caught before they had gone two blocks.

Holt pleaded guilty to armed robbery. She was sentenced to five years; with good behavior, she'd be out in "two years, eight months, twenty-one days," numbers she could recite years later. She was sent to the Louisiana Correctional Institute for Women, in St. Gabriel, prisoner 80367, another number etched into her psyche. She was assigned to work in the kitchen. She cut herself a lot. It wasn't suicidal. She was just numb; it was a way to feel something.

Those photography courses she had taken and excelled in at Houston Technical Institute now served her well. She was assigned to take mug shots of incoming inmates. The photo lab was next to the law library. Ellen Flood, who was serving a life sentence for killing her husband with arsenic, was in charge. She befriended Diana and persuaded the warden to let her work in the library.

Diana was beginning to develop an interest in the law, an instinct that had lain dormant since the sixth grade. She and Ellen became the prison's de facto legal aid office.

Donna Lee Peck Aucoin, convicted of robbery, came to them for help. Aucoin was retarded, possibly suffering from Down syndrome. How could she be held accountable for what she did? Diana thought. Why was she not in a mental institution? Diana wanted Aucoin's file. Displaying the boldness that would become her signature, she wrote directly to the judge (with a few spelling errors):

> On numerous occasions I have written to the Clerk of Court for the 16th Judicial District, asking for a copy of Ms. Aucoins Bill of Indictment and a full word for word copy of the minutes of the Court. I have continually been ignored. It is imperitive that I obtain true copy's of both documents. . . .
>
> . . . I do not understand why the Clerk of the Court has chosen to ignore my requests and I am very sorry that I had to disturb you as a result of it. I am in no position

to question your decision to send Ms. Aucoin to a penitentiary, but if you know of any information pertaining to Ms. Aucoin that would be of help to me, relating to such a decision would you please forward it to me. No disrespect whatsoever is intended towards you or the position you hold. I just find it hard to understand how a person in Ms. Aucoin mental condition was committed to this sort of institution.

It was an impressive document for a seventeen-year-old without a high school education.

In another case, on behalf of an inmate who was serving two consecutive sentences, Diana wrote the judge that the sentences should run concurrently. The judge agreed. It gave Diana a good feeling that she could make a difference.

Diana matured, got off drugs, and learned a lot in prison. She met the types most lawyers never meet, except as clients. She developed empathy. She realized how close she had come to going over the edge. A tall blond with hair to her waist, Catherine "Kitty" Dodds, drove the lesson home. Arrogant and mean as hell, Dodds had been convicted of hiring two teenagers to kill her husband, a New Orleans police officer. She was first sentenced to die, before her punishment was commuted to life. That could too easily be me, Diana understood. (Dodds later acquired international renown. After escaping from prison, she settled in a small town in Missouri, adopting a new name and life, until she was caught by the FBI and sent back to prison. She was released in 1992 and became the subject of a television movie, in which she was portrayed as a battered woman and victim.)

Prison officials liked Diana. They believed in rehabilitation, and Diana was their prize exhibit. They sent her to speak to sociology and criminology classes at Louisiana State University. She was a good public face—blond, blue-eyed, more educated than most, young and soft-looking. In her photo for the Louisiana Governor's Conference on Women in 1976, she had long hair and was wearing a low-cut dress and a white necklace—she could have been mistaken for a fun-loving coed.

Diana's mother retained a young lawyer fresh out of LSU, paying him $500 to get her daughter a pardon. The prison warden, who was fond of Diana, told her she would be better off appearing before the board with her mother and family friends, rather than being represented by a slick lawyer. Diana and her mother dismissed the lawyer, but it didn't hurt his career: C. James Carville Jr. went on to politics and fame.

On October 30, 1977, Diana was released from prison and boarded a Greyhound for Texas. Under the release terms, she was not allowed to leave the state of Louisiana until the thirty-first, and when the bus crossed the border before midnight, she had some nervous moments, fearing it would be pulled over and she would be sent back.

Diana got a full pardon, which Louisiana grants first offenders on completion of their jail time. All her rights were restored. The State Bar of Texas knew of Holt's conviction for armed robbery when it approved her application to take the bar exam. The South Carolina Bar knew of the conviction and likewise decided she was of sufficient moral character to be a lawyer. The State Bar of Georgia approved her as well.

But the attorney general of South Carolina and the chief of SLED didn't give a damn about the judgments of others. They had their own agenda.

As part of the investigation that the South Carolina Supreme Court had ordered in the Johnson case, Hess would be called to testify that she had lied at Johnson's trial. If she declined, which she well might, given the potential criminal charges she was facing, then John Blume would introduce into evidence the affidavit Hess had given Holt. Blume would have to put Holt on the stand to vouch for the affidavit's authenticity. The state would seek to undermine Holt's credibility with her felony conviction. The attorney general subpoenaed her for a deposition. On Friday, April 21, 2000, Holt and Blume walked to the attorney general's office, where Don Zelenka was waiting for them. He was going to take her deposition. Blume was representing his former protégé turned colleague. When Holt had first told John about the incident in New Orleans and her time in prison, he was not pleased. He worried that if the information became public, it would hurt the center's clients, that conservatives would say, in effect, What do you expect from death penalty lawyers? They're no better than their clients. For weeks, Blume and Holt barely spoke. Eventually, however, Blume came to see her story as one of redemption.

Walking into the deposition, Blume and Holt were not sure how much Zelenka knew about her past. The deposition began routinely. Zelenka asked her name, age, and date of birth.

"I always think I'm still eighteen," she said, never able to resist a quip.

"I keep thinking I'm forty," said Zelenka, who was over fifty. That brought some laughter. The last.

Zelenka began methodically asking her about her past— where she had gone to high school, where she had lived and worked in Texas.

Holt had trouble remembering all the dates in her turbulent past. "If I had known y'all were going to be asking about this stuff, I would have researched it," she said.

"Just general questions," Zelenka responded.

Abruptly, the mood changed.

"Description of anything in your background that could be used to discredit you or prejudice the court?" Zelenka asked in the cryptic way lawyers sometimes use in depositions. "For example, have you ever been arrested for DUI or other offenses?" He knew the answer, of course.

Blume objected. This was irrelevant. But he and Diana still weren't sure what Zelenka had.

"Did you go by the name of Diana Lynn Nerren in 1975?" Zelenka asked.

Now they knew. They looked at each other. What do you want to do? he asked. I'll answer, let's go, she said. "You're the bravest person I know," Blume said. The memory of his reaction, those words, moved her years after.

"I think all of this is irrelevant," Blume told Zelenka. "I also think it is unbelievably tacky." He said he would move to have the deposition sealed. Zelenka said he would not agree to seal the deposition or to any limitations on its use. This was down and dirty. He turned back to Diana and asked her about the conviction.

She started the answer where she thought she should, with the custody proceeding, where she'd been called as a witness by her mother, to tell the judge about the years of sexual abuse at the hands of her stepfather.

Zelenka interrupted. That wasn't necessary. He just wanted to know about the conviction.

"May I finish?" she said icily.

"But I'm telling you, you don't need to go into that."

Holt's attitude was, No, buddy, you want the story, you're going to get the whole story, not just the parts that suit you. She explained what had happened, the introduction of the nude pictures and, above all, the brutal cross-examination by her stepfather's lawyer.

"It was extraordinarily traumatic, as you can imagine," she told Zelenka. Never quite able to hold her tongue, she said, "It was not unlike some of the cross-examinations of some of the people who are sentenced to death."

She went on: "There were I don't know how many hundreds of nude photographs of myself and my little sister that were then introduced into that court record." Holt started to cry when she told about the judge ordering that child protective services take custody of her sister.

The deposition lasted nearly four hours.

That evening, Diana's husband, Kevin Bell, called Zelenka at home. Zelenka's wife answered. Bell identified himself and was surprised when Zelenka came to the phone. Bell was furious. "My mother would not have been proud of my language," he recalled. He yelled at Zelenka. He said his wife was in a corner, a basket case. What Zelenka was doing was unethical and unprofessional. How in the hell did he get the information? Bell demanded to know. Louisiana law prohibits authorities from releasing criminal records, except to other law enforcement agencies, and then only if it is part of a criminal investigation; that does not include using the information to impeach a witness.

Zelenka didn't have just photocopies of the Louisiana report; he had obtained the carbon copies directly from the files. What the hell did Zelenka tell the state of Louisiana? Bell accused him of lying. Zelenka didn't answer Bell's questions and charges. He didn't argue, and he didn't hang up. He just took it. Zelenka told Bell that a SLED agent had brought the information to him and that he had run a background check to confirm it. Zelenka also said that he was referring the matter to the head of the criminal division of the attorney general's office. The SLED agent, whoever he was, had probably violated federal and South Carolina privacy laws. Nothing ever happened.

When the hearing in the Johnson case took place, Blume, Holt, and Zelenka went together into the judge's chambers. Zelenka had a thirty-page memorandum, essentially portraying Holt as trailer-park trash. Zelenka told the judge, William P. Keesley, that he wanted to use the material, including the conviction, to impeach Holt.

Judge Keesley began reading. He was visibly disgusted.

He was not going to allow Zelenka to do this, he said. What happened took place twenty-five years ago, when Holt was young. She made it through the board of character and fitness in Texas and in South Carolina, the judge said. He advised Zelenka against proceeding as he planned, but if he wanted to make a record, he could. Zelenka said he would not.

Holt and Blume walked out. They sagged, hugged each other, and broke into tears.

THE SOUTH CAROLINA SUPREME COURT rejected Johnson's appeal. To get a new trial, the majority wrote, the defendant had to show that the new evidence—in this case, Hess's sworn confession—would "probably change the result" of the original trial. That standard had not been met. "We do not believe it is probable that a jury would find Hess credible given her prior inconsistent statements," Justice James E. Moore wrote for the court. He had been the judge at Elmore's second trial. Joining him in the opinion was Justice E. C. Burnett III. He had been the judge in the first Elmore trial.

The dissents were short but powerful. "I believe that to deny Johnson a new trial in the face of a confession by someone who was admittedly present when the murder was committed would constitute a denial of fundamental fairness shocking to the universal sense of justice," Justice Waller wrote in a three-paragraph opinion. "Our system of justice dictates that before Johnson is put to death he must be given an opportunity to present such evidence to a jury of his peers."

The United States Supreme Court rejected Johnson's appeal. Johnson's supporters mounted a campaign to persuade South Carolina governor James Hodges to grant him clemency. The mother of Bruce Smalls, the state trooper Johnson was convicted of murdering, issued a public letter urging clemency. Smalls's sister, Pat, and son, Kevin, asked the governor to uphold the sentence.

Governors rarely grant clemency in capital cases, the extraordinary exception being Illinois governor George Ryan. In January 2003, three years after he had declared a moratorium and appointed a blue-ribbon commission to examine how to reform the state's death penalty, he commuted the sentences of 167 death row inmates on a single day. It was a monumental step, all the more so because as a legislator, in 1977, Ryan had voted to reinstate the death penalty, and when he became governor, in 1999, he was "a firm believer in the American system of justice and the death penalty," he said in announcing the mass commutation. "I believed that the ultimate penalty for the taking of a life was administered in a just and fair manner."

He could no longer be so confident, not in light of "the systematic failures of our capital punishment system" two reporters at the *Chicago Tribune*, Steve Mills and Ken Armstrong, had revealed. The reporters had looked at some three hundred capital cases in Illinois. Nearly half had been reversed on appeal, for a new trial on guilt or innocence or for resentencing.

"Now, how many of you people here today that are professionals can call your life a success if you're only fifty percent successful?" Ryan asked rhetorically in his speech at Northwestern University Law School. "Certainly, I can't as a pharmacist. I don't think doctors can."

Ryan deliberately chose to make the announcement at Northwestern, where the work of the Center on Wrongful Convictions—a combined program of the law and journalism schools—had resulted in several men being released from Illinois's death row. The room was jammed with some five hundred law students, journalism students, and anti–death penalty activists.

Ryan said that more than two-thirds of the death row inmates were African Americans and that forty-six had been convicted on the basis of testimony from jailhouse informants.

"I can recall looking at these cases from the Mills/Armstrong series, and I asked myself and my staff: How does this happen? How in God's name does that happen? In America, how does it happen?"

Ryan said that he had been lobbied to end the death penalty by many international bodies and individuals, including the European Union, the Vatican, Nelson Mandela, and Archbishop Desmond Tutu.

"To take the life when a life has been lost is revenge. It's not justice," Bishop Tutu wrote.

Only the day before, Nelson Mandela had called. The essence of his message, Ryan told those gathered, was, "America is a beacon of fairness and justice and the death penalty really doesn't pay homage to that kind of operation."

Ryan noted that the death penalty had been abolished by every European country, as well as Canada, South Africa, and nearly every country in Latin America, including Mexico. That leaves the United States "in partners in death with several Third World countries," Ryan told the audience.

As Ryan neared the end of his often emotional speech, he borrowed from Justice Blackmun: "I shall no longer tinker with the machinery of death." (In 2010, Illinois abolished the death penalty. New Jersey had abolished it in 2007 and New Mexico in 2009.)

No South Carolina governor had ever granted clemency. And now it was an election year, with Hodges, a Democrat, facing a potential challenge from Don Zelenka's boss, Attorney General Charlie Condon, who once proposed that the electric chair be replaced by an electric couch so there could be simultaneous executions. Hodges refused clemency.

As Johnson faced death, Diana talked to him almost daily, sometimes for two hours. She was convinced he was innocent. On execution day, she went to death row to be with him. He was chain-smoking and went from talking a blue streak to being somber. Another lawyer, Fielding Pringle, who had worked on the clemency petition, came in. She was strikingly attractive, and Holt noticed how Johnson lit up. She had to smile. He's a red-blooded male and still kicking, she thought to herself.

Diana was with him for almost seven hours. As she left, his last words were, "I'll see you at the beach." He'd grown up on the North Carolina shore, and he and his sister Lori played there together. He had a favorite spot on the beach, where he loved watching the sun go down behind him. He had pictures his sister had taken at the beach, and he gave them to Diana. She told him she was going to sit at the beach for him one last time.

On May 3, 2002, Richard Charles Johnson, thirty-nine years old, ordered for his last meal fried shrimp, fried oysters, French fries, chocolate cake, and iced tea. When he finished, he was strapped to a gurney, needles were stuck in his arms, and his life was ended with a lethal injection. At his funeral, before the casket was closed, his sister managed to cut some locks from his hair. A few days later, she and Diana went to the beach in North Carolina, waded into the surf, and let them go.

The Johnson case was a turning point for Holt. She was convinced Johnson was innocent. The politics surrounding the case disgusted her. She had now made the journey to the position of firm opposition to capital punishment, though still not on moral grounds. She simply believed "there is no way to implement it fairly. Despite all legal safeguards, whether one gets death or not is dependent on geography, the elected official with the power to seek it, the color of his skin, gender, the color of the victim's skin, the victim's gender, wealth of any of those, poverty of the defendant, mental health of any of those, and judges with agendas, etc. I haven't begun to address the innocence or not question, the integrity of law enforcement, the competence of law enforcement, the competence of forensic analyst, and on and on and on."

Johnson was the twenty-eighth man Elmore had watched leave his cell and not return.

CHAPTER NINE

One Hair . . .

T HE SUMMER AND FALL of 2000 were nerve-racking for
Holt. In June, she sent Item T to the Laboratory Corpora-
tion of America, in Research Triangle Park, North Carolina, for
testing. By September, she was calling the lab practically every
day. Didn't they have the results yet? When were they going to
have them?

Twenty-three days before Christmas, the fax machine in her
office spit out three pages. It was the report from LabCorp. The
lab had tested nine hairs. Five were found to be "consistent
with these hairs originating from Dorothy Edwards or an individual that is maternally related to her," the lab reported. Three
had insufficient DNA for testing purposes.

That left one.

This hair "could not have originated from Dorothy Edwards or
an individual that is maternally related to her," the lab reported.

Holt was ecstatic.

Judge Kinard had promised a hearing when the DNA results
came in, and on December 21, Edward Lee Elmore was back
in the Greenwood County courtroom where he had first been
sentenced to death. He was barely twenty-three years old at
the first trial, with a full head of hair. He was three weeks shy
of forty-two now and bald, partly from age and partly because
he shaved his head. At the first trial, he had been saddled with
Anderson and Beasley. Now he had Holt and Blume. Elmore

had every reason to believe that Christmas 2000 would be the best he had celebrated in eighteen years. "He thought he had it made this time, after all these years, that people would see the light, that they just got the wrong man," said his sister Peggy, who was twenty-five at her brother's first trial and was now a grandmother. A female guard from the South Carolina Department of Corrections led Elmore, shackled and in a green prison-issue jumpsuit, into the courtroom; she had a pump-action shotgun. What she need that for, her finger on the trigger, Peggy said to herself. He ain't goin' nowhere.

"All rise," the bailiff intoned. Judge Kinard entered the courtroom, his judicial robes covering a loud plaid suit. "Okay, at ease," he said, taking his seat.

"I'd like to request that the shackles be removed from Mr. Elmore" were the first words from Holt. She was always trying to give Elmore as much dignity as possible. Judge Kinard, ever amiable, agreed.

Kinard, his morning coffee in a white Styrofoam cup next to his arm, acknowledged "the disproportionately large number of media present."

There were also some observers with considerable interest in the outcome. Townes Jones had walked over from his office across the street. Two of the policemen who had originally investigated the case were present—Jim Coursey, retired, now working in security for Pizza Hut, and Al Johnson, also retired, now an amateur thespian.

Elmore's family and supporters were there—Peggy, his brother James, and Reverend Spearman. Diana's best friend and colleague, Fielding Pringle, had gotten up early and driven from Columbia with her three-month-old son, which meant a lot to Diana. Fielding had also brought her mother to witness what she expected to be a historic event: Elmore getting a new trial after nearly two decades on death row. Rauch Wise came from his law office on the other side of Main Street; convinced of the outcome, he had called a friend who had a talk show on local radio station WLMA and suggested he come to the court. "You'll be the first with the news when Elmore gets a new trial," Wise said.

Holt, in a navy blue suit, stood and asked that several exhibits be admitted into evidence. One was an affidavit from Myron Scholberg, the retired FBI forensic expert who examined Item T. As the day for the hearing approached, Holt had remembered how upset he had been with SLED and Earl Wells. She called Scholberg and asked if he would be willing to sign an affidavit that could be submitted to the court stating his views. He agreed. "The presence of hair was immediately apparent and clearly visible, that is to say that hair was visible on these slides to the naked eye," he said in the affidavit. He hadn't even needed a microscope. He went on: "I do not know or see how Mr. Wells could have looked at the four microscope slides and honestly reported that the four Item T slides only contained blue fiber." (Out of court, Scholberg was more straightforward: "The report is a fraud.")

Holt went on to explain to Judge Kinard that Chris Jensen was unable to attend the hearing for medical reasons. She didn't want the court to think that perhaps Jensen was bailing out because he no longer believed in Elmore's innocence. "He's had heart problems, irregular heartbeat, and his doctor would not allow him to come today, prior to undergoing the testing the doctor ordered," she explained. "And that's the only reason Mr. Jensen is not here today."

Holt knew the case better than anyone, but she still lacked confidence in court. She was also uncomfortable about having to face so many reporters. John Blume would therefore argue the case. Not only was he skilled at presenting oral arguments, but he was good at concise analysis, sound bites, and snappy quotes for reporters.

His hair almost to his shoulders, wearing a double-breasted gray suit and rimless glasses, Blume addressed the court first. "In any fair system this gentleman is entitled, we believe, to a new trial," he told Kinard. A hair had been found on the victim's body, a white hair, which didn't belong to the victim, Blume pointed out. "That, in and of itself, we believe entitles Mr. Elmore to a new trial."

Before he could go on, a spectator shouted, "Holloway, confess." He was led from the courtroom, and the proceedings continued.

Blume and Holt had prepared a blowup of the statements officials had made under oath about Item T. They mounted it on an easel, easily visible to the television cameras and reporters as well as to Judge Kinard.

THE EIGHTEEN YEAR HISTORY OF "ITEM T"

JAN. 16, 1982: CONRADI AUTOPSY REPORT—TIGHTLY CURLED APPARENT PUBIC HAIR

APRIL 2, 1982: SLED REPORT—BLUE FIBERS

FEB. 14, 1995: WELLS, UNDER OATH—GAVE ITEM T BACK TO THE POLICE

MARCH 4, 1995: WELLS, UNDER OATH—"NO HAIR, JUST BLUE FIBERS." GAVE THEM TO POLICE

NOV. 8, 2000: ZELENKA DEPOSITION—WELLS FOUND ITEM T; HAD IT ALL THE TIME

Blume, looking at the history of Item T, saw only one conclusion. "There's no way to mince words about this. Agent Wells has clearly committed perjury," Blume said. "If this were a defense witness, or a defense expert, or a defense lawyer who had given the testimony he had, I have no doubt they would have been arrested." Wells was "like the proverbial child lying when they have their hand in the cookie jar," Blume went on.

Blume turned to other evidence. Gilliam, the jailhouse informant, had recanted; the state said there were no other fingerprints, but it was established that there was at least one unidentified print, on the underside of the toilet seat in the victim's bathroom; the prosecutor had argued graphically that Mrs. Edwards had reached up and grabbed hairs from Elmore's groin, yet he had no injury to his groin area, no cuts, no bruises; and there were no Negroid hairs found under Mrs. Edwards's fingernails, or anywhere else at the scene.

"The whole thing really stinks," Blume said, concluding with some blunt, if not exactly legal, language. He had addressed Kinard for just under thirty minutes.

Don Zelenka, in a dark suit and white shirt and wearing his rimless glasses, raised his lanky body and addressed the judge. Wells had been "incorrect" when he reported finding only blue fibers, Zelenka told the court; he had "misreported" his test data. Wells, in a natty dark suit, crisp white shirt, and red tie, sat just to Zelenka's right, listening intently. Still, this did not justify a new trial, Zelenka argued.

Yes, a white hair had been found on Mrs. Edwards's body that was not hers, Zelenka conceded. So what? Who knows how it got there? he said. It could have been a stray hair lying around the house, "completely unrelated to this crime," picked up by her body while she was being beaten, Zelenka argued. "It is merely another hair that was in the bedroom of Mrs. Edwards," he went on. "One stray hair."

Zelenka pointed to all the evidence that the state had introduced against Elmore: forty-some pubic hairs on the bed, the victim's blood type on Elmore's clothes, his fingerprint on the back door, Gilliam's testimony at three trials.

Zelenka finished, and Blume had another opportunity. He continued to focus on Wells. "I am not in the habit of coming in and saying that law enforcement agents lied, but in this case this is not a mistake, this is a lie. This is perjury."

In closing, Blume drew on his theological education, borrowing from Rabbi Hillel: "I think in the final analysis the question really is, If not now, when?" If it is not enough to grant somebody a new trial when material, exculpatory evidence has been withheld in violation of *Brady*, when there has been false testimony, "then when is post-conviction relief ever appropriate?"

A little more than an hour had passed since the hearing began. It was assumed Judge Kinard would return to Columbia, study the lawyers' briefs and oral arguments, and write an opinion. Then he began to speak. There were murmurings in the courtroom when it became clear that he was going to rule right then, from the bench, without further consideration.

"Obviously, it should have been disclosed to counsel," he said about Item T. But he agreed with the state that the failure to do so had not "unduly prejudiced" Elmore. "One hair is not enough," he said.

The disbelief was audible—gasps, followed by a stunned silence—when the import of what Judge Kinard had said registered.

Kinard quickly added. "Good luck to everybody, I'm out of here."

"We love you, Eddie," someone shouted.

"Eddie, chin up, hold your head up," came another voice.

"Keep your head up, bro."

Elmore registered no emotion. He did not understand what the judge had ruled. Diana whispered in his ear and started to cry. When Elmore understood, he said softly, "I bet if that one hair had been my hair, it would have been enough."

His sister Elease, wearing a red coat and a black beret, came up to embrace him but was blocked. The guard with the pump-action rifle led Elmore from the courtroom.

"The system's just not right for the black and the poor," Elease said in the corridor. "If you've got money and you're white, you can move a mountain."

Outside the courthouse, the family and Reverend Spearman hugged and prayed. They waved to Elmore as he was put into the white prison van and driven away.

Blume, shocked and angry, repeated for reporters what he had said in court: If any defense lawyer had lied like Wells had, he would be prosecuted.

Wise was dumbfounded. "You could have knocked me over with a feather," he said. He knew Kinard well, had argued many cases in front of him. "Of all the judges who would have done the right thing, I would have thought it would be him." The only explanation Wise could come up with was that Kinard looked at the fact that three juries, thirty-six men and women, had sentenced Elmore to death, and he just couldn't bring himself to overrule that. What this overlooked, Wise said, was that in reality there had been only one trial, replayed twice. If the evidence was flawed in the first trial, if there was prosecutorial misconduct, if there was ineffective assistance of counsel, then it permeated all the trials. James Bradford, one of the best defense lawyers in Greenwood, who had since moved to York, wasn't so surprised. It wasn't that he thought the evidence against Elmore was convincing, or because he thought Judge Kinard was right on the law. Rather, this case was like so many capital cases: there were bad defense lawyers and prosecutorial misconduct, but there was also a mindset among judges that once there is a conviction, "it is going to take Jesus walking on water to make me believe we screwed this thing up."

Holt was devastated, her feelings raw—"skin peeled with a paring knife kind of raw." She and Blume went to lunch but could hardly eat. There was some gallows humor; over and over they repeated, with disbelief, "One hair is not enough."

They drove back to Columbia in separate cars. As they approached the city and John turned off on the exit that would take him home, Diana looked over. He had a sad, painful look and made a thin effort to smile. "And then he was gone, and I was gone."

There was a Christmas party that night at Fielding's. Many revelers were from the public defender's office, young, still filled with idealistic enthusiasm. Fielding, John, and Diana were miserable, in no mood to party. As Diana was making her way out, David Bruck was coming in. She burst into tears.

To Bruck, Kinard's ruling was surprising on one level—ignoring the facts, the lies, and the law—but also spoke volumes about the death penalty: no one wants to take responsibility; everyone is always trying to pass the buck. He knew that judges say they're only enforcing the law given by the legislators; that juries think judges will overrule them; that trial judges look to the appellate judges to save a man, if he should be saved; and that appellate judges say if the man shouldn't be executed, then let the governor grant clemency. Kinard had effectively passed the buck to the South Carolina Supreme Court.

Holt had still not given up.

CHAPTER TEN

Digging Up the Dead

O N JANUARY 4, 2001, Diana Holt filed a motion that pushed the limits of the law, reached a new level of audacity, and tested the meaning of impudence. Moreover, the idea had come to her from a most improbable source, a SLED agent. She had invited the agent, David Caldwell, to lunch. She didn't want to talk about Elmore, but about another of her death row clients, whose case Caldwell had investigated. She didn't have much respect for Caldwell, had all but accused him of lying in one case, but Holt had been told by another SLED agent that Caldwell had doubts about her client's guilt, and she'd break bread with just about anyone if it would save a man from execution. Holt had been warned by David Bruck that Caldwell had a history of saying one thing to gain a defense lawyer's sympathy, then saying something entirely different when he was on the stand. Over lunch, Holt understood. Caldwell told Holt that her client was one of the most cold-blooded killers he'd ever seen. She abruptly changed the subject.

Now she mentioned Elmore. Caldwell hadn't been following the case, so Holt gave him a lengthy précis, going on for nearly an hour.

I'd bet my career Holloway did it, Caldwell said. It took a second or two for it to sink in with Diana what he'd said. Why don't you exhume his body, get his DNA, said Caldwell. That would determine if the Item T hair was his. And she could get

Holloway's fingerprints at the same time, to see if they matched the fingerprint on the underside of the toilet seat.

Holt was uneasy with the idea of exhuming Holloway. You just don't go around digging up the dead. But with Kinard having ruled against Elmore yet again, she felt she had no choice but to go to extremes.

Nineteen years to the month after Dorothy Edwards was murdered, Holt filed a short motion with Judge Kinard. It reflected her obvious exhaustion and impatience and was not smoothly written. She wanted a court order to "exhume the body of Mr. James Holloway in order to obtain a DNA sample (to determine if the hair belongs to him) and to see if it is possible to still obtain fingerprints (to check against the unidentified prints found on the toilet seat in the victim's private bathroom)." She also wanted DNA testing of the scrapings from under Mrs. Edward's fingernails. Surely that would reveal whether Elmore was her attacker and, if not, whether Holloway was (assuming she got to exhume his body).

Finally, she asked the court to order DNA testing of the blood spots on Elmore's shoes and blue jeans to determine whether the blood was the victim's, as the state argued. She didn't really want to do this, fearing that the blood spots might have been planted. "Applicant fully believes that the few small areas of Type A blood (the same ABO type that the victim and the applicant's brother shared) identified on the shoe and pants were either placed there when the items were inexplicably removed from SLED by former neighbor to James Holloway—former SLED agent Tom Henderson." Still, Holt couldn't let Elmore die and then later find out that the blood was not his, that no blood had been planted, so she asked for the testing.

Holt had several long talks with Elmore. He had to understand what she was going to request. If DNA tests were performed and it turned out that it was Dorothy Edwards's blood on the jeans and shoes, Eddie would be executed. Did he understand that? Yes. Did he still want to go ahead with the DNA testing? Yes.

Holt faxed the motion to Don Zelenka, with a one-sentence cover letter:

Dear Mr. Zelenka:
Since you have said many times that it is your duty to seek justice, I am sure you will have no opposition to the attached motion.

Very truly yours,
Diana L. Holt

She knew he would oppose the motion, and he did. Exhuming a body should not be allowed without a showing that it was "absolutely necessary to the fair administration of justice," Zelenka argued in a four-page legal brief (which is about as brief as lawyers ever get). Elmore's lawyers had not only failed to show absolute necessity, they had failed to show *any* necessity for this extraordinary step, he argued. His principal contention was that the request was too late. Elmore's lawyers should have requested DNA testing prior to the hearing in December.

Holt was disgusted. "It is inconceivable that the state opposes, based on a technicality, conducting DNA testing on the items which applicant seeks testing," she wrote in a letter she faxed to Judge Kinard. Zelenka could not "seriously object to the testing that could fully exonerate Mr. Elmore," she wrote. While the legal burden was on Elmore's lawyers to justify the motion, she noted, "the burden of truth is on the state of South Carolina."

Holt's daring had a consequence she did not foresee, and certainly didn't want. James Holloway Jr. learned about the request to dig up his father when a reporter called him for comment. He sent a searing letter to Zelenka. "For a decade my family has been subjected to all manner of rumor and innuendo crafted by Ms. Diana Holt," he began. "This request to violate the sanctity of the grave is utterly despicable. Ms. Holt's professional behavior is outrageous, exceeds the bounds of behavior in a civilized society."

Holloway had grown up next to the Edwardses. Little Jimmy, or Jimmy Junior as he was called until he became an adult and insisted on Jim, delighted in throwing stones at the fish in the Edwardses' pond. One day he found the bottle of liquor that Mr. Edwards kept secreted in his dad's garage, poured out the liquor, and filled it with pepper and vinegar; he watched from a safe distance when Mr. Edwards took a swig, gagged, and spit it out. Carolyn Edwards often babysat young Holloway. When he went to college at The Citadel, in the late 1960s, Mrs. Edwards painted him a Citadel bulldog standing in the stadium, with the campus in the background. He still has it. After college, he served as a supply officer in the navy, then moved to Columbia, opening his own accounting office. His office, cluttered with putters and golf balls, was in a single-story redbrick building on Henderson Street, only a few blocks from Holt's.

For years, Holloway had watched the case inconspicuously from the sidelines. Then, in the fall of 2000, a lengthy article about the case appeared in *The Charlotte Observer*. The reporter, Eric Frazier, had interviewed the police, the prosecutors, and several jurors, as well as John Blume and Chris Jensen. Holt had declined to talk to him. She is not only shy around strangers, but generally doesn't trust reporters, believing them too sympathetic to the state. (This was confirmed, in her mind, by the reporting on the Elmore case. An AP story, for instance, said that Mrs. Edwards "had been raped." She hadn't. The article went on to say that hairs found at the scene matched Elmore's pubic hairs. There was no mention of the possibility that the hairs might have been planted.)

Frazier's article was the first serious look at the Elmore case by a journalist. "Race Often a Key in Death-Penalty Cases" was the headline of his article. That was hardly an astonishing conclusion. Near the end of his lengthy story, however, in a section headed "The Defense Attacks," Frazier wrote that Elmore's lawyers considered Jimmy Holloway a suspect. Blume and Jensen had not told Frazier this directly. What they had done was direct him to the six-page affidavit Holt had prepared after interviewing Holloway Senior at his home in Greenwood in 1993, which was part of the record in the case. Citing the affidavit, Frazier wrote that Holloway had led the police to Elmore. Frazier also quoted from the affidavit that Holloway had told Holt, "I am the only one who could kill her and get away with it, the way she trusted me."

The *Observer* did not put the story on the front page, and the accusations against Holloway Senior would likely have evaporated. Jim Holloway Jr. gave them prominence. He began with an op-ed piece in *The State*, South Carolina's largest-circulation daily. "My dad died six years ago. Since he can't defend himself, that's now my job," he wrote. "Notwithstanding convictions by three separate juries, Elmore's latest defense counsel has its own suspect—my dad."

Unless someone in Greenwood had been following the case closely, so closely that they had been going to the courthouse to read the filings, this was probably the first anyone knew that Holloway Senior was a suspect. His son also told the largest newspaper audience in South Carolina that there were rumors his father had been having an affair with Mrs. Edwards. That made him laugh, he wrote. "That would have been a sight. A 75-year-old woman and a 66-year-old man, in the pre-Viagra days—right!"

Jim Holloway then introduced the public to a woman few had ever heard of, "an aspiring law student" who had showed up to interview his father—Diana Holt. Holloway wrote that Holt had asked his father hypothetical, "what if" questions. "What would you say if I told you a neighbor told me you might be having an affair with Mrs. Edwards?" "Are you the only person who could get away with the murder of Mrs. Edwards?"

The Monica Lewinsky–Bill Clinton affair, with Clinton's memorable redefining of the meaning of the words "sex" and "is," had not been forgotten. Holloway bunched Holt with Clinton. "We live in the age of Bill Clinton where a lawyer can say anything, redefine words and misrepresent their intentions with impunity."

Holloway concluded that there was "a lesson to be learned. It's the age-old story of a wolf in sheep's clothing. It's one I wish my dad had learned."

Holloway, fifty-two years old, continued to vent in other forums. He was against the death penalty, not on moral grounds but because it was dysfunctional and unduly expensive, he wrote in another op-ed piece. "What I find disgusting is the death penalty has given birth to an entire cottage industry that has learned how to feed on it." The death penalty lawyers, tax-exempt foundations that fund their work, even journalists were part of it. "Death row pimps," he called them, "people who use the bodies of convicted murderers for their economic enrichment." Holloway was so convinced that journalists and death row lawyers were in connivance that he ranted on that he had told a *New York Times* reporter that he would write a letter to the governor urging him to commute Elmore's death sentence to life imprisonment. "The reporter immediately rejected my offer on behalf of Diana Holt without so much as a telephone call to her," Holloway wrote. Holloway dismissed the reporter's explanation that it wasn't his role to serve as an intermediary between parties, much less act on behalf of one of them.

He found that the Greenwood *Index-Journal* was willing to carry his case when he wrote another op-ed piece, angrier and less restrained than the one published in *The State,* and more revealing in intimate details about his father. The paper had covered Elmore's arrest and his three trials on the front page, while completely ignoring his PCR hearing. The executive editor of *The Index-Journal,* Robert Bentley, now gave Holloway the front page. It was styled as "A Letter To Our Readers" from the executive editor. "Legal fight for convicted murderer's life at great cost to others" was the six-column headline. Bentley filled his readers in on the background of the case: Edward Lee Elmore was now the longest-serving inmate on South Carolina's death row, having been convicted, not once, but three times, for the murder of Dorothy Edwards; the case had attracted national media attention; Elmore's lawyers were now trying to blame

Holloway Senior, who, Bentley wrote, had been a "pillar of the community."

Then Bentley effectively turned the space over to Holloway. What had been intended as an op-ed ran as if Bentley had interviewed Holloway.

"The story's three main parts are sex, violence and racism," Holloway wrote. That was sure to keep any reader interested.

It would be hard for Holt to make a case that his father had carried out the violent act and raped Mrs. Edwards, he went on. He then laid out for the readers of *The Index-Journal* personal information about his father that they would not have found anywhere else, not even if they had read every page of the record from all three trials. His dad was five foot seven and weighed about 155 pounds, Holloway began. He "wore a hernia truss, similar to a man's athletic supporter in that it has a supporting undercarriage. The difference is that the truss has a six-inch-wide waistband made of heavy medical elastic designed to hold and support stomach muscles from rupture."

He went on to say that if it were a trial and Holt were the prosecutor, she would "have to overcome the jurists' mental picture of a smallish, elderly man gaining entrance by knocking an exterior door from its hinges.

"While using one hand to restrain a horrified woman fighting for her life, he uses the other to extract himself from his hernia truss. After a successful sexual encounter, he summons the energy to stab her 66 times and, without rupturing himself, drags the body to a closet."

Holloway Junior had taken some liberty with the facts—Mrs. Edwards had allowed the killer in, the door was not knocked off the hinges, there weren't sixty-six stab wounds, and she had not been raped. Holloway was entitled to these liberties, playing defense lawyer for his own father. But if he had been a witness in a courtroom and subject to cross-examination, his defense might not have persuaded a jury. In January 1982, Holloway Senior had been strong enough to lift a five-gallon canister of kerosene out of the trunk of Mrs. Edwards's car and lug it into her den. He was working in his woodshop regularly and was even building a boat. The onset of his illnesses, including diabetes and the need for kidney dialysis, wasn't until the late 1980s, his son said years later.

As Holloway came to the conclusion of his op-ed–cum–"A Letter To Our Readers," he turned on Holt. She had asked his father hypothetical questions, he said, and then proceeded with an argument that was somewhat hard to follow. "The word 'might' is a wonderfully permissive word," he wrote. "It allows one to say something without being responsible for its factual correctness. By saying something might be, you are also saying something might not be. Therein lies the protection." Holloway was building up.

"I could also probably find someone who would be willing to say Holt 'might' be a pedophile." Produce some documents, he said, "and I can publicly infer that she has had sex with little boys and girls."

Holloway wasn't trying to "tank her case," he would explain. "I had one objective: to keep my Daddy in the ground."

Whatever Holloway's objectives, Holt took it personally; she was hurt and angry. "Unadulterated horseshit," she said about his claim that she had asked his father hypothetical questions. She wanted to sue Holloway for libel. Her husband, and just about everyone else whose advice she sought, cautioned her against it. Her friend Marta Kahn said she shouldn't; but she understood why Diana felt she had to, and she knew that once Diana decided she was going to do something, there was no way to stop her. Diana sued Holloway. The statements made by Holloway "impugned my character and attacked my reputation for honesty, morality, and chastity," she alleged. "The statements also attacked my reputation and professionalism as an attorney and accused me of being unethical and dishonest in my actions as an attorney. One of the statements even went so far as to accuse me of being a pedophile."

IN ELMORE'S CASE, Holt lost the motion to have Holloway's father exhumed. It didn't matter that an unidentified Caucasian hair had been found on Mrs. Edwards's body, Judge Kinard said. "One hair from the victim's body from the bedroom floor that could have come from various sources does not mandate a new trial," he ruled. "Even if DNA testing showed the single hair to be Holloway's, the prior jury verdicts would not have been undermined." Kinard would also not allow Elmore's lawyers to test the blood on the jeans and shoes. "I will not now authorize further testing," Kinard asserted sternly.

Young Holloway adopted the same line of reasoning. "So what if that was my father's hair?" he said in an interview in his office. "I guarantee you, the first thing he would have done when he found that body was reach across, and that is when his hair could have fallen on her." This seemed a strange response, an indirect admission that it had been his father's hair. Further, there was nothing in the record that indicated his father had leaned across the body, that he had done anything more than open the door and look in. Told this, Holloway responded that there were plenty of other ways his dad's hair could have gotten on the body. "Everybody knows he was in that house, many times," he said. "How does it get on her body? I don't know. Open the door, whoof, the wind blows one of his hairs on her."

CHAPTER ELEVEN

Bizarre

Dear, Diana
I figure I'd write you instead of calling As always I hope you
are doing well I'm fine. I got the money you send me Think's
I really appreciate Also wanted you know how grateful and
appreciative I'm for you hanging in there with me all these
years, Diana I have every confidence in you when you argue
my case in the supreme court so go for it, take care,
Love Eddie

IT WAS SPRING 2004. Diana's emotions were stretched. Elmore's
fate was now in the hands of the justices of the South Carolina
Supreme Court. Her twenty-year-old son, Justin, was also facing death. Following the 9/11 attacks, in a burst of patriotism
he had joined the army. In March, Diana saw him off for Iraq,
a member of the Second Regiment of the Fifth Cavalry Division, out of Fort Hood, Texas. Even before reaching Iraq, while
still in Kuwait, he had cut and burned his hands when muni-
tions he was handling exploded. On the drive to Baghdad, one
of the men in his vehicle got out and into the vehicle in front. A
few miles later, Justin came upon his friend, his head and body
crushed; the vehicle had crashed. In Baghdad, Justin's unit was
assigned to Sadr City, where anti-Americanism seethed. Seven
men from his unit were killed in the first week. In e-mails and
phone conversations, Justin told his mom about searching for

body parts from men in his unit who had been blown away. He was scared. On guard duty, he worried about mortars, and when he went on patrol, he told his mom, he saw Iraqis who hated Americans.

In a conflict familiar to many Americans, Diana found that her love and support for her son clashed with her views about the war. On a towering pine in the front yard of her modest red-brick home on a leafy cul-de-sac, the Stars and Stripes flew from a pole at roughly forty-five degrees; a yellow bow was wrapped around the huge tree trunk. On Holt's black Volvo, the silver metallic license plate frame said "Army Mom." She had also affixed a bumper sticker: "Bush Is Lying. Soldiers Are Dying."

Holt worked at home, in the glassed-in porch with an idyllic view of a pond. There was a mimosa tree just outside her window, which she'd planted to remind her of the tree she escaped to as a child in Houston. In the spring, it yielded its wispy pom-poms; long-necked Canada geese, a blue heron, and baby mallards with their mother waddled about. "It's comforting," Diana said. Legal papers were scattered on the floor, along with a bag of chips. Dressed in Ralph Lauren blue jeans and a striped jersey, she fidgeted in front of a large flat-screen computer monitor. An e-mail came in from her daughter-in-law in Texas: Diana was about to become a grandmother.

Following the latest loss in front of Judge Kinard, Elmore's case was again headed to the South Carolina Supreme Court. Holt had already filed a petition for a writ of certiorari. In it she laid out the constitutional issues that the court needed to address. prosecutorial misconduct, ineffective assistance of counsel, withholding of evidence in violation of *Brady*, exclusion of blacks from the jury in violation of *Batson*. At least three of the five justices thought the case raised significant constitutional issues, and cert was granted. Now she was at work on the brief in support of their arguments. Holt wrote drafts and sent them to Jensen and Blume. Blume kept making changes that Holt didn't want. Blume wanted to ask the court for an extension of time to file the brief. Holt wanted no more delays: Elmore was innocent, and he had been on death row too long already. "If this were any other case, I'd tell you what to do and you'd do it," Blume said angrily one day. But Elmore was not just another case, not for Holt. This was her case. Blume knew it and backed off.

Holt filed her brief in September 2003. The state's reply was due thirty days later. Zelenka asked for an extension, then another and another. Finally, he filed, in January 2004. The court set oral arguments for May 27.

Making a supreme court appearance is the high point in many lawyers' careers, and there was some clashing of egos as Elmore's lawyers considered who would argue the case. Holt, Jensen, and Blume were all qualified in different ways, and each would have liked to. An outsider, Barry Scheck, was considered. Since gaining fame in the O. J. Simpson case, he had set up the Innocence Project at the law school at Yeshiva University, and his name had become synonymous with getting innocent men out of prison.

It was basically Holt's decision who would argue, and she went back and forth over whether she should do it herself. She knew the facts best, and her obvious passion might move the justices. Jensen agreed; besides, he knew he would be seen as a liberal northerner.

A couple of weeks before the hearing, Holt decided she'd argue and began preparing with moot courts. One was held before lawyers at her husband's firm; another before a panel of death penalty lawyers. They did not go well. "I'm going to give up my bar card," she moaned after one moot court. Her self-doubt grew. She knew she was not, as David Bruck put it gently, "a natural in the courtroom." A week before the hearing, steeling herself, she went into Blume's office and expressed her doubts. Blume said he was prepared to argue the case if she wanted him to. "Just give me twenty-four hours' notice," he said.

She called Elmore. She might not be the one to argue his case, she said. Mr. Blume might. Holt could sense that he was hurt. Was Diana giving up on him? No, she explained, this was in his best interests. In fact, she was still wavering. Saturday night, at home, eating a steak-and-vegetable kebab, pouring red wine, she argued with herself out loud. Finally, she said, "I'm going to do it." Two days later, shortly after noon on Monday, she went in to see Blume again.

Her voice cracking, she looked down, fighting tears. "I feel like I should be there for him, but, well, I think it is the right thing to do."

Are you talking about Elmore? Blume asked.

Yes, she said. "I know you'll hit it out of the park."

"Don't be so sure," he said. "You can think about it for another day."

Whatever the outcome, Diana knew she would blame herself. If she argued and lost, she would feel she should have let Blume argue. If Blume argued and lost, she would blame herself for not having argued the case.

She had finally made up her mind. Blume would argue.

THREE DAYS LATER, on the warm morning of May 27, the temperature pushing ninety degrees before noon, Holt, Blume, and Jensen walked from the death penalty resource center to the Supreme Court Building, which had been the post office until 1971. Jensen had flown down from New York the previous day. When Diana picked him up at the Columbia airport, the first thing she did when they got in the car was call Elmore on her Nokia. Once she had him on the line, she told him that Chris Jensen was with her, and she handed him the phone. The message was not lost on the New York lawyer: there is an individual involved in this case, and you have to make sure Elmore knows you care about him.

Townes Jones was one of the first to arrive for the argument. It is not unprecedented for a prosecutor to come for a supreme court argument, although it is unusual. But Jones had more at stake in this case than a typical prosecutor: his father's reputation was on the line, as was his own, as well as that of the Greenwood police force. He brought his eleven-year-old daughter, Gilland, with him, which Holt found bizarre. "I wanted to show her what her father does," Jones said, introducing Gilland to a reporter. Precocious and homeschooled, Gilland was a petite budding model and had already appeared in national ads, Jones proudly noted before going into the courtroom.

Several of Elmore's siblings had made the long drive from Abbeville. When they walked into the courtroom, they shook hands with Blume and Jensen. They hugged Diana, who wore a yellow ribbon on her checkered coat. Diana had a warm embrace for Salley Elliott, cocounsel to Don Zelenka on the case. She shook hands professionally with Zelenka. Holt sat at the counsel table between Jensen, in a pin-striped suit, and Blume, in a dark navy suit (during the proceedings she would occasionally hand Blume a note). She had her computer open in front of her; the screen saver was a picture of Justin.

There are five justices on the South Carolina Supreme Court. Two of them—E. C. Burnett and Jim Moore—had presided over Elmore trials, so they had to recuse themselves. The chief justice, Jean Toal, also recused herself at the last minute, for reasons she never explained. Three substitute justices would be hearing the case.

The justices filed in and took their seats. Blume stood, walked to the lectern, and addressed the court. His arguments were those that a good defense lawyer would have made at trial (and Anderson had not). How was it possible that the investigators had not taken the sheets from the bed where they claimed to have found Elmore's pubic hairs? "Do you know how much blood they found on the bed?" he asked. "Not a drop, not a bit." How could it be that there was no blood on Elmore's shirt? It should have been covered with blood, given the nature of the crime. How could it be that there was no hair found under the victim's fingernails, if she had reached up and pulled out his pubic hairs as the state argued so graphically? "Did trial counsel ever point this out?" Blume asked. "No." He again accused SLED agent Wells of lying about Item T. As for that hair that Wells now admitted was on Item T, "most likely it was the perpetrator's," Blume said. That fact alone justified a new trial, Blume argued.

"Three unfair trials don't make one fair trial," Blume said. "The fact that there have been three proceedings or thirty-six jurors, that doesn't mean a thing in this case because no jury has ever heard the evidence which should be heard, and which must be before a man can be dispatched to death."

Blume sat down. To his right, Donald Zelenka stood, buttoning his suit jacket. It was a gesture he always performed when he stood to address a court, "a crutch to focus my attention," he called it. "There were mistakes in this case," he conceded quickly. "But those mistakes do not undermine the confidence in the verdict."

Justice Costa M. Pleicones interrupted. "There are mistakes in every trial, and we don't require perfection," he said. But what about agent Wells's testimony about Item T, which Wells had said was blue fibers but when tested was found to indeed be hair? "Mr. Blume asserts it is flat out and out perjury," said Pleicones, who asked more questions than the other justices combined. "I'd like for you to address that."

Wells's report was an "error," Zelenka conceded, but he had not committed perjury. He went on: "The fact that there is one stray hair that was located on the victim's body at that time commingled with fibers and commingled with her hair" was not reason to grant a new trial. It was the same "stray hair" theory accepted by Judge Kinard.

Zelenka turned to the fingerprints. Yes, there were fingerprints in the house that weren't the victim's and weren't Elmore's. His answer was the same as for the hair. "The fact that another individual's prints may be in the victim's house does not turn this case into something that undermines the confidence of this proceeding."

Justice Clifton Newman, one of the substitutes, asked about the quality of representation Elmore had received from Geddes Anderson. "Did he challenge any of the state's witnesses?"

"No, not really," Zelenka acknowledged.

"You concede the quality of representation that Mr. Elmore received was maybe not the best in the world," Justice Pleicones said. "Are you willing to go further?" Did he concede that it did not meet the requirements set out by the Supreme Court for what constitutes effective representation of counsel?

"No," said Zelenka.

"You're not willing to concede that?"

"No."

Because the justices had asked so many questions, the chief justice allowed Zelenka a few extra minutes. "But wind it down," he said. Zelenka finished, Blume was allowed a short reply, the justices rose and left, and the lawyers shook hands and walked out of the courthouse.

Holt, Jensen, and Blume headed to lunch feeling positive. Townes Jones did not. He thought he had lost. Back in Greenwood, he told the public defender to get set to defend Elmore again.

From the defense point of view, it was possible for Holt to be almost giddy about the prospects for a new trial. It was exciting to imagine the police and SLED agents cross-examined by Chris Jensen and a more confident Diana Holt. Barry Scheck would do to Earl Wells what he had done to Dennis Fung, the LAPD criminologist whom Scheck witheringly cross-examined for eight days in the O. J. Simpson trial.

And if Elmore got a new trial, Holt would have a new witness.

The day she put her son on a plane for Iraq, she had returned home and found two messages on her answering machine. They were from a Kay Raborn in Augusta, Georgia. Holt recognized the name—the Raborns had lived on Melrose Terrace, a few doors from Mrs. Edwards; in her search for witnesses over the years, Holt had never been able to locate them. In her message, Mrs. Raborn said that she and her husband had just watched a Court TV show about the Elmore case. They had moved away from Greenwood many years ago and were surprised to learn that Elmore was still alive, that he had not been executed. They could not let him be executed, not knowing what they knew, she said in the voice message. She didn't give any details but invited Diana to come to Augusta to talk to them.

Holt thought the call might be a setup. Was Townes Jones using the Raborns to find out what she was planning? But she was left with so few options to save Elmore's life that she drove to Augusta. When she got there, she learned it was really Mr. Raborn who wanted to talk to her. He had been on the grand jury that had indicted Elmore. After watching the Court TV show and reading more about the case, he was convinced Jones had misled the grand jury. "The grand jury was never told anything about Holloway," Raborn said. It wasn't told that Holloway and Mrs. Edwards might have been having an affair. "If a sexual relationship is brought up, you get into motives right there," he said.

There was another, more powerful reason that Raborn had concluded Elmore was innocent. A year or so after the murder, Raborn had run into Charley Webber at a fraternity reunion. Webber was the SLED agent in Greenwood who had turned up at the crime scene and was told by Jim Coursey that he wasn't needed. "Charley had already put away a few drinks and beers when we spoke," Raborn said. "He whispered to me, 'He didn't do it.' I asked him, 'Who didn't do what?' He again whispered, 'You remember, Black Elmo, he didn't do it.'" (The Greenwood cops often referred to Elmore as "Black Elmo," which infuriated Holt.) "He didn't elaborate," Raborn said. "He just wanted to say it, because it was really bothering him."

For years, Raborn had kept the conversation to himself. Webber died in 2003. Raborn told Holt he was prepared to testify about what Webber had told him.

The odds against the State of South Carolina retrying the case were great. So many contentious issues would have to be revisited, some to the embarrassment of the South Carolina justice system. In a new trial, a jury would hear about the Caucasian hair found on Mrs. Edwards's abdomen, the fingerprint on the underside of the toilet, the absence of blood on the sheets, the failure of the police to take photographs of the bed. It was more likely the state would offer Elmore a deal: plead guilty to manslaughter, which is not a capital offense, and he would be released. How tempting that would be, to have Elmore finally out of jail after twenty-two years. The decision would be Elmore's. But everyone knew he would follow Diana's advice. Marta Kahn had no doubt Holt should take such a deal.

"In a heartbeat," she said. She didn't trust the system anymore; her approach was to take whatever you can to get your client off death row. But how could Diana let Elmore plead guilty to anything when she was convinced he was completely innocent?

THE SOUTH CAROLINA SUPREME COURT took only six weeks to issue its ruling, which was faster than most expected, given the complexity of the issues and the likelihood that there would be several opinions. But there were no opinions. There was only the court's ruling: "We granted a writ of certiorari to review the denial of Petitioner's application for post-conviction relief (PCR). After thoroughly reviewing the appendix in this case, we find there is probative evidence supporting the findings of the PCR judge. Accordingly, we dismiss the writ as improvidently granted."

The court was saying there were no legal issues, that it should not even have agreed to hear the case. It was a puzzling ruling, at best; an unfathomable one to many lawyers.

"Ain't that some shit," said David Bruck, abandoning his usual legal erudition. Rauch Wise called it a "crazy decision." Elmore would be "the only person in the country executed on the basis of evidence now considered perjury," he added, referring to Gilliam's trial testimony.

Maybe the explanation was that supreme court justices couldn't find there were constitutional errors when two of their colleagues had handled two of the trials.

Holt called Elmore immediately. She did not want him to hear the news on the TV or radio, or worse, from a prison guard. How do you start a conversation like this? she worried as she placed the call. She said she was sorry and tried to explain that not only had the South Carolina Supreme Court refused to give him a new trial, but it had simply dismissed his appeal. It was clear Elmore didn't know what it all meant. You're not the only one, Holt said to herself. She hung up, emotionally distraught.

A few minutes later the phone rang. It was Elmore. He said he hadn't understood her before because he'd been asleep when she called and was groggy. Diana knew it was his way of trying to conceal his intellectual limitations. She again tried to explain. He was dejected, but he said he knew she had done her best for him, he knew she cared about him.

A few days later, Elmore wrote to his sister, in block letters.

DEAR PEGGY
"HELLO" LET ME SAY I APOLOGIZE FOR NOT WRITEING YOU BEFOUR NOW THEY TURN ME DOWN IN COURT REALLY HIT ME IN A DEPRESS-ING STATE OF A KIND, I'M DOING BETTER NOW GETTING STRONGER EMOTIONALLY AND SPIRI-TUALLY BEEN PRAYING AND READING MY BIBLE SO"OO I'AM DOING JUST FINE NOW I'LL BE OK, AND YOU SIS HOW ARE YOU DOING? I PRAY YOU ARE IN GOOD HEALTH AND EVERYTHING IS GOING WELL, I MISS YOU EVERY DAY.
PEGGY I NEED YOUR HELP MY RADIO HAS BROKE COULD YOU SEND ME SOME MONEY TO BUY ANOTHER ONE I'LL APPRECIATED,
I CLOSE NOW YOU TAKE CARE TELL EVERY-ONE I" SAID HELLO, LOVE, TULIP.

Holt filed a petition for rehearing with the South Carolina Supreme Court, a routine step. But being Holt, she added a twist. She wanted DNA testing of the hair the state had said it found on the bed, and of the blood on the shoes and on the blue jeans.

"It is inconceivable that the respondent would object to definitive DNA testing," she added. "What is the State afraid of?" She knew the answer, of course.

Predictably, Zelenka opposed it. Elmore's lawyers should have made these requests earlier, at the PCR, Zelenka argued. His brief was short, only three pages. At the bottom of page 3, he wrote, "For this reason, the Petition must be denied."

Before Holt could cry or curse, she turned to the next page. At its top in bold letters, she read:

"SLED will complete testing on the hairs recovered from the victim's bed, the traces of blood found on blue jeans, and the defendant's shoes." Holt was taken aback. The state was refusing to agree to a rehearing but was agreeing to conduct the DNA testing, which was precisely what she sought in the petition for a rehearing. She wasn't surprised when the supreme court denied a rehearing. It said nothing about her request for DNA testing.

Elmore's execution was set: October 15, 2004, at 6:00 p.m.

CHAPTER TWELVE

Denouement

FOLLOWING THE DECISION by the South Carolina Supreme
Court, prison authorities put Edward Lee Elmore in "lock-
down," a kind of administrative segregation that death row
inmates are placed under thirty days before execution. His cell
had a heavy metal door, with only a small window, and the shut-
ter was closed most of the time. He was allowed out for just an
hour a day and then was kept in full chains. This was especially
hard on Elmore, who suffered from mild claustrophobia. Diana
wanted him back in his cell on death row.

Two days after the supreme court's adverse ruling, Holt
jumped into her Volvo, sped downtown, and walked briskly
into the sixteen-story Strom Thurmond Federal Building on
Assembly Street. Designed by the firm of Marcel Breuer, the
sixteen-story building has a stark concrete exterior and deeply
recessed windows. Holt went to the office for the federal district court and handed the clerk a motion for a stay of execution.
She took a seat, "in tears, sweating bullets." Cases are assigned
to federal judges randomly; Holt was nervous about whom she
would draw. As the tears welled, she watched the clock—2:40,
2:45, the minutes ticked by. At 3:00 p.m. the clerk informed her
the case had been assigned to Judge David C. Norton. George
H. W. Bush had appointed Norton to the bench in 1990, on the
recommendation of Senator Strom Thurmond, one of the most

conservative members of the Senate. Prosecutors liked him. One gave him a 9.7 rating out of a possible 10 on The Robing Room, a website where lawyers evaluate federal judges. "Judge Norton is a fantastic judge and a true gentleman," the prosecutor wrote. "South Carolina is lucky to have him." Holt happened to agree. He had granted a stay in an earlier case she had had before him, and her spirits were buoyed by the draw.

Thirteen days after she'd filed for the stay, Norton granted it. Elmore was back with the general death row population, and Holt had another chance to save his life.

She turned to the DNA testing. Zelenka had said he would do it voluntarily. Holt was having none of that. She wanted court supervision—Judge Norton, to be precise. Holt and Jensen requested a status conference, which is a meeting of the lawyers with the judge to discuss procedural matters in a case. On the afternoon of December 7, 2004, they arrived at the federal courthouse in Charleston, where Norton sat. The gray granite building is on the corner of Broad and Meeting Streets, on the site of what had been a gallows for public executions during British colonial days.

"Okay, Ms. Holt, just like Toyota, you asked for it, you got it," Judge Norton opened the proceedings good-naturedly. "Mr. Jensen, welcome," he said. It was as informal as a hearing in a federal court could be. "Sit, stand right there, or come up here, whatever you want," Norton said to Jensen.

Jensen explained that he and Holt wanted the court to oversee the DNA testing. Jensen assured Norton that he didn't anticipate any problems, but if there were—such as what would be tested, by whom, using what tests—they wanted to be able to come back to Judge Norton.

Zelenka listened to the exchange between Norton and Jensen, feeling more like a spectator than a participant. "I am not sure I am in this setting," he said lightly when it was his turn to speak. He argued that there was no need for Judge Norton to get involved; a state court could supervise. "I thought it would be more expeditious to go through Greenwood," he explained. Holt was shaking her head.

"I'm pretty expeditious," Norton said, smiling. As a legal matter, he added, he wasn't sure if a Greenwood judge still had jurisdiction over the case now that it had moved into federal court.

"He has control over the stuff that was involved in the case," Zelenka said.

"I have control over the whole thing," Norton countered. Holt was amazed and bemused. It was as if Norton were saying "My army is bigger than yours." She smiled.

Zelenka said that the state would test a sample of the hairs found on the bed. Holt's head jerked in disbelief. She wanted them all tested. She wasn't about to gamble that the hairs the state chose to test just happened to be Elmore's while others in the bag might belong to someone else.

After thirty minutes, both sides said they had nothing more. "Happy holiday," Judge Norton wished everyone.

Holt rose. She had one more thing to say: "Mr. Elmore asked me to thank you for granting his stay of execution." Spectators and court personnel smiled. They weren't accustomed to hearing such a personal sentiment from a lawyer in behalf of her client.

"Well, you're welcome," Judge Norton said.

Holt walked out of the courtroom, spirits soaring. Courts usually split the decisions or give the state everything. Here, she was getting everything she wanted. "I wanted to kiss the hem of his robe," she said, and then enjoy "this piece of justice, however small it is."

She soon had another reason to celebrate. "PVT. Holt and the mighty 2–5 Cav made it safely to Kuwait, which means they are almost HOME!" she wrote in a March 2005 e-mail to the families of the men in A Company, 115th Battalion of the Second Regiment of the Fifth Cavalry Division. "Apparently I had muscles clenched that I didn't even know I owned. We can all exhale now!"

DIANA WAS FILLED with joy that her son had survived Iraq when she got a call from a very worried Elmore. "Am I next?" he asked. She didn't know what he was talking about. He explained that Richard Longworth had been executed the previous evening. It was the thirty-third execution since Elmore had arrived on death row, but this one hit harder because Longworth was especially popular. He had been on death row for fourteen years; Elmore had just completed his twenty-third year. He had recently been taken to the hospital with a bad case of emphysema; after ten days, he was returned to his cell with two inhalers and an oxygen tank. Diana assured Elmore that no execution date had been set.

Holt filed for a writ of habeas corpus with Judge Norton on July 5, 2005. It was the beginning of the process that would have the federal courts address whether Elmore had been denied his constitutional rights. Much of the brief was written by Marta Kahn. After what Diana considered to be the South Carolina Supreme Court's inexplicable ruling against Elmore, Holt was distraught and generally exhausted. She asked Marta if she'd like to help with the case. Not yet forty, Marta had given up full-time work as a death penalty lawyer. In just two and a half years in Virginia, twenty-five men were executed. When she got married and had a child, she had stepped away from death penalty representation—it took too much out of her, physically and emotionally. The rage and anger she felt toward the system were not things she wanted to be carrying around while she was raising a child. But she remained deeply committed to fighting what she saw as injustice, and Elmore's case exemplified that as much as any she'd seen. Marta was a law lawyer, and her brief was a brilliant exposition of the constitutional issues. They were basically the same ones that had been presented to the South Carolina Supreme Court—ineffective assistance of counsel, prosecutorial misconduct, exclusion of blacks from the jury.

But there was one new claim as well: that Elmore was mentally retarded, and therefore his execution was barred in light of the recent Supreme Court ruling (in *Atkins v. Virginia*). This claim was buried three pages from the end of the forty-nine-page legal brief. At this point, Diana had all but given up on getting Elmore justice, which would mean complete exoneration for a crime she didn't believe he committed. She just wanted to keep him from being executed. A finding that he was mentally retarded would do that.

For years, opponents of the death penalty, unable to persuade the Supreme Court to abolish capital punishment altogether, sought to limit its use by expanding the categories of individuals whom the state could not execute. One exemption they sought was for the mentally retarded.

The issue of a criminal defendant's mental state is widely misunderstood, and mental retardation is often confused with insanity. "We should never execute the mentally retarded," President George W. Bush said in 2001, when the issue was being hotly debated. He added, "And our court system protects people who don't understand the nature of the crime they've committed nor the punishment they are about to receive."

But in this latter statement, Bush was talking about a person who is legally insane. Standards have changed over time and are not identical in every state, but the general test for insanity is whether the defendant was able to distinguish right from wrong at the time of the crime. Paranoid schizophrenia and severe psychosis rob the individual of the ability to know right from wrong. Most mentally retarded people are not insane, and vice versa. John W. Hinckley Jr., who shot President Reagan in 1981, was found not guilty by reason of insanity. He was not mentally retarded. Indeed, his IQ was 113.

In 1989, the court addressed the issue of executing the mentally retarded in the case of John Paul Penry. He had raped and stabbed to death—with a scissors—a twenty-two-year-old woman, Pamela Moseley Carpenter. His IQ was 60, and he had the functioning capacity of a seven-year-old; on death row, he spent his days coloring with crayons and looking at comic books he couldn't read. The State of Texas did not accept that he was retarded. He was a "sociopath," said a prosecutor in the case, and had been sent to schools for the mentally retarded because he was "an uncontrollable child." In a landmark decision, *Penry v. Lynaugh*, the Supreme Court reversed Penry's conviction on the grounds that the judge had failed to instruct the jury that it could consider his mental capacity as a factor in the sentencing. But the court held that it was not a violation of the Eighth Amendment ban on cruel and unusual punishment to execute someone who was mentally retarded. There was not a national consensus against doing so, the court said. At the time, of the thirty-eight capital punishment states, all but two permitted the execution of a person who was mentally retarded. Justice O'Connor wrote the majority opinion.

Thirteen years later, the issue was before the court again, in *Atkins v. Virginia*. Twenty-one death penalty states now banned executing an individual who was mentally retarded. Finding a "changing national consensus," the court overturned *Penry*. The execution of someone who was mentally retarded was proscribed by the Eighth Amendment, the court ruled in a 6–3 decision. Justice O'Connor, persuaded by the trend among the states, joined the majority. The court's conservative justices— Scalia, Thomas, and Rehnquist—disagreed. "The arrogance of this assumption of power takes one's breath away," Scalia wrote. The court was engaged in "incremental abolition" of the death penalty, he wrote (which was, of course, just what opponents of the death penalty wanted).

The Supreme Court left it up to the states to decide how to implement its decision, both for defendants in future capital cases and for men on death row, such as Elmore.

Holt raised Elmore's *Atkins* claim with a motion for another post-conviction review, which she filed in September 2005. The state's response was simple: too late. Under South Carolina law, legal claims in criminal cases have to be raised within one year after they become available. Since *Atkins* was decided in June 2002, that made the deadline for Elmore's lawyers June 2003. "Simply put," Zelenka said, the failure of Elmore's lawyers to file their mental retardation claim by June 20, 2003, required the court to deny their request.

After each side had argued their case in written briefs, Zelenka and Jensen squared off in court. It was two fine lawyers at their best. The hearing, in February, 2007, was held in a small courtroom in the Richland County Judicial Center, in downtown Columbia. Five armed guards watched over Elmore, wearing a green prison-issue jumpsuit with SCDC (South Carolina Department of Corrections) printed on the back, over a thermal undershirt. The judge was J. Mark Hayes II, a fifty-year-old Spartanburg native with fire-engine-red hair. His background did not bode well for Elmore. While at Wofford College, he had been an intern for Strom Thurmond, and he had begun his legal career as a clerk for Judge E. C. Burnett III, who had presided over Elmore's first trial (and who had also attended Wofford).

Zelenka was convinced that Holt and Jensen were manipulating the system. He argued that they had been aware that Elmore was mentally retarded in 1995, at the time of the first PCR. At that time, Zelenka said, Elmore's lawyers had retained Dr. Jonathan Venn, a psychologist, and he had testified that Elmore was not mentally retarded.

Zelenka finished his argument. With the law seemingly in the state's favor, Jensen abandoned juridical sophistication and adopted a colloquial approach. "I would like to introduce to you Edward Lee Elmore, who I have been representing fifteen years," Jensen said to Judge Hayes. Never in those fifteen years, in the many times Jensen had been in court with Elmore, had he made such a gesture; it was as if Holt had finally gotten through to him that there was more at stake in this than the legal issues.

Jensen was on his verbal knees, beseeching the court not to allow Elmore to be executed. "Just listen for a moment, okay? Listen for a moment. And I beg Your Honor's indulgence." Jensen proceeded to recite Elmore's biography: born to a woman who had thirteen children by five different men; living in squalor as a child, in houses without windows, without bathrooms; going to school without shoes; failing first and second grade, and third grade twice; tested in school with an IQ that established him as mentally retarded.

"This court's faced with this choice," Jensen said, invoking emotion more than law. "Say, look, I know he's mentally retarded, or I know there's a great likelihood that he's mentally retarded, that he meets all the requirements of the statute, but you know something? Too bad. Tough luck. There's a statute of limitations here. I'm not going to exercise any equity powers that I may have in this court to do anything about that." Was the court "going to walk in at the end of the day and say, Okay, you can be executed, Mr. Elmore? Too bad, too late, your lawyers didn't wake up in time and that's your tough luck."

Jensen was hanging from a precipice and had to explain Dr. Venn's testimony. Jensen asserted that Venn had addressed only the very narrow issue of Elmore's alleged statements to police officials Johnson and Henderson: "If I did it, I don't remember." Because of Elmore's limited mental capabilities, he might say something like that without it being true, Venn had testified. "That's all Dr. Venn opined on," Jensen said. "And as Mr. Zelenka knows, Dr. Venn did not give any opinion about mental retardation."

Jensen finished. He was wrong in his comment about Dr. Venn, and Zelenka was prepared to challenge it. He handed the judge volume 5 of the record in the Elmore case, and directed him to page 843. In response to a question from Jensen, Venn had said: "Mr. Elmore is not mentally retarded, but he's just a notch above being mentally retarded." Then Zelenka directed Judge Hayes to pages 1853 and 1854 of the record. In response to a question from Zelenka during cross-examination, Venn repeated what he had said to Jensen: "I do not consider him to be mentally retarded."

Zelenka reiterated to Judge Hayes that South Carolina law was unequivocal—the defense has one year to file a claim after it becomes available. "We're simply asserting that they're barred, they're barred from raising this action based upon what has occurred and what they knew and when they knew it."

Judge Hayes had listened carefully to the lawyers' arguments, and his questions demonstrated a greater intellect and search for the truth than any other state judge who had handled Elmore's case over the last twenty-five years. He bore in on Jensen.

"So far what I've heard is that there was a revelation to counsel that my client might suffer from mental retardation, that lo and behold I did not realize this in my twelve, fifteen years of representing him and now I need to bring it up," Hayes began, clearly skeptical. Where are the facts that would justify disregarding the very clear statute of limitations? Hayes asked Jensen.

Jensen knew his legal arguments were weak. He tried contrition. "I have to accept a large measure of the blame," he said. After Venn testified that Elmore was not mentally retarded, none of Elmore's lawyers had given much, if any, thought to the issue, Jensen said. It was only after spending more time with Elmore that "we became aware that he is truly mentally retarded." When the South Carolina Supreme Court ruled against Elmore, Jensen said, his lawyers "had begun to think about the issue of his mental condition in a way we had never thought about it before."

It wasn't terribly persuasive, and once more Jensen ramped up the emotion. "The bottom line is the court cannot carry out a miscarriage of justice. That's the bottom line. There can't be a miscarriage of justice. You don't execute people who are seventeen years old when they committed the crime. You don't execute people who are mentally retarded when they committed the crime. You can't do that. It's a miscarriage of justice. And that shouldn't hinge on the matter of months that, according to Mr. Zelenka, we were late in filing this petition."

Hayes was still troubled. "You've said to me, you've apologized to it, you've put it on the record that I should have done a better job, didn't recognize it earlier, and that in conversations while we were preparing the federal writ then realized that we really might have a case here, and I want to understand what your position is if you want me to apply equitable provisions to stop the statute of limitations," Hayes said to Jensen.

When considerations of equity or justice demand, judges may waive procedural requirements, such as the statute of limitations on filing a claim. But they are reluctant to do so and need to be persuaded by strong arguments. Hayes seemed to want to rule in Elmore's favor and was looking for something from his lawyers on which to hang his ruling. "I would love to have something to work with," he said.

Holt didn't have a good feeling when she left. Desperate for hope, she found some a few months after the hearing, when Hayes ruled that the state's Internet Crime Against Children Task Force had abused its authority by using a federal statute to force an Internet company to divulge a defendant's identity. South Carolina had a higher standard, Hayes ruled. Maybe Holt was grasping for anything, but the ruling suggested to her that Hayes was willing to make unpopular rulings, and against the establishment.

By the summer of 2007, Elmore's case had become a bungee cord for Holt. One court decision would send her plummeting, but before she crashed, another court decision would snap her back.

In May, Judge Norton denied Elmore's petition for habeas corpus.

The next month, Judge Hayes issued his ruling on the request for a hearing on the mental retardation issue. The state's arguments that the one-year statute of limitations barred Elmore's request were "reasonable and rational," he wrote in his three-page order. Nevertheless, he was denying the state's motion to dismiss. The Supreme Court in *Atkins* had made clear that states should engage in a substantive review of a claim that a death row inmate was mentally retarded. Consequently, he said, Elmore was to be evaluated by the South Carolina Department of Disabilities and Special Needs. It was the first court ruling in Elmore's favor in two decades, since he had been sentenced to death after his third trial, in 1987.

Then, on August 3, 2007, Don Zelenka filed the results of the DNA tests. The hairs had been mounted on slides for testing. Several of the slides had hair that matched Elmore's, which did not surprise Holt. She had always assumed the hair had been planted, and had only agreed to their being tested because Zelenka would not agree to DNA testing on any items unless she did. On the other hand, on two slides, the hairs were from a "male individual" other than Elmore, the examiners reported. It was not possible, they said, to know whose they were. The examiners also reported that nothing found under Mrs. Edwards's fingernails was connected to Elmore. Thus, as Holt would say, scoffing, "Mrs. Edwards had pulled pubic and head hairs from Elmore without getting anything under her carefully manicured fingernails."

All these findings were background noise. The critical finding was about the spots of blood on Elmore's shoes and blue jeans. And that finding was devastating: the blood matched Mrs. Edwards's.

Calming herself, Diana called Elmore. She spoke more sternly to him than she ever had, slowly, so that he could understand. Then she said, "You did it. You just don't remember, but you did it."

"No, I wasn't there," he said softly.

Holt, of course, didn't believe he had done it, and there was something strange about the manner in which Zelenka was handling the DNA results. He had waited to file until after Judge Norton had denied Elmore's habeas petition. Why? The results weren't going to help the state at that point. And why had Zelenka not put out a press release or said anything publicly about the results? He had trumpeted every other victory in the case. It was months before the police and lawyers in Greenwood, who had worked on the case, got word of the DNA results, and that was because a reporter began asking questions. Why had Zelenka been so silent? they wondered

Maybe Zelenka knew that the blood had been planted, Holt thought. She had no doubt that it had been. The blood spots on the jeans were pinprick size, not streaks or smears or dollops, which they would have been, given all the blood at the scene.

Holt wondered whether Henderson had planted the stains. It would have been easy. Blood had been drawn from Mrs. Edwards during the autopsy. Henderson would have had access to the vials, either in Greenwood or at SLED headquarters in Columbia. And he had taken the jeans and shoes out of the lab even though he was not involved in the forensics of the case. He had inexplicably kept them for sixteen days. Holt and Jensen now realized the error they had made in not calling Henderson as a witness during the PCR.

Henderson denies having planted the blood. He doesn't remember ever having possession of the blue jeans. "Where did I have them? Why did I have them? That's the question," he said years after the trial. It was a warm spring evening in May 2006, and Henderson, with short hair, a ruddy face, and a bulbous nose, was now retired from SLED, living in scenic Gowensville, South Carolina, at the foot of the Blue Ridge Mountains. He talked about the Elmore case for a couple of hours, in the kitchen of his farmhouse, which he had modernized. His red Honda pickup was parked in the driveway, in front of a three-car garage. He was wearing a bright green golf shirt, IZOD Bermuda shorts, and boat shoes. Henderson railed against Elmore's lawyers. "They don't care about him, they're just using him for their anti–death penalty cause," he said. "They picked him out because he's a nice-looking kid and he's black."

He agreed that it was hard to understand how there could have been so little blood on Elmore's blue jeans and shoes. "A rational person looking back at that would say he ought to be covered in blood." But he insisted he had not taken the blue jeans and shoes to plant any blood. "I've always had a set of ethics, and I've tried to live by them. I was not going to trump up anything on anybody. I never have and I never will." He knows, however, that some police officers do that. "They have the mentality, He might not be guilty of this, but he's guilty of a hell of a lot of other stuff."

After taking the blue jeans out of the lab, Henderson, rather than return them to the lab, had given them to the Greenwood police captain Jimmy Coursey, according to the notes made at the time by Solicitor Jones. Coursey, who was as convinced of Elmore's guilt as Henderson, doesn't recall Henderson giving him the blue jeans. "I have no idea why they would have been brought back from SLED and put up here," he said, sitting on the screened-in porch of his house on Lake Greenwood. "As God is my witness, if I am ever asked if I had those jeans in my hand, I'd swear I didn't." He is adamant he never planted any blood on them. "There wasn't shit planted on that boy," he said.

"I ain't gonna do one thing that would put my ass in jail to put his ass in jail."

As Elmore faced his twenty-fifth Christmas on death row, on December 19, 2007, he underwent a psychological evaluation by Dr. Donna Culley, a clinical psychologist with the Department of Disabilities and Special Needs. She interviewed Elmore for two hours at the prison. Elmore was dressed in a prison jumpsuit, wore a knitted sock hat, and had shackles on his ankles and wrists. Holt asked that the shackles be removed; Culley agreed. Elmore cried when he talked about his family. "I miss my momma," he said. She had died in 1998. Asked to name five cities, he said, "Georgia, Virginia, Tennessee." She asked him again, stressing *cities*. "Ain't that what that is?" he said. "Ain't that what that is?" Asked to name the directions on a map, he did not understand the concept. He said he had attended more than one school as a child, but he could remember the name of only one, "Abbeville Middle School." His records showed that he never attended a school by that name, Dr. Culley wrote in her report.

Dr. Culley concluded: "Based on the totality of the data, it is the opinion of this examiner that Mr. Elmore meets the diagnostic criteria for mental retardation as defined in the South Carolina Code of Laws. It is estimated that his level of functioning falls within the mild range of mental retardation."

Elmore was not off death row yet, however. There still had to be a hearing before Judge Hayes, in which the state could challenge Culley's findings.

Hayes decided to hold the hearing at the Broad River Correctional Institution, instead of in a courtroom, to make it easier for the prison personnel, who wouldn't have to travel back and forth to Spartanburg. Only one reporter was at the hearing, from *The Spartanburg Herald-Journal,* Hayes's hometown newspaper. Not a good omen, Holt thought. Elmore was brought in wearing a green prison jumpsuit and leg and wrist shackles. Holt requested that the shackles be removed, as usual, which every judge before had granted. In the ultrasecure prison courtroom, Hayes deferred to the prison officials. They insisted on keeping Elmore in full chains. Holt was furious. Zelenka was faced with having to discredit the findings of the state's own psychologist. He called a North Carolina psychologist, Roger B. Moore Jr., who suggested that Elmore might have purposefully performed poorly on the tests given to him by Dr. Culley. "No way that performing well was in Elmore's best interest," Moore testified. The sharpest moments of the hearing came when Dr. Culley took the stand. Her findings were tainted, Zelenka argued, because Diana Holt had been present during the evaluation. Judge Hayes expressed great concern about that. Holt left the hearing convinced she had lost.

On a personal level, Holt was preparing for a trial that would not be pleasant, her libel action against Jim Holloway. Holloway's lawyers had already taken a video deposition of Holt, in which many of the sordid details of her childhood had been dragged out again. Finally, Holloway and the newspaper agreed to pay Diana $25,000. In her impish way, before accepting the offer, she asked that Holloway agree to the exhumation of his father for DNA testing purposes. Of course, he said no. The case was settled. The video deposition was sealed.

Holt waited for Judge Hayes's ruling on Elmore's mental retardation claim for months. She couldn't imagine what was taking so long, and the longer it took, the more she was convinced she had lost, that Hayes was crafting his order and opinion with legal care so that it would not be reversed on appeal. Holt would have to appeal to the South Carolina Supreme Court, and she knew what her chances were there. She was still in federal court, with her habeas claim, but that would eventually have to go to the United States Supreme Court, and her chances there were nil, at least as long as there was a conservative majority. She wouldn't say it, but she felt Elmore was doomed to die for a crime he didn't commit. It was really only a question of how long she could keep him alive.

On September 30, 2009, Holt was sitting at her computer

when an e-mail arrived. It was from Judge Hayes. She had to read it twice before it was clear what he was saying.

Hayes had concluded that Edward Lee Elmore was mentally retarded, as defined by South Carolina law. Therefore, he could not be executed under *Atkins*.

Holt was delirious with joy.

She called the prison and asked for the warden, McKither Bodison. "Mr. Edward Lee Elmore is leaving death row," she said cheerfully when he came on the line. He almost started crying. "Ms. Holt, I know you'd never forgive me if something ever happened to him," Bodison said. Lately, other prisoners had been harassing Elmore, jealous of his relative freedom. They said he was acting like a slave, behaving well to please the prison authorities. Bodison said he would move Elmore to a special section of the prison for his protection.

Then she called Elmore.

"Hello, is this Eddie? Is this pokie wokie? Is this my Eddie, my little Brown Bear?" she said, using his prison nickname. "Well, I have something to tell you." She paused. "Tomorrow is October first. That's all."

She laughed, paused, then said: "Mr. Edward Lee Elmore, I am so pleased to inform you that the judge is going to enter an order vacating your death sentence for all time."

"Wow," he said softly.

"Wow!" she screamed.

She read from the e-mail from Judge Hayes that he had found him mentally retarded and therefore not subject to the death penalty. She explained the *Atkins* ruling and its connection to his case.

"Wow," he said.

"They cannot seek the death penalty against you, for any reason. All right, you knucklehead. Take care, sweetie."

When she hung up, she screamed. "It hasn't sunk in yet, I can fucking assure you."

Elmore would live. To almost anyone else, it might seem anticlimactic—after twenty-seven years, Elmore was off death row, but he hadn't been exonerated, and he was facing the rest of his life in jail. Nevertheless, for Diana Holt, her defense team partners, for all death penalty lawyers, keeping a man alive is about as good as it gets.

"I can exhale now," she said.

THOUGH EDWARD LEE ELMORE is off death row, for Holt justice requires that he be released from prison and that his conviction be expunged. The state should apologize and compensate him, she feels. She would also like an investigation into what happened. Under oath, Wells, Parnell, DeFreese, Johnson, and Henderson should be made to explain about the hairs on the bed, about Item T, about the fingerprint on the underside of the toilet seat. Justice would require that James Holloway Sr. be exhumed, she believes. All that might happen if the United States Justice Department decided to conduct an investigation, for surely Elmore's civil rights have been violated.

Diana Holt isn't a vindictive person. She would just like to see justice.

EPILOGUE

Diana Holt wasn't about to let Edward Lee Elmore remain in prison for a crime he didn't commit. She and Chris Jensen appealed to the U.S. Fourth Circuit Court of Appeals, in Richmond, Virginia, seeking a new trial, as they had all along. The three-judge panel heard oral arguments in September 2010.

Two days before Thanksgiving in 2011, a bitterly divided court ruled that Elmore was entitled to a new trial. In a staggeringly long 163-page opinion, the majority was searing in its criticism of the SLED agents and police, writing that there was "persuasive evidence that the agents were outright dishonest," and that there was "further evidence of police ineptitude and deceit." Judge Robert Bruce King, writing for himself and Judge Roger Gregory, suggested that "the real perpetrator was Holloway."

In his dissent, Judge J. Harvie Wilkinson III was equally stinging, but his rebuke was directed at his colleagues on the bench. He accused them of conjuring up a "fanciful conspiracy." "In spinning this tale of deceit, fabrication, perjury, and corruption," he wrote, "the majority has unduly impugned the South Carolina criminal justice system—directly in the case of its law enforcement officers and indirectly in the case of the prosecutors and judges who turned a blind eye to malfeasance of this magnitude."

Wilkinson was the most senior judge on the court, as well as one of its most conservative members, and his dissent gave added impetus to the state's determination to appeal rather than grant Elmore a new trial. Holt's marathon battle to get justice for Elmore would continue.

As expected, the state asked the Fourth Circuit for a rehearing by the entire court. Unexpectedly, it was turned down. The state then asked the United States Supreme Court for a stay of the Fourth Circuit's order for a new trial. Given the conservative nature of the court, it was widely assumed that the necessary four justices would vote to grant it. The Roberts Court turned down the request less than five hours after the state had filed the papers. Holt was ecstatic. "WOWOWOWOW," she wrote in an e-mail when the state's request for a stay was denied.

The state said it would appeal the Fourth Circuit's ruling to the Supreme Court. Meanwhile, in Greenwood, the current solicitor, Jerry Peace, announced that he intended to retry Elmore.

Holt wasn't about to let Elmore remain in prison a day longer than necessary, and she requested a bail hearing. After some back-and-forth, a hearing was scheduled for March 2, 2012.

At the end of February, Peace called Rauch Wise, the local attorney who had some involvement with the Elmore case and Holt over the years. Peace told Wise he had just finished reading *Anatomy of Injustice*. He didn't agree with everything in the book, but he was troubled, foremost by the evidence suggesting that, contrary to testimony by police officers and SLED investigators at Elmore's trial, no hairs had been found on the victim's bed.

During a conversation that lasted some ten to fifteen minutes, Peace also raised with Wise the matter of the blue jeans. He was uneasy because of the statements Greenwood police officer Jim Coursey and SLED agent Tom Henderson had made to me about the possibility that the victim's blood had been planted on the jeans after Henderson had removed them inexplicably from the SLED evidence locker. If there were another trial, the police officers and SLED agents would be subject to rigorous cross-examination by Holt and Jensen; the "deceit" and "outright dishonest[y]" the Fourth Circuit found would be exposed.

Peace wondered if there might be a way to resolve the case without another trial. Wise offered to call Holt, which he did immediately after hanging up with Peace.

The negotiations began. Holt wanted all charges dismissed. Peace said he wouldn't do that. Was Elmore willing to enter an Alford plea?

Epilogue

Peace asked. Named after a 1970 Supreme Court case, *North Carolina v. Alford*, the essence of an Alford plea is that a defendant maintains his innocence but pleads guilty in order to avoid a trial, and receives a reduction in his sentence. Holt agonized and had trouble sleeping as she pondered that possibility.

On Friday morning, March 2, Elmore was led into the Greenwood courtroom where he had first been convicted. As he waited for his case to be called, he sat where a jury does during trials. He was dressed in civilian clothes: a gray vest unbuttoned over a striped shirt and pleated blue trousers, which were too big now, reflecting that he was not in good health and had lost a considerable amount of weight in recent years. Eight of Elmore's brothers and sisters took seats in the front row.

Townes Jones, whose father had first convicted Elmore and who himself had been the prosecutor in the third trial, walked into the courtroom attired in a blue blazer over a white, broad-collared shirt. He shook hands with Donald Zelenka, from the attorney general's office, who for more than twenty years had fought ferociously to see Elmore executed. Having lost that battle when Judge Hayes declared Elmore was mentally retarded, Zelenka was now determined to keep him in prison for the rest of his life. He appeared glum and was trying to be as inconspicuous as possible.

Billy Garrett, who had defended Elmore in the third trial and believed he was innocent, was present. He said he would never speak to Zelenka again until he publicly apologized to Diana Holt for what he had done to her. Rauch Wise made the same vow. Before reading this book, neither had been aware of her life story, of what she had overcome, and how Zelenka had tried to smear her during the Johnson case.

At 11:12, Elmore's case was called. Prison guards removed the shackles from his ankles and wrists, and he walked to the podium in front of Judge Frank R. Addy Jr. Holt, in a pin-striped suit, stood on Elmore's right. She introduced Chris Jensen, standing to Elmore's left, who had flown down from New York, and Marta Kahn, to Elmore's right, who had flown in the night before from Baltimore. Holt explained that John Blume, who had first assigned Holt the Elmore case in 1993, and who had been a guiding voice when needed, could not be present because of a commitment in another case.

Holt asked for all the charges to be dismissed. Judge Addy denied the motion, as Holt knew he would. Peace then advised the court that Elmore was prepared to enter an Alford plea.

Elmore didn't like it one bit. Nor did Holt. But she had come to believe it was the best course of action. The State of South Carolina had tried Elmore three times based on perjured testimony and evidence that had been manufactured. And no South Carolina court, with the exception of Judge Hayes's, had been willing to deliver justice.

Elmore's lawyers felt they simply could not take the chance that the State of South Carolina would now play fair. If there was only a 1 percent chance that the state could manage to get another conviction, it was too great a risk to take. And the lawyers did not want Elmore to spend another day in prison. He had spent more than half his life on death row, altogether more than eleven thousand days in jail since his arrest. He had seen more than thirty men led from their death row cells, never to return. During his entire time in prison, Elmore had not received a single write-up for any infraction of any kind, an almost unbelievable record of good conduct.

Peace laid out the evidence the state would introduce if there were a new trial, including the fingerprint by the back door and the "hairs on the bed." (He did not, however, mention a specific number of hairs.)

Judge Addy explained to Elmore that if he pleaded guilty, it did not mean he was admitting to the truth of this evidence but only that it would be the evidence the state would introduce.

"Are you satisfied with your lawyers?" Judge Addy asked.

"Oh, yes, sir!" the normally hesitant Elmore answered assertively. Diana patted him on the back. Jensen placed his hand on Elmore's shoulder.

"I will accept this plea," Judge Addy said. It was 11:32.

Holt wanted another word. "He did not do it. He wasn't there," she said to Addy, choking back tears. The Fourth Circuit's opinion had "dismantled" the state's case and dealt a blow to the "architects of injustice," she asserted.

"The question we had to ask: Is there any justice for Mr. Elmore?" She went on: "Freedom is justice, and that is why we have entered this plea."

Epilogue

Peace spoke again, insisting Elmore was guilty.

There was a long silence while Judge Addy made some notes. Then the case was over.

"I wish you luck, sir," the judge said to Elmore. It was 11:39. Elmore was free.

There were hugs and tears among the lawyers, Elmore, and Elmore's brothers and sisters. Then court officials led Elmore through the back door to the Greenwood jail. It would take four hours to process him out, they said. Holt was furious. At her request, Judge Addy had ordered that Elmore be released immediately and that he walk out the front door. Someone now notified Judge Addy of what was happening, and he called the jail and repeated his order, standing at the back door to be sure it was fulfilled. Minutes later, Edward Lee Elmore walked out the front door of the Greenwood County Courthouse a free man, head held high.

For the first time in thirty years, he got into a car, and Holt drove him to Abbeville, the town in which he had grown up and which he had not seen in thirty years. Standing in the town square, with the memorial to the Confederate soldiers, Elmore gaped at all the new restaurants and stores. They went to lunch at the Village Grill. It was the first time Elmore had made a choice about what to eat in three decades; he copied Jensen and ordered a prime rib sandwich.

While Elmore was eating, Holt received calls from Lieber Correctional Institution near Charleston, from her clients still on death row. They had no idea that their friend was now free. There were verbal high fives and expressions of astonishment coming down the line.

"Hey man, you won't believe where I'm at," Elmore said to the first caller, who was on speakerphone so other inmates could hear. "Sitting in a restaurant in my hometown!"

"Your joy is our joy," said one man still on the row. "It gives us hope all the way across the board. It brings light to the darkness."

Another call, another row inmate. "This is the news we've been waiting, hoping, praying for."

"Thanks for your prayers," Elmore said. Diana cried.

"Oh, man," said his friend. Then he added, "That's what happens when you got the best attorney in the world: Miss Diana Holt."

Edward Lee Elmore is free, but, to borrow a line from the Barry Gold-water campaign, "none dare call it justice." To get out of prison, he had to plead guilty to a crime he did not commit.

"It's bittersweet," Holt said during lunch. "The fact that the judge treated him with respect and dignity sweetened the day." She knows, of course, that it is not full justice. "It's more justice than we had," she said.

By pleading guilty, Elmore has given up the right to sue the state for wrongful conviction and incarceration. If there is going to be any justice in this case, it will happen only if the U.S. Justice Department launches an investigation and requires police officers Alvin Johnson and Jim Coursey and SLED investigators Tom Henderson, Ira Parnell, and Earl Wells to testify under oath.

A NOTE ON SOURCES
AND ACKNOWLEDGMENTS

This book is based primarily on the record in the Elmore case—transcripts from three trials; legal briefs, depositions, oral arguments, and transcript from the post-conviction relief hearing; and other hearings in state and federal court. I also interviewed all the principals in the case—police officers, prosecutors, Elmore's lawyers, jurors, witnesses, Elmore's family—most of them several times. I am deeply grateful for the courtesies they extended, even those who did not like the direction of my questions. Jimmy Holloway Jr. never declined to talk to me, even though he said at one time, "You think my father did it, don't you?" Tom Henderson didn't throw me out of his house but offered me a home-brewed peach schnapps after I asked if he had planted blood on Elmore's blue jeans. Only two persons declined to be interviewed—Greenwood police sergeant Alvin Johnson and Donald Zelenka. When I knocked on Johnson's door in Greenwood, his son answered. He is a former marine, as am I, and we chatted about the corps. His father wasn't home. When I later called his father, he thanked me for being kind to his son, but he told me that he would not talk to me about the case, and that I should never knock on his door or call him again. "Enjoy your stay in Greenwood," he said. It was chilling. Mr. Zelenka said he could not give me an interview because it was a violation of ethical standards while Elmore's appeals were pending. I reminded him that he had talked to me on one or two occasions when I was writing articles about the case for *The New York Times*, and that one time he had initiated the contact. He wasn't swayed, but he did answer some questions about his background in an e-mail.

If this book had footnotes, it would be replete with references to articles about Supreme Court decisions written by Linda Greenhouse for the *Times*. Linda has a lawyer's mind and a journalist's pen, giving her an ability to explain legal nuances in concise language that the non-lawyer can understand. She was also a dear colleague during my years at the newspaper. I am also deeply indebted to her biography *Becoming Justice Blackmun: Harry Blackmun's Supreme Court Journey*.

I would like to recommend two other books. *Capital Punishment on Trial:* Furman v. Georgia *and the Death Penalty in Modern America* by David Oshinksy is a fluidly written account of how the case reached the court and why the justices decided as they did. Though *Furman* is a landmark decision, in the pantheon with *Roe v. Wade* and *Brown v. Board of Education,* and is the subject of uncountable law review articles, the popular literature on the case is almost nonexistent, making Oshinsky's book even more useful and important.

The other book is *The Origins of Adversary Criminal Trial* by John H. Langbein. The book is part of a series covering legal history since 1750. Though academic in presentation, it is an utterly fascinating account of the evolution of criminal trials, from a time when there were, astonishingly, no lawyers—no prosecutors, no defense counsel. It was "altercation trial that pitted citizen accuser against citizen accused," Langbein writes.

The Death Penalty Information Center is the best single source of facts, figures, and other information about capital punishment in America.

In the beginning, as it were, there was Jill Abramson; as deputy Washington bureau chief for the *Times,* she gave me a chance, and assigned me to write about the death penalty. This book was ten years in the making, and I had the benefit of many readers of the many drafts and iterations through which it progressed: Geraldine Brooks, Julie Empson, Doug Frantz, Alma Guillermoprieto, Denise Leith, and Laura Wilson. Thea Garland applied her exceptional literary talent and gave me moral support. Steve Engelberg, a friend, colleague, and editor, came through with a critical critique at a critical moment. A special thanks to Alan Riding, who has been editing me since I wrote my first article for the *Times* (from Guatemala). George Kendall, who is one of the most accomplished and honored death penalty lawyers, offered me invaluable assistance in understanding Supreme Court decisions and the law, and saved me from numerous errors. David Bruck and Joe Margulies, both law professors, also tutored me. Any errors or legal misinterpretations that remain are my responsibility. Rauch Wise and James Bradford guided me in the ways and history of Greenwood, even as they wondered if I was ever going to produce a finished book. I thank Amber Landsman, Margaret O'Shea, Muktita Suhartono, and Margot Williams for their research assistance, and Laura Raphael for computer assistance in times of dire need.

I want to pay particular tribute to Ruth Fecych, who was an editor on two of my previous books. At one point, I sent the manuscript to Ruth as a friend, asking her if she thought it was worth my continuing or if I should drop it. She read the manuscript carefully, made suggestions, and encouraged me to keep going.

Thanks to tireless research, Mary Panzer managed to locate elusive photos. At Knopf, Joey McGarvey was unfailingly pleasant in assisting me in so many ways, large and small. Louise Collazo copyedited the manuscript, fixing my grammar, saving me from embarrassing inconsistencies, and correcting errors of fact. She has real pride in her work.

It is hard to know where to begin, or end, to express my admiration and respect for Jonathan Segal, my editor on this, our fourth book together. He is, succinctly put, a brilliant editor. I still have the notes from our earliest conversation about the book, scribbled by me on a yellow legal pad over lunch at an Indian restaurant in Manhattan, and I referred to them often while writing. Jonathan pushed and prodded me to make the book not just about one death row inmate and one lawyer, but to explore the broader legal questions as well. I owe him a great deal.

Continuing twenty-five years of loyalty, Gloria Loomis was my agent. I value her advice and wisdom, but above all, I cherish her friendship. My heartfelt thanks to Jane, who has endured again, with love. Finally, this book is dedicated to my mother because somehow she instilled in me the sense of right and wrong that kept me going for a decade in the dissection of an anatomy of injustice.

INDEX

Index

Index

Index

Index

Index

Index

Index

Index

Index

Index